Women Rapping Revolution

Women Rapping Revolution

Hip Hop and Community Building in Detroit

Rebekah Farrugia and Kellie D. Hay

Forewords by Piper Carter and Mahogany Jones

UNIVERSITY OF CALIFORNIA PRESS

University of California Press
Oakland, California

© 2020 by Rebekah Farrugia and Kellie D. Hay

California Series in Hip Hop Studies, 1

Library of Congress Cataloging-in-Publication Data

Names: Farrugia, Rebekah, author. | Hay, Kellie D.,
    1965– author. | Carter, Piper, writer of foreword. |
    Jones, Mahogany, writer of foreword.
Title: Women rapping revolution : hip hop and
    community building in Detroit / Rebekah Farrugia and
    Kellie D. Hay ; forewords by Piper Carter and
    Mahogany Jones.
Other titles: California series in hip hop studies ; 1.
Description: Oakland, California : University of
    California Press, [2020] | Series: California series in
    hip hop studies ; 1 | Includes bibliographical references
    and index.
Identifiers: LCCN 2020004029 (print) | LCCN 2020004030
    (ebook) | ISBN 9780520305311 (cloth) |
    ISBN 9780520305328 (paperback) |
    ISBN 9780520973367 (epub)
Subjects: LCSH: Foundation of Women in Hip Hop. |
    Hip hop feminism—Michigan—Detroit. | African
    American women—Michigan—Detroit.
Classification: LCC HQ1111 .F37 2020 (print) | LCC
    HQ1111 (ebook) | DDC 305.48/896073077434—dc23
LC record available at https://lccn.loc.gov/2020004029
LC ebook record available at https://lccn.loc.gov
    /2020004030

Manufactured in the United States of America

28 27 26 25 24 23 22 21 20
10 9 8 7 6 5 4 3 2 1

Rebekah—
For my husband, Matt, and my sons,
Leeland and Huxley

Kellie—
To Karen A.J. Miller and
Tanya Copeland Stanford

Contents

Foreword

PIPER CARTER

Who knew that the work I'd been doing along with other folks would be immortalized in a scholarly publication?!

When I started the Foundation of Women in Hip Hop back in 2009, I hadn't intended to do any kind of social justice, I hadn't even heard of the term yet.

After we (the 5e Hip Hop Gallery) had been doing our no misogyny open mic for about three years, I met Dr. Kellie Hay and Dr. Rebekah Farrugia when they asked if they could study "our work." They were actually the first ones to point out to me that we were utilizing hip hop culture to create positive social change.

We were just living our culture and honestly I just wanted to be around other women who enjoyed hip hop and identified as hip hop artists and I didn't want to hear the negative lyrics and I wanted everyone to feel safe to enjoy themselves without being groped and grabbed on.

They were college professors so they would ask us all kinds of questions and we would have lengthy conversations about all kinds of issues. After speaking with them I'd contemplate: how do we bring community folks into the conversation around engaging in the struggle against the incinerator and the fight for clean air, water affordability and water safety, public transit and transit justice, food justice/food security/food sovereignty, climate change, and clean power?

They introduced me to hip hop feminist authors such as Dr. Aisha Durham and Dr. Ruth Nicole Brown. We had debates about Black feminism, hip hop feminism, feminism, and Black women.

All of this reading and debating led me to lasting relationships across the country and to work with all kinds of women in hip hop making the connection to Mother Earth and motherhood and our role in protecting Her, as well as "real life" solutions that have been created to do things very differently, using imagination as the driving force behind creative expression in community organizing.

Through our exchanges over the years, mostly in loving struggle around ideas and really digging into questions, and through their continued unwavering consistent support of our work, we were able to really uplift our resistance, asking the question: what role does hip hop play in movement building?

There are so many stories I could tell about the learning that took place, from that very first encounter to the various conferences they invited us to participate in to the many late night and lengthy sessions we've had over time. But honestly, I would need an entire book to explain how important their capturing and documenting our process has been to us.

Our no-misogyny open mic lasted five years. It was hugely successful and attracted international press and attention. Since it ended we are now a complete reconfiguration of members and participants and have become an organization that offers services to women in hip hop. Our mission and vision have expanded.

In reflection, I appreciate the authenticity with which they approached the process of their research. From the very beginning they were more than respectful. They literally took the time to learn from us and be led by us (Black Women). All along the way they were open to critique, criticism, opposition, redefining, and relabeling, as well as unlearning. They practiced deep listening and made changes accordingly when asked and more often self-checked without being asked to do so.

For us, we were just folks in community who wanted to shift the paradigm, and we did. Many of the young folks who attended our open mic are young adults now and organizing their own events and because the "rules" of engagement were natural to them they now have the same guidelines at their events. That's pretty profound. And it's more than what we imagined as an outcome.

I hope that after reading this book folks will reach out to us and invite us to perform or speak or conduct a workshop. I hope that folks will listen to our mixtape series featuring women's voices. I hope folks will open themselves up to listening to women emcees, and hire women music producers and women graffiti artists and b-girls, and . . .

Foreword

MAHOGANY JONES

I was a NYC transplant and for the years I had been in Detroit (since 2004), I had yet to experience a hip hop open mic scene that came close to mirroring the magic of what I encountered in the late 90s/early 2000s in New York City. Most of the open mics that I attended were chock full of aggression, and cats trying to get "put on." Not that the scene in NYC didn't have its fair share of that, but there was a sense of community and connectivity, service and purpose that was the driving force behind why we religiously showed up every week, that I hadn't quite been able to place in the hip hop scene in Detroit just yet.

It was the spring of 2011 when I received a text'ed flyer from a Detroit legend then known as "Invincible," inviting me to check out this women in hip hop open mic night "the Foundation." She (at the time) said it was every Tuesday and she knew I was kinda new to the "D" and thought it would be great for me. I had been waiting for something like what she mentioned. It sounded perfect. I was hungry to connect with a community of artists and fellow emcees to build with.

At the Foundation, I stepped into what felt like an alternate world—the vibes were high and just right. I walked in to see a woman on the turntables, "DJ Lajedi," who was spinning nothing but classics. An all-women band was playing along as the DJ was spinning, b-boys and b-girls were on the dance floor, writers were practicing graffiti in a corner, and a few children were with their mothers "catching the vibe." The environment was warm, sincere, electric, and connected.

I was drawn, and what was just a once-in-a-while let-me-drop-by became a weekly practice, especially once I met the gallery owners, DJ Sicari and our founder, fearless leader, and a woman I'm honored to call sister, Piper Carter.

Coming weekly was more than just keeping my skills sharp. We had a mission: to become a presence in the community and a resource center, where we could encourage one another to grow as artists, but also as humans. The heart of the Foundation was about celebrating women in hip hop. It was about honoring the presence, voices, and contribution of women in media in efforts to bring restoration to our sense of identity as a whole. The Foundation had become my *Cheers;* we all knew each other's names and hearts. Pipe's ambition to maintain a weekly open mic on a week night was often met with criticism and resistance, as was her premise—that our open mic night be one that didn't tolerate misogyny, at all! That was tough. What was hip hop culture without the disrespect and oversexualization of women? I had quickly gone from an attendee to a co-host (alongside Nik-Nak), in order to be a part of finding the answer to that question.

The Foundation found a home at the 5e Gallery. Its purpose was to serve as both art gallery and community center, both maker space and lounge. It was multipurpose in every sense—a space to come and get a meal when needed or catch a multimedia fashion show. Piper and Sicari had created not just an art gallery space, but a movement.

Unfortunately, like most movements, there was red tape and push-back. The Gallery had building violations and therefore, it would not be available for public use, which meant a relocation. This relocation, to Detroit's famed veterans' bar the Old Miami, initially felt like a curse, because nothing about it said "hip-hop feminism." But it quickly evolved into one of the most renowned open mic nights in the city for about three years, where I had the pleasure of meeting our authors and now close friends, sisters, and comrades, Rebekah and Kellie. These professors not only came to the open mic nights but toiled in the trenches with us, faithfully attending planning meetings for the night and special events and serving as partial sponsors for events. They have celebrated birthdays alongside us and literally did and do life with us, and have invited us to do the same with them.

Hip hop culture is not a spectator sport; it's best experienced as a participant. It would have been easy for Kellie and Rebekah to have entered our world and comfortably posted their tents on the edges, looking from the outside in. Instead we have grown together as artists, educators, advocates, some of us academics, but most importantly as women and sisters. This journey has not been a comfortable one; it has been full, rich, thick, and provided plenty of moments for both professional and personal growth. There are no two other individuals, aside from Piper Carter herself, who I feel are more qualified to lend voice and insight into what was the Foundation, what is now We Found Hip Hop, and what ultimately became a piece of Detroit's hip hop historical landscape, and will be a capstone for Detroit women in hip hop.

Preface

There is a lack of research that examines Black women's contributions to the hip hop underground. *Women Rapping Revolution* begins to fill this gap, opening conversations about Black women's cultural production and community building work. Our project is the product of seven years of immersion in a women-centered hip hop collective in Detroit. Created by cultural organizer and hip hop aficionado Piper Carter, the Foundation's initial purpose aspired to provide a stage where women could showcase their talent and create a community to foster their development. Over the course of our engagement with the Foundation we witnessed the evolution of the collective's artistic and political growth. In this context cultural work often constitutes political work.

Historically, the dominant narrative about hip hop's development was drenched in New York and Los Angeles, which came to define East Coast and West Coast rap. Following the coastal paradigm, cities like Miami, New Orleans, and Atlanta led the South to emerge as a dominant player in hip hop cultural production. While the Midwest has produced its fair share of artists, including Kanye West, Chance the Rapper, and Lupe Fiasco from Chicago and artists like Eminem and Big Sean from Detroit, as a region it remains an understudied site of US hip hop. A study of Detroit hip hop has much to contribute to this narrative. Its industrial past, musical heritage, and social movement history situate Detroit as a unique site. It is an ideal neoliberal city that has much in common with other postindustrial cities like Pittsburgh,

Buffalo, and Cleveland. Detroit's economic, racial, and cultural particularities produce a distinct aesthetic, sound, and politic that shape the ways that hip hop's five elements are lived in the city.[1]

Neoliberalism, whether it is imagined as a worldview, a mechanism to ameliorate economic issues, or an idealistic conception of market and consumer behavior, reproduces the unevenness between rich and poor, often white and Black. We view it as a stage in late capitalism that radically departs from earlier formations of the welfare state where government was felt to be obliged to care for its citizens. Instead, neoliberalism places stock in radical individualism. That is, citizens are independent and responsible for their own welfare. Big government is viewed as threatening and ill-conceived, and any form of regulation that limits market activity is considered dangerous. In this philosophy, the market replaces the state. Instead of providing programming, training, or subsidized schooling, medicine, or housing, neoliberals believe in individual responsibility. Since markets are deemed to be the best way to create capital, jobs, and profit, the function of government shifts from welfare to business management. Corporations have a lot at stake in this shifting modality of capitalism as they become the role models and stakeholders after which government models itself. Risk management becomes a high priority, akin to the way actuaries forecast profit and risk potential in insurance companies. Profit, business, and managed populations are high priorities in this iteration of capitalism. In contemporary Detroit, neoliberal planning has taken the form of urban renewal. Foundation artists actively push against these ideologies and practices, especially as they impact urban planning; they expose the displacements and political distress that they see as urban removal rather than urban renewal.

Black people constitute more than 80 percent of Detroit's population, making it one of the blackest cities in the United States. Racial pride and politics are at stake in the cultural production we analyze. We think it is powerful to highlight women's particular contributions to hip hop culture as well as their organizing strategies. We simply do not know enough about Black women's contributions to the hip hop underground. Similarly, outside of the concrete boundaries of neighborhood associations and activist organizations Black women's cultural work is virtually unknown.

A shared interest in hip hop music and culture led us to pursue this project together. Our differing working-class backgrounds, ethnic identities, and academic training also shaped how we imagined the project. While we are both white women, we are shaped by structures of whiteness and class location in different ways. Given the population shifts going on in Detroit and its racial history, understanding how we came to this project and what the stakes are when white women study predominantly Black populations matters—methodologically and politically. Describing key moments in our histories situates our interest in pursuing the Foundation as a rich and worthy site of investigation.

REBEKAH

Growing up in Windsor in the 1980s and 90s, I saw Detroit as a mysterious and dangerous place whose tall buildings I observed from a safe distance across the river. I was a product of a racist culture that propagated stereotypical views about Detroit and its people. I learned about its gun violence, Devil's Night destruction, and designation as a murder capital from the nightly local news. By the time I was fifteen, in the early 1990s, I was taking the tunnel bus across to explore a limited area of downtown that was home to concert venues like Saint Andrew's Hall and The Shelter where I'd check out punk and alternative bands. I would roam the blighted streets of Detroit unsupervised, dreaming about what Woodward Ave must have been like in decades past. I imagined the mostly deserted and boarded-up shops I wandered past to be selling fine clothing and furniture, full of customers—Black and white—while Martha and the Vandellas played from the transistor radios of Cadillacs and Fairlanes cruising down the country's first highway, their drivers proud to live in the city that birthed both the auto industry and Motown. It was a romanticized imagining, but I was young and the city—both its past and present—fascinated me. It was an Other world that I mostly imagined from a distance and sometimes stumbled into, but rarely interacted with.

At nineteen I discovered Detroit techno and Chicago house. I fell in love with electronic music after my first rave experience and was euphoric upon learning that the DJs and producers I made my way across the river to dance to on Saturday nights were locals with worldwide notoriety. They were pioneers, repurposing synthesizers and drum machines, whose experimentation culminated in the creation of Detroit techno. Long before cellphones, let alone smartphones, it was exhilarating to pull up to a venue and be assured by a banging bass line that we'd finally found the spot. But this was the mid-nineties, and by then white suburban youth dominated warehouse parties in the city. Occasionally DJs would throw down ghettotech sets. Combining elements of various subgenres of electronic music including electro, Chicago house, and

Miami bass, but sped up to 160 beats per minute, ghettotech could be heard every Friday night on the local hip hop and R&B station WJLB. Tracks often included repetitive and at times sexually provocative lyrics. Live broadcasting from the club Legends sparked my interest in Detroit's Black dance music and hip hop scene. However, as a young white woman from Windsor without any connections to Detroiters, I felt like this wasn't a world that was available for me to explore beyond the bins of record stores and radio play. Three months after the first Detroit Electronic Music festival in 2000 I left the area for graduate school. Nine years later I would return, this time settling on the US side of the border and determined to find my way into Detroit: its people, complexities, and relationship to hip hop.

KELLIE

I grew up as an Okie-identified white girl. Both of my parents were raised on country music, but only my father was passionate about country and bluegrass. Billy Crash Craddock's "Cajun Baby" spun daily in my house, along with Loretta Lyn, Johnny Cash, Tammy Wynette, and Conway Twitty. Only old country pleased my dad—other genres and new forms of country did not matter to him. My mother also grew up around country music; however, she loved to dance and country was not her style. Fats Domino, Chuck Berry, and Little Richard were her favorite artists. She was a dope swing/jitterbug dancer. In my childhood, I remember her singing and dancing around in the kitchen to Fats Domino's "Blueberry Hill"—her all-time favorite song—when she did chores. R&B, soul, and artists like the Jackson 5 offered acceptable styles of music; they crossed over just like my mother's favorite Black entertainers.[2] Everything I thought my mother loved about Black music changed when hip hop hit the radio.

Like many white kids uneducated in hip hop culture, I thought I was down with rap music when the Sugar Hill Gang's 1979 hit "Rapper's Delight" rippled across commercial radio. My parents had no patience; in their minds rap was talk over phony sounds, not real music. I had to sneak my new fascination with music that I did not know, but loved anyway. And even though I listened to whatever commercial rap radio offered from age fourteen onward, in 1994 my worldview changed when Tricia Rose published *Black Noise,* one of hip hop's foundational scholarly texts, and Nas dropped his first album, *Illmatic.* Both artifacts opened my eyes and my heart. So too did my immersion in graduate school, where postcolonial theory, Black feminist theory, and the god-like figures who created British cultural studies turned everything I was raised to think inside out. I had to learn the conditions that birthed hip hop's history, the repurposing of technology, all the elements that form the culture. Most of all, I learned that in the absence of forming relationships with hip hop heads and the communities living hip hop, I was no different than what my parents learned to be: Okie crossover consumers of Black music. I was a reader of hip hop, not a maker, far away from anything that resembled a hip hop community. And then came our immersion in the Foundation. I let my shy poet-self out of a box. Mahogany Jones and Miz Korona, two well-known Detroit emcees, graciously took me on as their poetry student; they encouraged me to perform in public and propelled me onto the Foundation's stage.

FEMINIST CO-ETHNOGRAPHY

Our stories and experiences illustrate how our intersecting identity locations are advantaged by structures of whiteness and simultaneously fall through its cracks; that is, as white women with working class backgrounds, one of whom identifies as queer, there are many points of intersection that we came to share with Foundation members and Detroit's broader hip hop underground. Race, however, has been the stickiest point of connection. In Detroit, the anxiety about who speaks for hip hop is amplified because of the city's racial history and contemporary uphill battles. Whether we asked for it or not, like it or not, we are assigned and possess obvious racial privilege that we have had to constantly work to navigate. We are aware of the power dynamics that are always at play. These underlying forces are as embodied as they are conceptual.

Our commitment to document what the women in our study find culturally relevant in their lives connects to the larger agenda of feminist activist ethnography.[3] This methodology encourages reflexive research strategies and intersectional understandings of social identity. It also requires the researcher to question power dynamics in a myriad of ways, including those between researcher and researched. Additionally, feminist activist ethnography identifies the connections researchers share with participants that collectively push back against the disparities produced in neoliberal economics and cultural values. What is more, Craven and Davis locate this project within the confines of neoliberalism as it is effected in North America.[4] To this end, we practice feminist activist ethnography from the perspective of collaboration. That is, as ethnographers we are co-creators of this and other research work; at the same time, we often co-create with Foundation members—planning events and making art. This bond brings cultural practice and political resistance together. Unlike the classical ethnography produced within a positivist scientific gaze, we do not accept any notion that objectivity is attainable and desirable in ethnographic fieldwork, or in the writing practices of scholars doing ethnography. Intersubjective, relational work produces what counts as data in our scholarship. In each move we make, problematizing power differences is at stake, whether they exist between us as co-ethnographers, between us and our research partners, or whether they are those that beset all of us involved in this study.

Throughout *Women Rapping Revolution* we link micro racial moments produced in talk, music, and hip hop culture to larger structures so as not to risk pathologizing Blackness, Black women's relationship to gender disparities, and/or their roles in creating inclusive Black communities. Scholars like Lila Abu-Lughod who critique and advance openly activist methodology question the ways that researchers who study marginalized populations have crafted their subjects as oppressed victims, resulting in frozen-in-time "universalized and romanticized women."[5] Foundation women reject the category of victim. Moreover, we employ the language of oppression cautiously, to aptly point at social structures and living conditions. We have come to learn that these women imagine themselves as revolutionaries, and in some cases organizers who fight against both material and affective conditions. Feminist ethnography articulates well with Anthony Kwame Harrison's conception of ethnographic comportment.[6] His embodied, mobile construct captures the power dynamics that we are obliged to address. For Harrison, ethnographic comportment "is both historically informed and future oriented; it includes familiarity with ethnography's problematic past and a disposition of accountability for one's role in advancing ethnographic practices."[7] Taking stock of how white liberal ethnographers have historically sensationalized Black urban culture through one-dimensional reports, we endeavor to write a more dialogic narrative that invites our participants to speak in their own idiom, on their terms. In spite of our efforts to earn/achieve transparency, however, we own our agency; that is, our hands, hearts, and heads fashioned this text. Inasmuch as ethnography is relational, it is also rhetorical. We make aesthetic decisions writing ethnography, just as the artists we engage intentionally fashion their lyrics, music, visual art, dance, and turntabling. Texture, layering, and flow are not only embraced by emcees; they are rhetorical/aesthetic tools for the hip hop ethnographer. Texture exceeds reporting. It requires aesthetic choices and discursive strategies to juxtapose ideas, practices, and disruptions into the form of ethnographic writing, whereas flow can mean cadence and timing or signifying on what is overly familiar.

Suspicion and concern about white women studying predominately Black communities may never be ameliorated, but we can't stop and won't stop trying to create an ethical, politically conscious strategy for ethnographic practice. This project engages and works to lift up the stories and cultural production of women and the men who support them. *Women Rapping Revolution* documents a significant collective that opened space for women in Detroit's hip hop underground to shine, showcasing their aesthetics, practices, and musical genius. Artists who come through and participate in Foundation events offer cultural production plus; that is, aesthetics and politics are difficult to disentangle in the work. One cannot listen to music in the underground without learning about Detroit—its history, politics, uneven urban development, and environmental conditions. What is more, the city's racial footprints are like semiotic musical indexes: the material is enmeshed into the symbolic forms of cultural production.

This study is a different kind of collaborative ethnography, one that departs from the current literature that is shaping duoethnography.[8] Duoethnographers insist that the researcher's life and reflections are sites of knowledge production. The approach presupposes that two people ought to push themselves into reflection that then leads to changes in research strategy, underlying assumptions, blind spots, and acknowledging when productive practices work. We agree that this type of work is important and necessary, and yet, it does not constitute the spectrum of our methodological practice. Indeed, we take our reflections seriously, but the intention of the project is not merely to process our experience, frustrations, learning curve, limits, and mistakes; instead our fieldwork, ruminations, and disagreements are but one layer of a larger set of interpretive work. Our study is an ethnography that we are doing together. It works from some of the same assumptions and practices that guide duoethnography but does not mimic its frameworks. We tell our stories in relation to the community that produced us as a duo-team. That is, they produced us and our awareness of us inasmuch as we engaged them as participants who provided important lessons and sites of inquiry. We have overlapping layers of narrative, both as a unit and in relation to the Foundation.

Between 2011 and 2018 we conducted over forty interviews, attended dozens of Foundation Tuesday open mic nights as well as events featuring or hosted by individual artists, and engaged in countless conversations. We also attended conferences and collaborated on panels together with Foundation artists. Over the course of our work we traveled to performances at galleries, street festivals, art exhibitions, album release parties, protests, and fundraisers, in addition to community-building events produced by and/or featuring Foundation artists. Immersed in music and community, we documented the sonic, discursive, and material practices performers employ in making claims to the city.

Forgoing any pretense that conducting fieldwork alone would somehow confirm our competence as ethnographic researchers, we also learned early on that the advantages of having a research partner extended to issues relating to safety. Because of Detroit's intense population decline, large portions of the city are sparsely populated and many neighborhoods are dimly lit. On some occasions, in particular locations, men would walk us back to our cars at the end of the night; at the Old Miami it was common for at least one of the doormen to be stationed out front, policing the area. Women conducting fieldwork in electronic dance music settings have articulated instances where they have been threatened with rape, groped, solicited for sexual acts, and experienced intense emotional anxiety and fear.[9] For us, attending events together assuaged much of the concern about the dangers that nighttime fieldwork can pose, especially when we often found ourselves in unfamiliar locations for one-time events, though most of the time we felt quite safe.

Our ethnographic comportment led us to places we never would have gone to otherwise. Some of these spaces include the Afrikan-centered, community-based organization Alkebu-Lan Village on the Eastside, Nandi's Knowledge Café in Highland Park, the resurrected Hip Hop Shop on Detroit's Westside, the Baltimore Gallery, fundraisers, rent parties, and a smattering of outdoor cafes, galleries, street fairs and festivals, public parks, bars, and clubs. Along the way, we also attended events at houses repurposed into performance spaces in Highland Park, Midtown, and the Boston-Edison neighborhood. We have strategized with the Foundation to help fund the organization, save 5e Gallery spaces, sponsor headlining artists at Foundation anniversary parties, and assisted with the production of key Foundation events, including Detroit's first women in hip hop conference and concert. Alongside

other members, we experienced direct sexism, gentrification, environmental decline, and the overwhelming stress that artists in the hip hop
underground must live as they dance the neoliberal hustle. As researchers and members of the Foundation we experienced "the struggles, joys,
and defeats" that follow from feminist ethnographic engagement.[10] Our
shared time with Foundation members led us to understand a wider
range of hip hop aesthetics, the fluidity of community politics, and
women's visions for a citizen-centered Detroit.

Acknowledgments

REBEKAH FARRUGIA

In May 2011 I found a listing in the *Metro Times* for a women and hip hop event in Detroit. Driving down I-75 to the Old Miami I had no idea what a life-altering decision I had made in deciding to check out this open mic night or the prolonged journey I was embarking on (and into which I'd soon bring Kellie). Researching and writing this book brought us into contact with an incredible cast of performers, places, and perspectives that we will forever be grateful for, all of which nurtured our thinking, scholarship, and personal lives. The inspiration and commitment of the members of The Foundation and every other artist, organizer, visionary, and supporter we came into contact with over the years served as both the catalyst and the steady beat that kept this work alive for the years it has taken to complete it. We are forever in your debt and thankful for your contributions to hip hop music, culture, and community, and for your support, without which this book could not have been written.

There are so many people in my life who help keep me balanced. I am especially grateful to my grad school writing groupmates Evelyn Ho, Kate Cady, and Vesti Silva for their unremitting support in my professional and personal life. Thank you for all the phone calls, texts, for working through ideas, reading drafts, and for chilling me out and making me laugh when I need it most.

Thank you, Kembrew McLeod, for all of your support since my grad school days. Your matter-of-fact, of-course-you-can-and-should-write-this-book attitude early on helped light the fire for this project.

I also owe a great deal to many of my IASPM-US colleagues. Justin Adams Burton, in particular, has been an invaluable colleague and friend throughout this entire journey. It was his suggestion that we submit to the Ecomusicology Listening Room session at the American Musicological Society's Annual Meeting in Pittsburgh in 2013 that launched the production of "Legendary" and chapter 5 of this book. He is also an exceptional and dedicated peer reviewer. The insightful feedback he provided on our chapter for the *Oxford Handbook of Hip Hop Studies* (that formed the basis for chapter 2 here) encouraged us to think more critically about the relationships between sound, space, and the concept of self-care. Thank you for being around to push and play with ideas and for all of the listening you've done over the years. I am also grateful to so many others for sitting through my conference presentations, reading drafts of my work, offering feedback, and just being all-around great people to talk to and learn from, especially: Luis-Manuel Garcia, Murray Forman, Kwame Harrison, Ali Colleen Neff, Mike D'Errico, and Norma Coates.

Sometimes ideas come when we least expect them. Thank you Michelle Habell-Pallán for answering my email inquiry and giving me the opportunity to sit in on a workshop at the Women Who Rock conference at the University of Washington in 2011. It was here that I first had the privilege of hearing women speak openly about their experiences as hip hop artists and organizers in Seattle and the ways that their participation built community and fostered healing. This was also the first time that I heard Invisible/ill Weaver speak about their hip hop and organizing efforts, which motivated me to look into the Detroit underground.

Oakland University Faculty Research Fellowship Awards gave me the time to focus exclusively on this work in the summers of 2015 and 2018. I'm grateful to the Research Committee for seeing the potential and significance of interdisciplinary work that sometimes is cast aside as trivial.

It is in the machinations of everyday life that culture and community are created. Matt Dunlop has been faithfully sending musical lifelines my way in the form of tracks, DJ sets, articles, and links through all of life's ups and downs for decades. Thanks for sticking around and and thank you Stephanie for being cool with it. In a world of so many uncertainties I am indebted to Kim Alexander, Joanna Chapman, Sandy

Soave, Penny Saunders, Danielle Leek and Catherine Veeser for making time for conversations about kids, music, everyday life stresses, and how to keep on keeping on. And Nancy, you were the very best friend one could ever hope for. You were around for the start of this project but regrettably not its end. You played a starring role in my life for 35 years. I miss you every day.

Also thanks to Karen Miller for reading draft upon draft of our work, for imparting to us your historical knowledge of Detroit, and for attending dozens of shows with us over the years, often into the wee hours of the night. Your personal and professional support has meant so much to me over the years.

My exploration and study of Detroit hip hop grew right along with my journey into motherhood. I am so blessed to be the mother of two amazing boys, Leeland and Huxley. I am grateful for their patience with my unconventional work schedule and for their appreciation for the people, music, and culture that have become part of our lives as I worked on this project over the duration of their young lives.

My husband Matt Dunstone has been instrumental in every stage required for this book to make it to print. His endless patience, support, and flexibility made it possible for me to spend years in the field conducting interviews, participating in organizing meetings, attending so many late-night events, and writing, writing, writing. Matt, your ability to radiate composure and confidence even in the most trying times continues to amaze me. Thank you for believing in me and for being so encouraging every step of the way.

Thank you to my dad Anthony Farrugia for instilling in me a passion for music at a young age. From my mother Doreen Farrugia I learned the importance of speaking up when I had something to say. Mum, your strength, perseverance, and courage while on this earth continue to amaze and inspire me. I love and miss you so much. My brother Konrad's deep knowledge of all things pop culture related, tech support, and unconditional love are always welcomed and needed. Thanks bro.

And finally, Kellie, I don't even know where to begin. This project has been an incredible journey on so many levels. It took a minute for us to find our way but you never let that stop us. In my many moments of stress you calmed me down and in my flashes of doubt you brought me up and cooked us yet another meal. You possessed a staunch faith in our ability to do this work from the very beginning despite the challenges we were up against. Our ongoing joke that "it takes two" is no joke. I couldn't have completed this project without you.

KELLIE D. HAY

Many people in my family supported me during this project, yet no one gave me more love, solace, and confidence than my cousin, Tanya Copeland Stanford. She read every page of the manuscript, offered comments and praise, but most of all she kept me going when obstacles emerged. My niece and nephew, Gloria Abbate and Matt Abbate, were supportive during this entire project. At 15 my niece posted our first publication on her Facebook page and Matt went with me to meet our editor, Raina, in Oakland. He got a real taste of academic life. My niblings are my pride and joy. That they care about this project is deeply meaningful.

As a newer member to IASPM-US, I am thankful for the guidance and support of Justin Adams Burton, Murray Forman, Anthony Kwame Harrison, and Steve Waksman.

Karen Miller was my silent partner during this project. She attended shows, developed her own relationships with artists in the community, shared her vast knowledge about Detroit's history, and read so many drafts of this book—so many drafts. She picked me up when I was exhausted and calmed me down when stress peaked. She loved me in a "self-care" kind of way everyday; for that I am forever grateful. She is a source of inspiration for what we develop as the "Vulnerable Maverick" in this book.

This project happened because Rebekah Farrugia took a risk and invited me to study The Foundation with her. It was a risk because she did not know me well and had never seen my writing when she asked me to join her. Lucky for Bekka, writing and ethnographies of performance are my passions. Together, we became "the two that roll together." And so we did. Interviews, daily writing, researching articles and books, attending shows, traveling to conferences, making art, reflecting on and discussing what we experienced and learned—all of this work we did together. Literally, we sat side-by-side and wrote the manuscript. We spent nearly as much time in each other's kitchens and dining rooms as we did at work or any form of leisure time. I watched her nurse a child while typing up conference abstracts and working on early ideas. She is the guru of multitasking. During our journey Rebekah became one of my closest friends and confidants—a kindred spirt. She is much more than my research partner. We have become part of one another's family, including children, in-laws, and dogs. She was the boss of me at times, and I hers. We life-coached one another and ate more sandwiches in my dining room than I can count. I am indelibly marked by our force as a writing team.

BEKKA AND KELLIE

So many artists touched our lives during the course of our study; however, Piper Carter, Miz Korona, Mahogany Jones, Nique Love Rhodes, Deidre "D.S. Sense" Smith, and Stacyé J will forever remain in the center of our friendship circles. Piper is a mover and a shaker but she is also a loyal, caring friend. We will be her hip hop soldiers throughout our lifetimes. Thank you for your vision, motivation, time, and effort. We also thank Miz Korona and Invincible/ill Weaver for being founding members of The Foundation and for paving the way for aspiring artists struggling to find their stage. We are especially grateful to ill for reading and commenting on our entire manuscript. Miz Korona is not only Kellie's poetry mentor, but she has become family. She traveled to California with her mother Debra Robinson for Kellie's wedding and served as the photographer. We are indebted for the time, support, and conversation that Mahogany Jones and Nique Love Rhodes shared with us over the years. Mahogany Jones is Kellie's other poetry teacher, as well as a comrade and dear friend to both of us. Anytime we had a question or shot her a text she got back to us within moments. Now in Florida, Mahogany stays in touch and finds us when she returns to Detroit. Kellie was so touched when Nique asked her to be the bartender at her wedding. We all have side hustles! Deidre "D.S. Sense" Smith not only gave us invaluable time and perspective but she also contributed significantly to our study of her work. We all have a deep, enduring bond that began at The Foundation and then seeped into our personal lives; it carries on into the next iteration and phase of our lives. We are better humans with these women in our lives.

We thank Insite the Riot for her generosity with her time and lyrics. DJ Los shared with us his Detroit hip hop archival mind. We also appreciate the endless hours of performance time he has committed to women making hip hop in the city. We thank Supa Emcee for his enduring support, his tenacity, and his generous community spirit. We are grateful for Valid's reflections on the 5e Gallery and the state of Detroit hip hop, and his dedication to Detroit artistry. We thank Will See for his powerful insights about cultural organizing and for his generous reads of our manuscript and his thoughts on masculinity, and Bryce Detroit for teaching us about Entertainment Justice and Afrocentric philosophies of gender. We thank DJ Sicari for his commitment to Detroit's hip hop underground and the 5e Gallery.

There were other artists we interviewed who contributed to our understanding of Detroit's vast hip hop underground and social justice networks. Thank you Abstract Jazz, Christina "Lady Firefly" El-Perez, Consuela Lopez, Cye, Diana J. Nucera, Dion Burroughs, DJ Lajedi, Intellect, Jayce Caprice, Jenny Lee, Mary Mar Ar-Rasheed aka b-girl Ma-Ma, Mel Wonder, Nicole Carter, Nik Nak, Ron "iRonic" Lee, Jr., Tawana "Honeycomb" Petty, and Steve Furray.

Many thanks to our editor Raina Polivka for her careful reading and direction in shaping our manuscript, our series editors H. Samy Alim and Jeff Chang, as well as the rest of the staff at University of California Press for giving us a platform to not only share our stories and findings but also the voices and artistry of so many Detroiters the world deserves to know about. Our anonymous reviewers overloaded their already busy schedules by agreeing to take on the laborious and time consuming task of reviewing our manuscript. Your passion and insightful feedback made our work sounder and led us to other fascinating studies. We hope to pay it forward. We also thank Meaghan Berry and Lilian Crum from Unsold Studio for designing our funky cover art.

We are also grateful to the Michigan Interdisciplinary Music Society (MIMS) at the University of Michigan for inviting us to present our work on women and hip hop when it was in its infancy. Thank you also to Naomi André who was in the audience that day and equated our project with finding gold. Thank you for your ongoing support and for inviting us back to present our work to your students.

To our colleagues at Oakland University, especially our FUBU (for us and by us) research group. Shea Howell, Valerie Palmer-Mehta, and Tom Discenna read multiple drafts and provided invaluable commentary. We are also grateful to Kathleen Battles, Erin Meyers, Lily Mendoza, and Adina Schneeweis for their comments and resources. We thank our former chair Jenn Heisler and current chair Jeff Youngquist for their ability to create harmonious work environments and teaching schedules conducive to writing. Many thanks to our hip hop colleague and friend Emery Petchauer for reading the entire manuscript and providing invaluable comments and support. You're part of our Kendrick Lamar family for life. Thank you Marty Shafer, who transcribed interviews for us while he was a graduate student.

We are indebted to Shea Howell for much more than reading drafts of our manuscript. She has been a vital resource and mentor over the course of this project. Dedicating her life to being a public intellectual and political organizer for the past fifty years, she embodies a living sense of Detroit's cultural memory. We are grateful for her willingness to share her knowledge and experience with us, and for introducing us to Detroit's network of community organizers. Shea also introduced us to Stephen Ward, who embraced our project and gave us invaluable comments.

Introduction

Intersections of Detroit, Women, and Hip Hop

May 14, 2013, Tangent Gallery. We pull up to the Tangent Gallery on Detroit's Eastside; decades of automotive manufacturing decline have transformed this once thriving business district into a desolate space. Empty, pothole laden parking lots and a few dilapidated bars keep the gallery company on East Milwaukee Avenue. It's hot, sunny, and humid enough to draw sweat out of a rock. We are here to celebrate the four-year anniversary of the Foundation, a nonprofit hip hop collective that provides women and their allies a safe and accepting space to perform. This party is a big event that's been in the making for months and is sure to draw a loyal crowd. We arrive early to help set up. Once inside, the building's bare-bones, warehouse-like exterior gives way to an atmosphere bustling with activity. A long bar lies to the left of the entrance. The room just past it is where the night's performances will take place. It is huge and unencumbered, with the exception of a stage and speaker stacks, waiting to be filled with the night's patrons and performers. We spot Foundation organizer Piper Carter in the next room over, making sure that vendors have everything they need. Sellers of everything from African glass pyramids to hair products and face creams, jewelry, t-shirts, and Afrocentric clothing are present. Months of meetings and labor have gone into organizing this night: reaching out to sponsors, agreeing on performers, and designing publicity.

Always on the go, Piper greets us with hugs and directions: we are responsible for "taking care of the performing artists." This is code for "take yourselves to the liquor store and get them what they want." As the night wears on we are sent to fetch Jameson, Hennessey, mixers and ice—Detroiters' drinks of choice. There is a lot riding on this night, which is stressing us out. In the absence of sponsors, Foundation members—Piper in particular—invested personal financial capital to secure the event. Of course, we want everyone to recoup their money but more importantly we feel like the Foundation's reputation for hosting dope events is on the line. It took years to cultivate a space where women in hip hop could do their thing and build an audience. This anniversary party is intended to signal the Foundation's success and growth. As much as we are stressed, relief calms our bodies as people flow in. From eight to nine they get drinks and mingle while the DJs build up the crowd's energy.

The lineup is rich and includes internationally renowned Detroit poet jessica Care moore as the host. At around 9:30 Invincible takes the stage with their Outer Spaces project collaborators Las Krudas and Climbing Poetree. Collectively, Outer Spaces self-identify as "a brigade of shape-shifting, gender-bending artists and activists."[1] Queer-identified, these artists aimed at taking audiences to the outer limits of their experience. The crowd embodies multiple hip hop aesthetics, including call and response, context specific dance forms, and rhyming along with familiar lyrics, while artists use Spanish and English interchangeably. The audience flocks to the floor; anytime a Detroit artist, song, or sound is referenced, the crowd hollers. Likewise, when Outer Spaces makes statements about queering hip hop, the audience responds with hoots, grooves, and snaps.

Other times, the crowd pushes back on the hosts and emcees. When jessica Care moore feels ignored as she performs, she throws pages of her poetry at the audience. Locals communicate nonverbal sentiments like "my bad" by touching their chests and sporting a hip hop style bow. Newcomers use their hands, crudely gesturing dismay about moore's flying poetry. Attitude is met with both resistance and respect. Similar audience behavior has been documented in ethnographic theorizing about rap battles in LA's hip hop underground. H. Samy Alim, Jooyoung Lee, and Lauren Masson Carris document how emcees not only rhyme skillfully, but also monitor audiences and survey them strategically.[2] Emcees surveil audiences to smash support for other artists. While we did not witness this practice, we do see the crowd answer and refuse the emcee's call. This moment that crashes over the crowd like a wave embodies Simon Frith's argument that music has a life of its own that is always shared by artist and audience and supports his insistence that affect is central to the production of sound and the feelings that audiences attach to it.[3] We see this in action; we feel the tensions just as we become caught up in the audience-artist synergy that produces embodied, poetic energy.

By this time the space is packed and one can't avoid the sway. Adults of all ages, from hippies to hipsters, with diverse racial and ethnic backgrounds are present. Next, Foundation artists Mahogany Jones, Nique Love Rhodes, Insite the Riot and Deidre "D.S. Sense" Smith perform a set together. The beats are bangin' and each artist features their favorite tracks off their latest projects. In typical Detroit style, hands are in the air doing the Errol Flynn[4] and feet are two-steppin'. Shortly after midnight hip hop and R&B artist Mae Day takes the stage to close out the night. Again, the crowd does not respond to the vibe of her call, exiting the dance floor. Mae Day draws her own fan base, but it is not the the Foundation's sustaining audience. The energy dipped after Foundation artists left the stage. As in many hip hop crowds, when people are not feeling it, they head to the bar, or to other gathering spaces.

Throughout the night, all of hip hop's elements are at play. Mary Mar, aka B-Girl Ma-Ma of Hardcore Detroit, and Martha Quezada of Motor City Rockers tear up the floor with their crews. Foundation member Nicole Carter has easels and corkboard canvases set up all over the space. To the beat of the music she paints Afrocentric women in different hip hop poses on the sides of the dance floor. Stacyé J and DJ XO work the ones and twos while we stand amazed at how the evening has come together—so many women, queer, and gender-nonconforming artists and fans rocking all the elements of hip hop. The fifth element, Knowledge of self and community, is emphasized not only in the music, but in the community-building messages that come through jessica Care moore's hype, artists' stories, and Piper's words throughout the night. This evening marks a peak point in the Foundation's life, both artistically and organizationally. Hundreds of people, twenty vendors, and one local television station attend the anniversary party. The event will be felt and remembered as one of the best that the community produced.

THIS BOOK

This book is about the Foundation, a nonprofit arts and culture organization that sought to change the gendered practices at work in Detroit's hip hop underground from 2009 to 2016. Before the Foundation's emergence women struggled to get on stage, to be taken seriously, and to be appreciated by industry forces, local promoters, and audiences. Our work focuses on the sites where the collective existed as well as the larger context of Detroit that grounds the lives of its performing artists. Planning, organizing, and performing took place all over the city. To fully understand the work of the Foundation and the artists who supported it, one has to grasp the current conditions that Detroit is facing. Given that Detroit is a Black city, our book makes explicit the multiple intersections of identity that shape the cultural productions of the artists we came to know over seven years of engagement. *Women Rapping Revolution* argues that the hip hop underground is a crucial site where Black women forge new subjectivities and claim self-care as a principle of community organizing. The Foundation's community-building practices operated from the assumption that self-care is a form of cultural welfare in the lives of its artists. Hip hop and activism are intersecting forces that shape a vital, vibrant sector of Detroit's hip hop underground.

This ethnography embodies hip hop's roots as a community-building enterprise. We provide alternative narratives that question the relations of power, patriarchy, consumerism, and violence that have come to dominate the commercial hip hop industry. We argue that the emergence of the Foundation created conditions where women organized and strategized ways to create stages for themselves and other artists: the collective showcased skills, aesthetics, and identities in the making and yet the Foundation was "bigger than hip hop."[5] Many members were and remain cultural workers. Their cultural production opens new ways to imagine what counts as community organizing and political work. In other words, cultural performance creates avenues where new world views can emerge. Our work with the Foundation articulates the dynamics of grassroots organizing situated within an arts community. In so doing, we reframe both popular and scholarly conceptualizations of women in hip hop. We contribute a much needed focus on Black women's subjectivity in the life and making of hip hop culture.

Over time, we came to understand that self-care shapes Black female subjectivity in the hip hop underground. For many, it is both a philosophy and a toolkit for survival—a form of cultural welfare.[6] This concept generates acts of self-other love and messages that sustain the possibilities of relational life, rather than sour, ideologically produced excoriations of "the welfare state" that dominate neoliberal public discourse. Self-care reclaims welfare as community-based practices that function as wellsprings of personal, social, and cultural health in the broadest sense. In many ways, our book shows readers in vivid detail what self-care looks like and how the practices that sustain it ultimately reach to community and larger social forces. Given that so much of the work that women in the hip hop community do is tied to care of youth, elders, and bringing the neighbor back into the hood, we ask, how does self-care become a politics of survival? In contemporary neoliberal Detroit, the politics of survival creates the conditions for resistance. In this context, self-care is far from solipsistic; it is a politics based on "waging love"[7] and getting "On My Detroit Everything."[8]

Although we focus predominantly on emcees, we also interviewed and illustrate how poets, DJs, organizers, b-girls, and others contribute to the aesthetic and political dimensions of Detroit's hip hop underground. This diverse community of cultural revolutionaries is messy. The Foundation centered on women, but not all members were/are women identified. Some embrace the language of feminism, while others prefer a gender-justice orientation that creates space for gender-nonconforming participants. Others support women but do not see their work as necessarily for or about women. However, all of the individuals that we have come to know see gender as one among many issues that needs more thought in hip hop communities. The Foundation used art and activism to construct, articulate, and disseminate ideologies about identity, community, difference, nation, and environment. They forged new social formations that assumed cooperative collaborative economics with a new social imaginary for what social relations can mean in public life. In all of its endeavors, members lived along an ethic that renowned local activist Grace Lee Boggs endorsed: "The idea that the world is 'made'—in a very extended and complex sense, of course—through the actions of ordinary people also meant that it could be unmade and remade."[9] In other words, everyday people have the power and responsibility to change existing problems, but it takes courage and imagination to foster hope and a willingness to unthink and reimagine old structures that continue to reproduce themselves.

WOMEN IN HIP HOP

Women's battles for respect and recognition are not unique to Detroit but tied to the larger history of women's systemic marginalization in hip hop. Born on the streets of the South Bronx in the 1970s, hip hop emerged from block parties organized by Black and Brown youth, many of whom struggled against unemployment, poverty, and gang violence. The elements of these parties collectively defined hip hop culture. DJs kept the beats going while emcees hyped up the crowd, b-boys/b-girls rocked the dance floor, and graffiti artists created flyers and beautified spaces with their signature artwork. Afrika Bambaataa's Zulu Nation popularized Knowledge—of self and community—as hip hop's fifth element. For many of its innovators, this DIY culture was a creative outlet and productive alternative to gang culture and violence. Hip hop historian Jeff Chang describes it as "an expression of a new generation of outcast youth whose worldview felt authentic, original and liberating."[10] Despite their involvement from the culture's inception, women's contributions are routinely marginalized if not altogether written out of hip hop histories. This is not only true in the mainstream but also in the hip hop underground.

In our work with the Foundation we have witnessed the ramifications of women being sidelined in hip hop for nearly half a century. They range from young women feeling apprehensive about getting on the mic for the first time, to blanket statements like "I just don't like female emcees," to outright contempt for the collective daring to host a night dedicated to women in hip hop in the first place. Scholars like Gwendolyn Pough, Marcyliena Morgan, and Jessica Nydia Pabón-Colón document varying ways that women's contributions to hip hop are devalued.[11] In the early oughts, Pough called into question Nelson George's overall assessment of women's contributions to hip hop. In his book *Hip Hop America,* George makes a provocative claim. Despite his discussion of the artistic output of rappers MC Lyte, Queen Latifah, Lauryn Hill, and Foxy Brown, he candidly remarks, "if none of these female artists had ever made a record, hip hop's development would have been no different."[12] If anything, Nelson's claim motivated artists, practitioners, and scholars alike to respond and bring into view performance, aesthetics, and politics that address not only racial disparities but also gendered practices that need rethinking. The battle for legitimacy continues across all the elements, and especially in women-centered spaces. Examining such spaces, graffiti scholar Pabón-Colón contends that "the tenor of dismissals ranges from neoliberal postfeminist discourse (the event is passé, girls and women have equal rights) to condescension (girls aren't good enough to participate in major jams, so these spaces are tolerable) to hostility (events are separatist or ghettoizing) to total lack of interest."[13] We have also witnessed that women are welcomed as consumers and supporters, but they face opposition as cultural producers in their own right.

Writing in 1987, Nancy Guevara was an early critic of the gender discrimination women in hip hop faced from their male peers as well as from mainstream media sources that omitted or distorted their contributions to hip hop culture.[14] To counter the male-centered narratives that had already taken hold, she documented the contributions of women graffiti writers like Lady Pink and Lady Heart, rappers including the US Girls and Roxanne Shanté, as well as B-Girl Baby Love and the Dynamic Dolls. Over the course of our seven years of fieldwork, we have seen women engaging with all of hip hop's elements in Detroit. They are rappers, DJs, b-girls, graffiti writers, and organizers, and yet, as Guevara and Pabón-Colón writing thirty years apart assert, the creative roles of women in hip hop continue to be challenged and dismissed in both commercial arenas and the hip hop underground.[15] Foundation artists provide complex ways to think about social issues while pushing the boundaries of hip hop's aesthetics in terms of lyrics, beats, and presentation of self. Their unique aesthetics, politics, and gender work are grounded in and respond to the contemporary forces reshaping Detroit.

DETROIT'S CONTEMPORARY CRISIS

Our study is located in a Black city; as such, facing race is both necessary and fruitful. The artists and organizers who form the basis of our work shake off old logics that produced insidious forms of racial reasoning. They choke out ideas that came to fruition during the United States's history of settler colonialism, like eugenics, social darwinism, and redlining policies, and which have taken on new forms in contemporary "postracial" imaginations. Race is but one of the amalgam of social identity categories that shape the struggle of Foundation members. Surviving race is a reality given the historical oppressions that shape the nation—and Detroit in particular. Race theory produced under the guise of science during late colonialism led to egregious white supremacist practices that have morphed into subtleties that dehumanize Blackness to this day. In the face of continuing struggle, Black women continue to speak out against racist practices and about the need for social transformation. In 2013, Alicia Garza, Opal Tometi, and Patrisse Cullors created the Black Lives Matter social media platform that has brought together dozens of organizations. Barbara Ransby[16] describes what has become the Black Lives Matter Movement [BLMM] as a "Black-led class struggle—informed by, grounded in, and bolstered by Black feminist politics."[17] Even before BLMM and the #MeToo movements gained traction, the women of the Foundation were fighting for women's legitimacy on many levels including their roles in hip hop and cultural politics. Their goals, artistic output, and community work respond directly to Detroit's contemporary context.

The gender, race, and class issues that women in the hip hop underground experience are intrinsically linked to the city's history. At its population peak in 1950, Detroit had 1.85 million residents and was a mixed-race city. Its population now hovers around 677,000, and it is 83 percent Black. Women making hip hop not only have to deal with the cis-male heteromasculinity that dominates in the hip hop underground, but also navigating daily life in a city that reflects the consequences of institutionalized racism, white flight, postindustrial economic decline, and gentrification. This constellation of conditions find form in urban renewal plans. There is a disconnect between the social actors who create urban renewal plans versus the residents and citizens who have to live their consequences. The Foundation fought against these ideological practices in two ways: one, they were actively involved in organizations that resist and reframe unacceptable conditions; and second, their artistry provided aesthetic narratives that gave voice to their world views. In this sense artists become organic intellectuals and cultural diplomats.[18] It is ironic that as the city mourned the effects of the 1967 rebellion,[19] corporate elites were planning a new, whitewashed vision for Detroit.

On the eve of the fiftieth anniversary of the 1967 rebellion, billionaire Dan Gilbert's Bedrock real estate company elected to publish a telling ad. The sign filled windows along the ground level of a historic twelve-story building on Woodward Ave. It consisted of the company's logo and a photograph of mostly white people, along with the phrase "See Detroit Like We Do" in large white lettering. In a city that is overwhelmingly Black, recovering from imposed bankruptcy, and what the United Nations deemed inhumane practices of ongoing water shutoffs, this ad is telling. It provides a striking example of the machinations of gentrification; as such, it is no surprise that immediate and vehement critique followed its release. The display was installed on a Friday and by Monday morning Gilbert had apologized and killed the marketing slogan. Despite his backtracking, the advertisement raises red flags about Gilbert's intentions. It is another layer of evidence that reveals the workings of institutionalized power; it fueled citizens' concerns that revitalization efforts are exclusively focused on attracting young, educated, white suburbanites to the city's downtown and midtown centers.

Detroit is not a blank slate, and yet, the colonial myth that its people need wealthy white men to save them continues to reproduce itself. At the 2019 Oscars ceremony, for example, Green Book director Peter Farrelly gave a shout out to Shinola as he accepted his award for Best Original Screenplay, exclaiming, "Shinola watches! Unbelievable! They're saving Detroit!" The luxury goods maker from Texas had no history with the city prior to launching the company in 2011. In the country's poorest big city, where 35 percent of the population lives in poverty, claims that the white billionaires from Texas behind the Shinola brand and its thousand-dollar wristwatches are saving Detroit are offensive. These revitalization practices, steeped in racially-motivated ideologies, are not lost on Detroiters. The city's Black and Latinx populations are paying the price for neoliberal governmentality and corporate recovery. Gentrification practices are wreaking havoc on their lives, displacing them to corners of the city where they lack transportation and community.

Knowledge of this history and the contemporary forces at play in Detroit are necessary to understand the relationships between the people, politics, music, and community building practices we engage in *Women Rapping Revolution*. Our work is grounded in an understanding of the larger structures that govern regulations and relationships between the state, citizens, private enterprise, and policymakers. Currently, there are two sociopolitical imaginaries competing for legitimacy and resources in Detroit: a top-down, for-profit capitalist view and a ground-up, citizen-driven one. The first includes the people who operate the institutional dynamics of urban planning, foundations, utility distribution, housing, and public space at large; the Other Detroit lives the consequences of these social engineering tactics of neoliberal whiteness. Members of the Foundation, its supporters, and the populations that are continuously being pushed away from the city's center of commerce and luxury experience the ramifications affecting today's Detroit. We have come to know artists who have been affected and whose children have been harmed by school closings, bad rental property agreements, and water shutoffs. One of the members of the Foundation was arrested when she defended her neighbor, trying to stop the city from turning off her water.

In the early 2000s, ruin porn was the face of Detroit; the city was the center of projects of exploitation and sensationalized media. Filmmakers, photographers, and pundits from near and far regularly journeyed to the city to sensationalize, exploit, and capitalize off of its misfortunes. Their obsession with the aestheticization of poverty came at the expense of the people who lived here.[20] Foundation artists are not only aware of ruin-porn representations, but they are also conscious of language and images that sustain the new face of Detroit's "come back." They resist obvious abasement and the coded language of neoliberalism. Words like "safety," "security," "resilience," and urban renewal" are used to signify that the new Detroit is sanitized for upwardly mobile professionals, most of whom are white.

In the aftermath of bankruptcy, a complex and contradictory set of narratives about revitalization emerged. They reflect two competing visions for what the city's future should be. Detroit's redevelopment plans have undermined and ignored the city's Black population as far back as the 1950s, when the Black Bottom and Paradise Valley neighborhoods were destroyed to make way for interstate construction. Racist practices including redlining, targeted tax foreclosures and water shutoffs continue to be aggressively instigated to displace poorer, older, mostly Black and Brown populations in an effort to make way for more desirable residents: younger, whiter, and wealthier. The same capitalist forces that performers Invincible and Finale accuse of contributing to Detroit's systemic demise in the 1990s and early 2000s on their track "Locusts"—which we analyze in chapter 2—returned to buy back property once its value hit rock bottom and was a safe bet for maximum return on investment. These financial transactions are proving to have massive payoffs. At their helm are financiers and developers like Dan Gilbert, John Hantz, and the Ilitch Family. Headquartered in the Fox Theater building in Detroit, Ilitch Holdings Inc.'s businesses include Little Caesars Pizza, the Detroit Red Wings, and the Detroit Tigers. The parent company's subsidiaries also manage a number of theaters and professional sports facilities. The Hantz Group owns a myriad of financial services firms, from banking to health insurance. Of them all, Gilbert, founder of Quicken Loans and Rock Ventures, is Detroit's wealthiest entrepreneur and the mover and shaker of the city's urban development.

Taking advantage of cheap real estate, Dan Gilbert relocated Quicken Loans and thousands of its employees from the suburbs to downtown in 2010. The mortgage company's relocation jumpstarted the development of "Detroit 2.0"—an initiative to rebrand the city as a Midwestern hub of tech-savvy entrepreneurial startups. It was estimated that Detroit had nearly 150,000 vacant and abandoned land parcels and that approximately twenty square miles of the city's occupiable land was vacant.[21] As the city was falling into bankruptcy in 2012, the city council approved the sale of 140 aces of public land (some of which was inhabited by residents) to the controversial Hantz Farms. The corporation paid eight cents per square foot ($300.00 per lot) for one of the largest urban land acquisitions in the history of any US city. There was widespread opposition to the deal from those involved with Detroit's urban agriculture movement, who felt the city should support smaller farmers who grow food for their livelihoods. Food justice advocates have declared the deal a "case of top-down environmental renewal versus bottom-up environmental justice and self-determination."[22] Artists we have come to work with have made food justice one of the many commitments that they speak on in their music. The track "Legendary," on which we focus in chapter 5, juxtaposes urban life with urban farming.

There is substantial evidence backing up the claim that redevelopment strategies in Detroit are driving both gentrification and abandonment. In early 2013, Governor Rick Snyder appointed Kevyn Orr as Emergency Financial Manager to oversee the city's Chapter 9 bankruptcy filing. Detroit's claim is the largest municipal bankruptcy filing in US history and Orr was given carte blanche to make decisions through his tenure, which lasted until December 2014. In his role, he attempted but failed to privatize the Detroit Institute of Arts [DIA], the key iconic institution for public art in the city; and succeeded in handing Belle Isle—a recreational landmark in the city—to the state. As with all state parks, vehicles now have to pay to enter. Prior to this shift, it was a free-to-the-public, popular recreational facility and on hot summer days it was populated by Detroiters picnicking and dancing to music emanating from sound system after sound system. The city's bankruptcy settlement also included pension cuts and reduced health insurance coverage for retired city workers. Bankruptcy became the means to displace African American political power, attack unions, and shift city assets into private hands.

Detroit land that has not been privatized outright is increasingly under surveillance. With the procurement of over one hundred properties in the city, Gilbert's Bedrock Real Estate Services has developed a state-of-the-art surveillance system that consists of more than five hundred cameras in downtown Detroit. This includes the policing of the Federal Reserve Building which houses the *Detroit Free Press*. In some cases, surveillance equipment has also been installed without permission on buildings that Gilbert does not own.[23] The net effect of Gilbert's efforts to surveil his sprawling downtown footprint is that cameras and private security guards now dominate public space in the city's bustling downtown. Activists Antonio Rafael and Matthew Irwin note how even the QLINE/M-1 Rail streetcar, constructed in 2017, was not built for Detroiters; rather, Gilbert's investment in it enabled his Rocket Fiber company to install gigabit internet technology underneath the streetcar line in an effort to attract tech workers and "self-styled urban pioneers eager to

gentrify/settle the city."[24] Those who challenge design-intensive development and surveillance are cast as naïve people who do not understand
business and the protection that public-private sanctioned spying fosters.

Clearly, Detroit's revitalization is extremely complex. In the eyes of
many city officials, urban planners, and private developers, attracting
tech entrepreneurs and other members of the creative class is key to
rebuilding. Most people understand the benefits of bringing new people
and corporations to the city, but the exclusive investment of resources
into the 7.2 square miles of the city's downtown and midtown core dis-
enfranchises the citizens who do not live along this corridor. In our conversations with poet/activist Tawana "Honeycomb" Petty, she disclosed
some of her recent everyday experiences at neighborhood restaurants
and cafes that she has been going to for years. Before it was rebranded
as Midtown in 2000, the neighborhood just north of downtown was
known as the Cass Corridor. Historically, the Corridor was an artists'
haven where writers and rockers lived and *Creem* magazine was born in
the 1960s. Since its renaming, the area has been refashioned with trendy
micro-breweries, restaurants, luxury baby clothing stores, and boutique
bookshops and yoga studios. For long-term residents the area has
become unrecognizable. Petty shared with us her experience of feeling
out of place at sites that she has frequented for many years:

> We used to go there every morning. I ordered my food to go, and I was sitting
> there waiting for my food. I said, 'good morning.' [The waitress] came back
> and slipped the receipt to me and I said, 'good morning.' She looked at me and
> kept walking. The person brought the food out and she said, 'is this for her!?'
> He said, 'I think so.' She goes through the boxes, hands me my change, and
> then she says to the person next to me, 'Is everything good?' I said, 'I said good
> morning three times.' I said 'What is your problem?!' She didn't say anything.
> 'I've come in here fifty times, what is your problem? Did I do something wrong?'
> She didn't say anything and people were looking at me like the angry black
> woman. I was mad at myself later for letting her get under my skin like that.
>
> All of the changes are bad like that because all of our history is being
> wiped out. There are schools I went to that aren't there anymore. There are
> places I can't google anymore, and I'm only thirty-eight. It's schools, institu-
> tions, streets. They changed names of streets and whole communities. My
> thing is, you know, at least archive it somewhere to where we can find it. It's
> hard to deal with it. But if people treat you with dignity and respect, then we
> can try to figure this out. But when you walk into a space and people treat
> you like a [different] species, it makes it that much more difficult.[25]

To be a life-long resident and be treated as an invisible imposter is part
of the breakdown of neighborhood continuity. The renaming of neigh-

borhoods and influx of new business and residents changes the dynamic of a community, especially in a site with a history of racial tension and violence and government sanctioned redlining practices that protected white interests. Such gentrification practices write over place, identity, and economic exchanges as well as erase memory. The end result is a problematic palimpsest.

Foundation member Nique Love Rhodes's experiences living and working in and around the city during this time of transition adds another layer to the story:

> I was just having a chat with Insite [the Riot] about this last week and we were talking about how like, yeah it's cool. I can go pick up a kale salad and that's cool and in the summer I'm going to be riding my bike around and that's cool and all but at what expense, you know? People, businesses have been kicked out for this shop to be. You know what I'm saying? It's about being aware of that and a lot of people aren't aware . . . . The worst part is that people don't think it's a problem. Or the conversation that, well, nobody's doing anything with that space to begin with. Well, let's analyze why they couldn't do anything with that space because of how banks treat small business owners of color and with loans and all these other opportunities.[26]

Rhodes weighs in on the practices through which Black Detroiters are left out of the decision making of redevelopment plans and processes, although they are the very people who live the consequences of urban renewal.

The Foundation, as well as its partnership with the 5e Gallery, cultivated community-centered citizenship. They created spaces and conditions that brought together a multigenerational nexus of practitioners and fans in the midst of these changes. Artists and organizers who were connected to them have continued to foster community through their music, art, and ongoing organizing efforts. In summer 2018 Nique Love Rhodes and Insite the Riot hosted the "D.Cipher Music Series" in the Lafayette Park neighborhood just east of downtown. The ten-week music series created a platform for a diverse range of local artists to perform. By example, the series uplifted women and Blackness across genres including blues, jazz, rock, hip hop, R&B, soul, neo-soul, future soul, house, and reggae. The audience was multigenerational and diverse.

MUSIC AND POLITICS

In the track "Shapeshifters," Detroit emcee Invincible insists that "music's not a mirror to reflect reality/It's a hammer with which we shape it." Their assumption that music makers shape culture, including aesthetic sensibilities and political action, is akin to Simon Frith's argument that music is not so much an expression of any internal idea or reality, but a mode of production. Musical practices create lyrical structure, sonic cacophony, and audience action. Invincible speaks on what we see as a circuit of sonic pleasure, the articulation of ideology and/or its critique, and affect. Affect is often what binds audience and artist; thus chants, call and response, and dance moves are practices that exist in circulation. Artists produce the outline of action while audiences produce energy, clapbacks, and calls of their own. In other words, music and culture, artists and audiences, are both produced by and producers of particular social and political visions.

The multitude and magnitude of political struggles that African Americans have experienced have inevitably bled into the art that Black Detroiters produce, from the early blues to bebop jazz, Motown's pop-inflected soul music, the synthesized sounds of techno, and present-day hip hop. We use the term "inevitably" because of the extensive history of African American music and culture's deep-seated relationship to social and political movements. Shana Redmond insists that "within the African diaspora, music functions as a method of rebellion, revolution, and future visions that disrupt and challenge the manufactured differences used to dismiss, detain, and destroy communities."[27] Since the time of slavery, to the Civil Rights era, and the present day hip hop movement, Black music "has served as a laboratory for the interplay of racial solidarity and struggle."[28] Reiland Rabaka goes so far as to say that African American music has consistently functioned as "the *mouthpieces* for [Blacks'] socio-political aspirations and frustrations, their socio-political organizations and nationally-networked movements."[29] Here, we illuminate the varied relationships between music, politics, and community-building efforts that Detroiters have cultivated over time. While not always overt and, in the case of Motown, not necessarily intended, the innovative sounds that have and continue to emanate from the city have often reflected the material realities, struggles, and hope of its people. Through telling the stories of communities, music documents everyday struggles, suggests alternative ways of being,[30] and gives people the power to envision what Jayna Brown describes as material possibility.[31] As we demonstrate throughout *Women Rapping Revolution,* the hip hop music and culture that the participants in our study make and support are intimately connected to their material and political realities as Black women who live, work, and create in the city. They are unequivocal in their assertions that Detroit's unique conditions have influenced their consciousness and artistry.[32] In other words, the state of the city, their worldviews, and the change they are working towards, are all embodied in the form, feel, and messaging of their music.

Writing on bebop jazz innovations in the 1940s and 1950s, Anthony Macías notes that "on the whole, the Motor City musical milieu nurtured a range of African American expressive forms and practices and community-based cultural work."[33] Detailing the connections between the two, he explains that "the music, style, and philosophy of Bebop musicians critiqued the ideological justifications used to naturalize an economic system that perpetuated racial and social inequities."[34] Like many Detroit-based hip hop artists today, bebop musicians also purposefully rejected the racist, commercial industry in favor of experimentation that pushed artistic and political boundaries.

A decade later Motown Records redefined the sonic and racial contours of popular music on a national level, positioning African Americans at its center. Berry Gordy purposefully distanced the label from overtly political messages; musically, his intentions were to create songs that would appeal to the masses, namely white audiences. And yet, by the summer of 1967 Martha and the Vandellas' hit "Dancing in the Street" had been appropriated as a civil rights anthem, not only in the context of the rebellion that ensued in the city that summer but nationwide. Suzanne E. Smith likens the bind Motown was in from this point on to "a tightrope that the company walked between its allegiance to the black struggle and its desire to establish itself in corporate America."[35] Even though commercial success was the label's top priority, Smith writes that by 1970 "the 'commercial' and the 'political' aspects of any black cultural product could no longer be mutually exclusive—even at Motown."[36] Consequently, Motown created a new imprint, Black Forum, as a place where African American spoken word artists could document and voice Black struggles.

In the 1980s and 1990s, Detroit's musical innovations were most famously heard in the melodies, beats, and bass lines emitting from synthesizers and drum machines that reflected the city's post-industrial landscape. The groundbreaking duo Cybotron, consisting of techno producers Juan Atkins and Richard Davis, were electronic music pioneers who merged (white) electro and (Black) funk in ways that marked "a negotiation and subversion of whiteness and black cultural expectations."[37] In the 1990s, the techno collective and independent label Underground Resistance [UR] continued Detroit's legacy of producing electronic music that was not only sonically innovative but also politically engaged. It characterized itself as

> a label for a movement. A movement that wants change by sonic revolution. We urge you to join the resistance and help us combat the mediocre audio and visual programming that is being fed to the inhabitants of Earth, this programming is stagnating the minds of the people; building a wall between races and preventing world peace. It is this wall we are going to smash. By using the untapped energy potential of sound we are going to destroy this wall much the same as certain frequencies shatter glass.[38]

Not only did the group/label take an anti-commercial stance, but aesthetically they fused early techno and industrial music to produce a more aggressive sound that was a stark contrast to early Detroit Techno. The group openly claimed an "allegiance with the hood" which they worked into some of their releases, including *Message to the Majors,* which included, printed on the record's label, a "Message to all murderers on the Detroit Police Force—We'll see you in hell!" It was also dedicated to Malice Green, a Black Detroiter who has recently died in police custody.[39] This provocative track was in play long before the explosion of the BLMM. Though committed to fighting police brutality and racial injustice, UR's all-male membership and aggressive sound, in tandem with its militaristic vocabulary and imagery, also contributed to techno's developing masculine narratives. Few doors were opened to women in electronic dance music at the time; if anything, one could easily argue that the group reinforced dominant hegemonic norms regarding gendered assumptions about technology and the production of electronic music.

In a city without major label investment, techno's DIY aesthetic and business acumen also fueled a burgeoning hip hop scene which saw the rise of acts like Kalimah "Nikki D./Eboni and Her Business" Johnson, EZ-B and DJ Los, Kaos & Mystro, Red Bone, A. W. O. L., Esham, Boss, Detroit's Most Wanted, Slum Village, J Dilla, and Eminem.[40] Today, it is impossible to talk about one hip hop community in Detroit. Some artists have been inspired to produce more experimental or politically motivated music and events, while others gravitate to more commercial sounds and messages. This is not to say that the two are mutually exclusive, but that divides exist. As we describe in detail in chapter 1, overall conditions make it difficult for women to participate as cultural producers in their own right. Presently, a range of women support the sexist culture that inspired Piper Carter to start the Foundation, while others are committed to its overhaul. Even within the Foundation and its orbit, artists' political interests and the degrees to which they are committed to them vary. They include gender and race issues, concerns about the environment, gentrification, and the politics of violence and police brutality. Like the artists and organizers that preceded them, Foundation members and supporters continue a Detroit arts legacy committed to the preservation of history, mentorship, and sharing their visions for change. Our work helps illuminate the deep relationship that music and other forms of cultural production share with politics through the lives, art, and activism that Foundation members bring to their communities.

THE FOUNDATION

The Foundation constituted a hip hop collective in a hyper-local movement working to uplift women and the larger community through sonic, aesthetic, and bodily warfare in spaces across the city. On stages, dance floors, parks, bars, restaurants, galleries, fundraisers, and community centers, its members shaped new forms of awareness, reminded the world that Detroit is still a chocolate city, and all the while made space for women to produce their style of hip hop. Its mission statement reads,

> This weekly event [is part of] a movement [that] focuses on redefining the vital role of women in hip hop. Our mission is to educate and empower the community through sharing love of the arts, inspiring change and growth, building leadership, and influencing the perceptions and roles of women in hip hop for current and future generations.[41]

The Great Recession of 2008 was the context in which the Foundation emerged. The loss that came from economic collapse was deeply felt among the poorest populations of Detroit. Foreclosures were commonplace and property values plummeted. Emergency financial management was yet to unfold. The city was already selling off its holdings and services. These practices paved the way for entrenchment of neoliberal privatization. This is the context that Piper Carter returned to when she moved back to Detroit from New York City to take care of her mother.

Reacquainting herself with Detroit's hip hop scene, Piper asked her friends, "where the women at?" Men commanded all the elements in the underground. Motivated to change hip hop's gender dynamics, she sought out emcees who were well-known in the community. Piper contacted established emcees Invincible/ill Weaver and Miz Korona. Both artists offered to help organize an open mic night dedicated to women in hip hop. Miz Korona agreed to be the first host and Piper solicited the all-women band Ying to perform. Over time, a range of performers who practiced all of the elements of hip hop claimed the Foundation's stage. While getting women onstage was always the goal, men, youth, and elders all participated regularly at Foundation events.

After one year of weekly open mic nights Piper expanded the vision of the collective. She recruited a multigenerational pool of women involved in local activism in her efforts to cultivate relationships with other like-minded community organizers. Most Foundation members were African American, though some Latina, white, and Asian American women were also members of the group. Most were emcees, though some were DJs, visual artists, and b-girls. While the ages of members ranged from early twenties to mid-fifties, the collective devoted special attention to youth activism. The Foundation was a culturally relevant, political and social resource center for youth and adults who love and live hip hop culture. Each artist that we have come to know has a fierce bond with the city; they have deeply personal and collective identifications with Detroit and its history. The chapters that follow illustrate the intricate role that Detroit plays in Foundation artists' work. Detroit's well-being is a community effort and Foundation artists are vocal about their visions and those of Black Detroiters who have weathered its storms. Removing Detroit from the work of Foundation artists is akin to making hip hop without a bass line or a sixteen-bar verse—it is inconceivable.

The work of the Foundation is much "bigger than hip hop." At base, this project illuminates the cultural production of the artists affiliated with the Foundation. It also documents the relationships the collective advances between cultural production and community building. Operating from principles of self-care, Foundation members weave community building into their cultural practices—the product of which yields a new paradigm for cultural organizing. Cultural workers are those that employ self-care to build relationships, heal communities, and cultivate cooperative communication practices.

Drawing on seven years of fieldwork, we detail Foundation artists' relationships to Detroit and their right to claim it. In the chapters that follow, Detroit is akin to a character in a novel much more than a backdrop. This is true not only for our work but also for the artists we feature. Mobilizing hip hop's aesthetics and revolutionary toolkits, the artists witness and testify to issues that the city and its people face. They speak on urban decay and renewal as well as neoliberal planning tactics that privilege upwardly mobile, white professionals. The escalating investment in businesses like fine dining establishments, new sports arenas, as well as loft and condo real estate leave longterm Detroiters displaced and outside the reach of urban renewal.

Self-care is one response to urban removal. It leads to reclaiming subjectivity so as to include vulnerability in the form of power; thus, a major construct we contribute is the notion of the Vulnerable Maverick, which stretches the contemporary literature about scripts that control and open doors for women in hip hop. The Vulnerable Maverick is a framework for analyzing Black women's subjectivity in their roles as cultural citizens and producers. The pairing of vulnerability with a maverick's attitude and power rescues vulnerability from weakness. It is a response and contrast to the controlling image known as the Strong Black Woman, which forecloses the possibility of vulnerability. We expound on this concept in chapter 4 to create a deeper understanding of the complexities of Black female subjectivity within the context of Detroit's hip hop underground.

Chapter 1, "Detroit Hip Hop and the Rise of the Foundation," provides a detailed history of Detroit's poorly documented hip hop underground and the conditions that led to the birth of the Foundation. In chapter 2, "Hip Hop Sounds and Sensibilities in Post-Bankruptcy Detroit," we locate the specific ways that women emcees are making claims to the city. Using neoliberalism as a framework, this chapter examines anthem songs that critique the politics of abandonment ideologically framed as "urban renewal." Given that gender figures so prominently in this book, chapter 3, "Negotiating Gender Queer Identity Formation," considers the ways that members of the Foundation and the men who support them navigate institutional and relational pressures that bear on gender politics. Examining beats, rhymes, and processes of production, we dive deep into the concept of the Vulnerable Maverick in chapter 4. The topics these emcees address and the identities they forge serve as productive, complex, intersectional routes that reveal the deep layers of subjectivity that women making hip hop live. Chapter 5, "'Legendary,' Environmental Justice, and Collaborative Cultural Production," pivots from earlier chapters in that it documents the collaborative production of the track and video for "Legendary." Grounded in the emergent literature of eco-musicology, we situate Black female subjectivity and hip hop in the heart of environmental justice. Hip hop aesthetics are mobilized to provides viewers with a different understanding of the city, one that is gendered female and encourages positive solutions rooted in creativity, strength, and solidarity. Our final chapter, "Hip Hop Activism in Action," details specific ways in which hip hop's Knowledge element is deeply entrenched in the local work of Detroit's cultural organizers. Focusing on three events—Dilla Youth Day, Denim Day, and the Foundation's Women in Hip Hop Conference—we showcase the community work that artists accomplish in and through their cultural practices.

Detroit Hip Hop and the Rise of the Foundation

Detroit's musical history is rich and hip hop figures prominently in its evolution. This chapter situates the Foundation in the context of the local hip hop underground and in particular, the development of inclusive spaces like the 5e Gallery that privileged hip hop's Knowledge element. We illustrate how these changes in the late 2000s were in contrast to the hard, raw, and male-centered battle rap culture that dominated in the 1990s and made it difficult for Black women like Miz Korona and Red Bone, as well as white male artists like Eminem, to be accepted at venues like the influential Hip Hop Shop. From here we move on to the Foundation's efforts to create more inclusive spaces for women and the dynamics of its weekly open night, which the collective hosted for five years, from 2009–2014. We conclude with discussion of the objections, struggles, and successes of the Foundation during their years of operation between 2009 and 2016.

In the 1980s and 1990s the city garnered an international musical reputation for its innovative electro and techno sounds. It took some time for hip hop to gain momentum in this musical milieu, but over time hip hop music and culture began to permeate the city and its people. Local emcees and producers drew on influences from East and West Coast rap as well as the legendary radio sets of local DJs The Electrifying Mojo and Jeff "The Wizard" Mills. In a time before mass media conglomeration and conformity, Mojo and Mills's sets featured everything from new wave and soul to classic rock.[1] Their eclecticism, along with

Detroit's rich musical history, inspired its hip hop trajectory. During this period, Detroit artists received some national attention and radio play but chart-topping hits from the region were sparse.[2] As the nineties wore on, the hip hop acts who garnered the most accolades were white and included the likes of Kid Rock, Insane Clown Posse, and Eminem.

The standardization of radio programming and the collapse of national rap tours were two conditions that led to the cultivation of hip hop scenes outside of Los Angeles and New York. Carleton Gholz[3] singles out several venues for producing early artists like Slum Village and Eminem who are now canonized as Detroit legends. We came to know sites like Saint Andrew's Hall downtown, the Rhythm Kitchen on the Eastside, and the Hip Hop Shop on the Westside as having the most impact. It was at fashion designer Maurice Malone and his partner Jerome Mongo's Hip Hop Shop on Seven Mile Road that legendary producer J Dilla hung out with emcees like Eminem and Proof. Gholz explains,

> The blueprint for the shop was the sale of Malone's jeans and other hip hop culture specific commodities with open mic battles on Saturday afternoon. B-boys danced in the shop, while on Saturday evenings from 5 to 7 p.m. rap battles raged, overseen by long-time employee Proof. Shoppers came from everywhere since the shop was, according to Malone, unique in the entire world in the early 1990s.[4]

More important that the products for sale, the Shop was the community headquarters for networking, honing skills, and hard-core competition. Hip hop artist Leaf Erikson sums it up, saying, "on the mic, if you could survive at the Shop, you could survive anywhere at anytime. This was the era when open mic meant freestyle."[5] This period was the height of the gangsta rap era and that vibe permeated Detroit hip hop. The character and nature of the Shop was decidedly masculine. Men dominated these early years but women emcees like Lynette "Smiley" Michaels and Kalimah in the late 1980s, along with Lichelle "Boss" Laws, Red Bone, and Miz Korona in the 1990s challenged the gendered norms that relegated women to hip hop's sidelines.

In our conversations with them, pioneers often begin their stories with institutional memory of places like the Hip Hop Shop. DJ Los is one of the city's hip hop legends. Under the direction of his father Carl Butch Small, master percussionist for artists including Ice Cube, Nas, and Snoop Dogg, he took up DJing as a teenager. In 1988, DJ Los and emcee EZB released *Untouchable* on World One Records, the first hip hop album to come out of Detroit. Los continues to be actively involved in Detroit's hip hop underground, working with artists such as the Almighty Dread-naughts, Supa Emcee, and Kid Vicious. In 2019, he toured with Kid Vicious as part of Eminem's Australia and New Zealand Rapture Tour. During the 5e Gallery's years of operation it was commonplace to see Los DJing its events and hanging out in support of 5e and Foundation artists. He is a mentor in the community who frequently supports Foundation artists, be it serving as Miz Korona's long-time DJ or scratching over the beats in Mahogany Jones's track/video "Blue Collar Logic."

DJ Los's connection to other key hip hop players in Detroit's underground goes back to the Hip Hop Shop days. The environment at the Shop was particularly brutal for women. As Los recalls, "It was raw, rugged and threatening; only a battle rapper like Miz Korona could feel comfortable on its stage."[6] It is no accident that during the Hip Hop Shop era Miz Korona's emcee moniker was Pimpette. As one of her mentors, Proof was adamant that she change her name. He had no problem with her hard style but found her moniker troubling. Los reflects that "the Hip Hop Shop was the proving grounds and birth spot of the most talented, passionate, and biggest lovers of hip hop culture in Detroit! It is the one place that all of Detroit's most recognized and most successful hip hop artists/DJs and producers of that era would meet to spar and collaborate with one another."[7] We cannot underestimate the intensity of the sparring. Community was indeed present, but for those on the mic it was also a brutal battleground.

Amazingly, while emcees were expected to spit skillful trash-talking rhymes, the beats underneath them were multidimensional. The jazzy, bass-heavy, horn-accented sounds trumped the killer context in which emcees abused one another with rhythmic, rhyming verbal assaults. Here we are reminded of Tricia Rose's challenge to listeners to not give in to the beat when lyrical content is drenched in misogyny and other forms of contempt.[8] When we met at the Cass Café to discuss his work with Mahogany Jones we asked producer Ronald "iRonic" Lee Jr. what he thought about the idea of conscious beats. After pausing to think he ruminated,

> Music does speak. Music has its own language. Music can make you feel a certain way, whether it's happy, sad, glad. [It can] make you more pensive, get you more amped and hyper. For me, I'm a revolutionary, you know what I'm saying, so music does have its own language and can evoke certain things.[9]

In addition to the relationship between music and revolutionary thinking, the influence of jazz also runs deep in Detroit. Motown's house band the

Funk Brothers brought their unique jazz-inflected pop sounds to the masses, and its influence can be heard on everything from Detroit techno records to the production of local hip hop. Most, if not all, of the producers we met come from musical families and homes where jazz, among other Black music genres, was a consistent soundtrack to daily life growing up. Traces and samples of these sounds continue to circulate in Detroit's musical underground, leading some to define jazz-inflected hip hop as "conscious," but consciousness implies awareness. The universal application of the descriptor to any jazz-inflected beat discourages thoughtful lyrical critique and enables emcees to evade responsibility for the content of their rhymes. More recent hip hop galleries and spaces continue to shape a full range of artistic styles within Detroit's hip hop underground.

Detroit's early hip hop scene left an imprint on the Foundation and the artists that supported it. The older pioneer figures came up in the Hip Hop Shop, whereas the next generation found their stage at the 5e Gallery. Inspired by his experiences at the Hip Hop Shop and his inter-elemental vision, DJ Sicari founded the 5e Gallery in 2008 as a sacred space where hip hop's fifth element—Knowledge of community and self—was a pedagogical principle. DJing, emceeing, breaking, and graffiti are widely embraced elements. A commitment to Knowledge of self and community distinguishes people in the underground who support the Foundation, the 5e Gallery, and the organizing networks that they are connected to from the commercial market. Emcee Valid, a 5e protégé, spoke to us about the Gallery's impact on his development:

> I was like, oh this is really the core of hip hop. DJ Head was there, Fat Cat, DJ Dez, Slum Village people . . . this is the core of the Detroit hip hop community . . . . That was my dojo, 5e Gallery. When you talk about J Dilla, Eminem, Fat Cat, and Royce the 5' 9" they say the Hip Hop Shop. Then there was a generation after that that talks about the Lush Lounge. And now to me, my spot in Detroit hip hop where I learned my craft, at least really where I fell in love with it and it made me a better emcee, and I worked on my stage craft—5e Gallery.[10]

In our conversation, not only did Valid map out a significant lineage of Detroit's hip hop history, but he also emphasized the cultivation of artistry and community that happens in these spaces.

The Hip Hop Shop and the 5e Gallery were central sites where artists honed their craft and identities. They provided crucial gathering spaces for the hip hop community. The Old Miami and the Cass Corridor Commons also figure prominently in our study as key sites where Foundation open mic nights and special events took place. Once Sicari met

Piper Carter and their worldviews coalesced the 5e Gallery became the first home and sponsor of the Foundation.

From 2008 until its closing in 2015, the 5e Gallery had a migrant existence. At the time of our interview in June 2012 Sicari was running his second gallery in the city's Corktown neighborhood just west of downtown and had been in this location for two years. He opened the first location in a warehouse just down the street in 2009 but was evicted when the owner sold the building to a courier service. The first and second spaces were lost as a result of entering land grant contracts with building owners. As the neighborhood began to gentrify hungry for-profit business owners sold their buildings to cash rich buyers. In the summer of 2013 the 5e moved from the Southwest neighborhood to the Cass Corridor. In its third location, the Gallery occupied the lower level of the Cass Corridor Commons—a charming nineteenth-century limestone building that was once the exclusive property of the First Unitarian-Universalist Church of Detroit but is now home to the East Michigan Environmental Action Council. Shortly after the Foundation open mic night came to an end in 2014, Sicari opened the final site of the Gallery on West Grand Boulevard. Lack of funding and affordable space factored into its closing within a few months. Whereas the Hip Hop Shop launched the careers of gangsta style artists, the 5e returned to the Knowledge element and hip hop's history as a community building culture. It was inclusive and fertile ground where women commanded many stages.

WHAT'S IN A NAME?

We understood early on that there were not a lot of places for women to hone their craft in Detroit; however, we didn't know the extent to which gender issues were paramount until we experienced deep hanging out with Piper Carter and the Foundation. Struggles ranged from deciding on a name, to building an audience, to producing supportive, mentoring communities.

We first interviewed Piper on a bone-chilling cold January morning in 2012. We arrived early, eager for the interview after attending the Foundation's Tuesday night open mic events for six months. In casual conversations we had learned that she loves coffee so we stopped by Avalon Bakery for lattés and scones on our way. As we pulled up to park, Piper was waiting for us on the steps of the Cass Corridor Commons building at the corner of Cass and Forest Avenues, just a few miles north of downtown.

We said our hellos as the building manager let the three of us to a comfortable, quiet room. It was furnished with couches, a long dining-room-like table, and was adorned with intricate bay windows—symbols from a bygone era of material wealth. Piper began her story with an overview of her educational history and family background. She grew up living between Detroit and New York and was educated at Howard University in Washington, DC, and the Fashion Institute of Technology in New York. She went on to relay industry stories from her time as a professional fashion photographer in New York where she had been working for the last several years. Sadly, the overt sexism that she experienced gave her endless examples of the exploitation of girls and women. More than anything she said she missed sites in New York's hip hop scene that offered reprieves from the banal monotony of misogyny: places where intellectual cultural play was at work and where it was common for women to command stages. When Piper returned to Detroit, she observed that women were virtually absent from the stage, and often the audience as well. These experiences led Piper to act. She explains,

> So I'm going to everyone in the community like this is what I want to do, build a hip hop community where women can get on. Tell me what you think. So they'd tell me what they think and I'd say, hmm this doesn't sound very community [oriented]. So then I started to really realize A) no one cared, B) not only did they not care, but they thought it was a dumb and horrible idea. Until I got support from already established emcees Invincible and Miz Korona . . . then it changed a little.[11]

The support of these two well-known and highly regarded emcees was a catalyst to reach out to the community. Piper anticipated enthusiastic support and so was shocked when a group of women she had reached out to for feedback suggested ideas and practices steeped in traditional misogynist stereotypes. She recalls,

> So I went back to this collective body with idea of calling the women and hip hop group the Foundation and the first thing—and I thought everyone would think it's genius—and the first thing I heard was that's the dumbest name. Why don't you call it Bitches Ain't Shit? It was this thing that stunned me. They were like, you should have girls in bikinis with Jello shots. I was like blown back. These were coming from women! At first, I was so hurt I went home and cried. It doesn't sound like something to cry over but . . . I cried more because I thought: here we are so far and I remember all the strides of women and it's like these younger women were upset because I wanted to do something that would empower them. They actually wanted to do the misogyny and they preferred that. Not only did they suggest it, they were

actually fighting me and pissed off because I didn't want to do that stuff. Now this proves the need. I'm definitely calling it this. If it's upsetting them that much, it's going to be called that.[12]

Piper's ruminations reveal how the younger women she tried to recruit had internalized sexism far beyond their consciousness or care. Her frustration is bound up in ironic contradiction. Piper imagines a women-centered, healing stage, while her young recruits desire Jello shots for bitches who ain't shit. Self-deprecation and at-risk behaviors become molding agents.

Without saying the words, Piper made tension productive. A perceptive trickster, she capitalized on the nerve she hit in her attempt to challenge taken-for-granted acts of misogyny. What is in a name and who decides is a material question. The pushback that Piper experienced when she offered up the name "the Foundation" is telling. Bakari Kitwana, exploring the tensions that men and women face in the Black community, considers the lack of exposure to feminism one of the conditions that leads Black men to misunderstand and resent Black women.[13] However, men are not alone. Many of the women in Piper's community upheld misogyny with the same vigor as men. In the absence of conversations that come from family, other women role models, and possibly formal education, women turn to their peers and popular culture for education. The young women Piper attempted to recruit to her cause were entrenched in hip hop's raunchiest scripts. The name they proposed, "Bitches Ain't Shit," is reminiscent of rap songs that have dominated commercial radio and television for decades. The bitch/ho scripts and video vixen roles that women are relegated to, along with the excessive materialism and consumption that much commercial rap promotes, implicates strip club culture. We address these scripts and their limits in fuller detail in chapter 4.

For Piper, strip club culture is undesirable. Others in hip hop studies go in alternative directions within strip club culture. Hip hop scholar Bettina Love develops the Black rachet imagination as a methodological perspective, arguing for a nuanced reading of racialized, street coded terms like "rachet."[14] She links the concept and its embodiment to the strip club scene that Piper bemoans above; however, rachet methodologies lift up hitherto understudied populations, like queer fans and artists who are invested in hip hop. The strip club is a space where queer blends with otherwise unacceptable sexual expression. Artists like Big Freedia, a New Orleanian transgender emcee, set off new possibilities for queer artists who desire space, place, and recognition in hip hop culture. In a conjunctural move, Bettina Love's theorizing questions the politics of respectability underlying common critiques of concepts like rachetness. Piper's experience in Detroit is not commensurable with queer readings of women in bikinis serving shots or Big Freedia bouncing on queer dance floors. This is not to say that Piper is against queer interventions in strip club culture; rather, the dominant way that it plays out in the Detroit hip hop scene is not as progressive as the contexts that Love describes in cities like New Orleans and Atlanta.

Opting to call the collective "the Foundation" as opposed to "Bitches Ain't Shit" is one type of battle Piper encountered. Gaining access to hip hop stages in the city was another material struggle. The 5e Gallery was one site where women could cultivate their skills as DJs, producers, emcees, visual artists, or whatever element they desired to practice. Supportive men mentored young women who aspired to DJ. Illuminating the struggles of women who wanted to be hip hop DJs, Piper shared the story of Mel Wonder.

> I was at the [5e] Gallery one day and Mel walks in the door, and she has a crate of records and her pocketbook and coat hanging off, and she's in tears. I'm like, what's wrong? She said, 'There was this event called open decks. I just came from open decks.' It's early, probably like 11 or midnight and she's crying. What's wrong? 'I just came from open decks and they won't let me spin!' I'm like what are you talking about!? It's open decks; it's supposed to be that anybody can spin. She said it was her third or fourth time going and every time she never had a chance to spin. She said each time she went she would go earlier and earlier. So whatever time the event started, she went in the middle the first time, then she went earlier, and that day got there at six or seven—whenever it first started. She said she waited all that time and was asking and they told her to wait. That's when I was like, that's it. You can be our DJ![15]

By the time we started attending the Foundation's Tuesday open mic night at the Old Miami Mel was one of the regular DJs. Her experience was also helping her land gigs elsewhere. When we had the opportunity, we asked Mel about her open decks experience at a local bar and how she connected with the Foundation and the 5e Gallery.

> I found that open decks were at a particular place and I would go. I wasn't good at all; that was obvious but I wanted the chance everyone else had. I wanted to hear my own records. They wouldn't let me play. That was hard. Then I asked Sicari if he could really start teaching me and helping me develop a skill for what I'm doing and so I said I don't wanna hurt people's ears and he did. He told me I needed to play and that's exactly what I did. He would tell me to take breaks and I wouldn't take them. I was stubborn

about it 'cause I felt better about what I was doing. It felt good too. I said I could do this forever and I was sorry that I waited so late but I thought maybe now's the time.[16]

When she started DJing Mel Wonder was in her thirties, and although she was an aspiring hip hop DJ her experiences have much in common with women DJs and producers in electronic dance music (EDM) culture. They experience unique challenges in an environment "where the taken-for-granted notion is that knowledgeable men produce the culture/industry that less informed women may participate in."[17] Nitasha Tamar Sharma also found that South Asian women in San Francisco's East Bay hip hop scene in the late oughts, the same locale where Too Short and EM-40 reigned a decade earlier, also experienced resistance when they entered DJ battles.[18] While it has become more commonplace to see women DJing and producing music, be it EDM or hip hop, parity in the industry and culture has a long way to go. Skill-sharing is an important strategy for women to gain entry but, as Mel Wonder's experience demonstrates, women continue to face difficulties gaining access to learning environments. Her story also echoes the importance of women-centered collectives and spaces because "boys' club" mentalities continue to thrive across genres. Such environments foster skill-sharing, mentoring, and networking opportunities that positively impact knowledge production, skills development and participation.[19]

TUESDAY NIGHTS AT THE FOUNDATION

When she established the Foundation in 2009, Piper Carter's main objectives were to foster confidence in women and encourage more of them to actively engage with and participate in Detroit's hip hop underground. Creating a weekly open mic night dedicated to women was central to achieving these goals. It was clear early on that finding artists and building an audience would be an uphill battle in a scene where, up until this point, women emcees or DJs were exceptions. The first official Foundation event was a Cinco de Mayo celebration. It was also Mel Wonder's first public appearance as a DJ. Piper recalled,

> Only about thirty people came the whole night. Sicari was pretty upset because they couldn't believe the hip hop community didn't support it. He was in disbelief. He couldn't believe nobody would come out for a night celebrating women in hip hop. He was like we're not going to do this here again. It's not going to make money. I was like, this isn't about making money, that's not what it's about. He was looking at it as an event. I was like

no, no, no it's not about that, it's about what we're building. We're building an audience.

She added,

> With my theatre background, and being a choreographer, and being in the business 'making' stars as a photographer, I was used to talking to girls, models, to do things. I was used to getting into the psyche of how to help build people up and everything. I was really aggressive. Then I started to realize how much dysfunction was in the women because they would have this thing like I want to, but I don't think I can because I don't sound like this guy.[20]

Piper navigated open mic nights and moments like the one above with both patience and pushiness, handing mics to young women before they could back away, or gently urging people in the audience to get in the cypher.

At its peak the Foundation attracted somewhere in the neighborhood of one to two hundred people to its weekly open mic night, many of whom were men, and its yearly anniversary parties were much bigger events. Attendance fluctuated over the course of the open mic night's five year run, with strong crowds some weeks and low attendance at other times. Throughout, Piper fielded objections. Both men and women grumbled about its focus on consciousness raising and the lack of hook-up potential. Their discontent was often couched in explicitly homophobic terms. Piper shared that a common reaction was "There's so many lesbians here. Who we gonna hook up with?!" Explaining these objections to the night—especially early on—Piper reasoned,

> There wasn't the sexual energy that people were looking for in going out at night. That's why people initially, they weren't feeling it. For them women in hip hop was guys going out to meet girls and everyone's having sex or hooking up or some version of that or the girls were there to support guys. That's where people were bucking it. 'Wait a minute, I'm a dude and I rap and do my thing and I'm in a room full of women and no one wants to have sex with me? This shit is wack!'[21]

Piper often complained that "educated, grown-ass women" whom she considered peers did not question the status quo of gender norms. When the Foundation was at the Old Miami some people came to party and get on stage while others were drawn to the alternative Knowledge element.

Every Foundation open mic night started off with a cypher. Unless she was out of town, Mahogany Jones ran the show, sometimes with a co-host. They would ask for a few volunteers to join them on the stage, then solicit four words from the crowd that would become themes for

FIGURE 1. Foundation Flyer.
Created by Piper Carter.

the cypher. Terms like freedom, money, justice, love, cannabis, and hustle were audience picks. The freestyle generally lasted for ten to fifteen minutes and drew on hip hop's most improvisational principles. The crowd was hyped and invested in the success of the emcees on the stage and the beats, many of which were also produced locally. Snaps, whistles, shout-outs, and other responses punctuated the cypher's flow. The call and response feedback loop produced both the calling feature of the emcee and the response character of the audience. The emcees' and DJs' skills were intoxicating to the body and exhilarating to the mind.

While many emcees, beat-makers, and instrumentalists embraced the open mic night's guiding principles, others begrudgingly followed along. The first rule was no misogyny of any kind, especially of the bitch/ho variety. Second, artists could only perform one piece and it had to be original work. And third, they had to go with whatever the DJ played; they could not supply their own beats. Given these three rules, we found it ironic that men and women who had issues with the Foundation boycotted because they believed that a night dedicated to women was not inclusive and having their free speech disciplined was not cool. Pushback came from people of all ages, from those in their twenties to their fifties. For the Foundation, the no-misogyny rule was seen as the first step in changing the culture in Detroit's hip hop underground. When Mahogany Jones or DJ Sicari called them out on their use of words like "bitch" or "ho" some were left speechless, unable to articulate a rhyme in conditions that they considered censorship. Early on, Bryce Detroit spearheaded the addition of the "no clap" policy for artists on stage who did not abide by the rules.

FIGURE 2. DJ Los, Piper Carter, Nik Nak, Mel Wonder, Drake Phiefer. Photo: Alias Pknukkle.

FIGURE 3. Open Mic Night at Old Miami. Photo: Nikki Kopytek.

The night drew the largest crowds the years it was at the Old Miami, from 2011–2013. People could drink there and the worn aesthetic of the old veterans' bar included tattered couches, televisions, and pool tables at the back. Its outdoor space was massive and when the temperature was right the tiki bar, barbecue pit, and bonfires sparked impromptu cyphers. It was mostly men, standing around the fire passing around a blunt or two, who broke into freestyles. A built-in audience was there to cheer them on and serve as emergent judges. Inside, the night cultivated a space where performers were willing to be more vulnerable than they typically are in hip hop performance spaces. The night fostered a vibe that was the opposite of the raw and rugged spirit at the Hip Hop Shop. Here, men articulated a range of vulnerabilities and emotional intelligence on stage through their raps but also spoken word poetry.

May 22, 2012, Old Miami. The first performer, a Black man who looks to be about thirty years old, introduces his piece by telling the audience that twenty-seven years ago today "lady heroin" took the life of his mother, and she is here again tonight for his aunt who is fighting for her life in a hospital around the corner. The next performer we saw outside in the back by the bonfire a little earlier in the evening. He was one of a group of six or so guys participating in an informal cypher. It's unusual for men to perform spoken word poetry at the Foundation. Normally they rap, often hard lyrics, over music, but this particular gentleman has Mel Wonder cut the beats before proceeding with his poetry. He speaks emotionally of being a mixed-race, bastard child whose parents had abandoned him when he was very young. In both cases the crowd is receptive and its hoots and hollers show support for the men on stage. The tone of the evening is heavier than most Tuesday nights but the crowd is supportive.

It is through these performances that the complexity of the Foundation comes to life. They embody all of hip hop's principles—peace, love, unity, and having fun. However, sometimes the heaviness of life overshadows the fun. This particular performance highlights the complexity of emotion, material reality, and aesthetics that often coalesce on the stage.

In 2013, when the Foundation's open mic night left the Old Miami and moved along with the 5e Gallery to the Cass Corridor Commons in Midtown, the pressures of securing space and raising money became insurmountable. This material pressure signaled the beginning of the end of the weekly event. Crowds were smaller, alcohol wasn't served, and Knowledge was the reigning principle. Youth and elders participated, which raised expectations for civic behavior. Some of the people willing to abide by the Foundation's rules at the bar were less eager to travel to gallery spaces where club culture was not in play even on the faintest of levels.

While in operation from 2008–2016 the Foundation and the 5e Gallery were the home of a new generation of hip hop heads in the city who desired a more intellectually uplifting hip hop than what the music industry continues to produce. Piper Carter imagined a hip hop environment that was as inclusive as possible; in her efforts to make this a reality she highlighted women's contributions to the culture at every opportunity. She played music and videos that featured women artists with inspiring messages and hung women's art on the walls at the 5e. This music and imagery created a warm and inviting atmosphere for women. With this sensibility came a commitment to celebrating all of the elements of hip hop. Piper drew in b-girls like Martha Quezada, aka B-Girl Snapshot of Motor City Rockers, and Mary Mar, aka B-Girl Ma-Ma of Hardcore Detroit, who brought members of their well-established crews to Foundation nights. Anniversary parties intentionally featured b-girls/b-boys, visual artists, and occasionally graffiti writers, as DJs dropped beats and emcees spat rhymes. Once a month the open mic night hosted a popular beat battle that drew in men we did not see on other nights.

The collective's five-year anniversary party in the summer of 2014 celebrated both its achievements and its struggles as it marked the end of the weekly open mic night that Mahogany Jones, along with a rotating list of emcees, had hosted for five years. The 5e Gallery also permanently shut its doors shortly after. However, it is still common to see hip hop heads sporting 5e t-shirts and hoodies in the streets and at events including Dilla Youth Day—an annual event we discuss in detail in chapter 6. Though they are no longer active, the 5e Gallery and the Foundation's commitment to developing hip hop skills, knowledge, and community continues to reverberate throughout Detroit; in particular, Piper Carter continues her mission of celebrating women in hip hop in her current project, We Found Hip Hop.

2

Hip Hop Sounds and Sensibilities
in Post-Bankruptcy Detroit

It was a dreary, wet Saturday evening in May, typical for Detroit. Insite the Riot and Nique Love Rhodes were kicking off their 2015 "Riots & Revolutions" tour at the Underground, a basement venue in the newly established Detroit Institute for Music Education [DIME]. When we arrived forty or so people were milling around; some chatted while others staked out their seats. Nique's mom was selling her t-shirts and CDs at a table at the back of the room. Next to her, local poet and emcee Deidre "D.S. Sense" Smith was also selling t-shirts. These featured the slogan "On My Detroit Everything," adapted from the title of one of her popular spoken word pieces. Over the past few years, we've seen an acceleration in the number of local hip hop artists creating brands and selling merchandise that reflects the people of Detroit's hustling, activism, and community sensibilities. In D.S. Sense's words, "'On My Detroit Everything' is a brand, initiative and movement [that] focuses on Detroit's emergence from disparity into promise and prosperity as told and seen through the eyes of residents, entrepreneurs, and supporters of the city."[1] Over the course of the night, the music, performances, and overall vibe underscored the sense of urgency and energy that Detroiters are putting forth in their efforts to enact meaningful, positive change in this distressed city.

This chapter locates the specific ways that local hip hop artists are making claims to the city: sonically, discursively, and materially. Articulating the larger role this music plays in the effort to mobilize citizens is especially important in the wake of recent tensions tied to Detroit's redevelopment strategies. Detroit's difficulties have much in common with those of other predominantly Black Michigan cities. The application of neoliberal tactics by wealthy elites and the state in the name of redevelopment has eroded the quality of life for local Black citizens in these communities while fortifying the financial portfolios of its instigators. Pinpointing the articulations between hip hop and cultural organizing in the city also contributes to the historical legacy of Detroit as a movement city. This music reclaims urban space, filling it with muted voices and the rhythmic, melodic, and driving sounds of hip hop. It also functions as a primary means for organizing and practicing both community care and individual ethics of self-care in a city where neoliberal policies are punishing its population. Racist government policies and practices are not unique to Detroit. They put people of color at risk the world over and thus self-care is a survival strategy, if not a precondition to community care and action. As we state in the introduction, self-care reclaims welfare as community-based practices that function as wellsprings of personal, social, and cultural health. The self-care practices that Black women who are cultural workers in Detroit employ build relationships, heal communities, and cultivate cooperative communication practices.

We explore the ways emcees use the art of rap to amplify their voices and those of community members who are too often marginalized and forgotten in neoliberal projects of urban renewal and gentrification. Ultimately, we argue that these tracks and the artists behind them are 1) reclaiming what it means to be a Detroiter; 2) questioning in whose best interests are the redevelopment processes and practices underway in the city; and 3) mobilizing citizens whose communities have been the target of gentrification. While the three dimensions that underwrite these musical practices are entrenched in neoliberal logics of development and renewal, the artists maneuver its forces like tricksters. They are social actors and stakeholders who spin and spit the language of neoliberalism as they remix their terms of play. With a system as complex and hegemonic as neoliberalism, responses to it take many different forms. The four tracks we examine below make audible the politics and ethics of self-care that Foundation artists live. In so doing, they provide multiple platforms of resistance.

CITIES AND SPACES

Sound, especially the ordered and ordering sound known as music, is overlooked as a force that constitutes spaces and places. Whereas visual maps represent the more stable aspects of places, with occasional revisions for shifting boundaries, musical maps can better represent place as a social product. Music represents space in terms of movement—as it moves through space—and as a process rather than an object, with locales experienced as ever-shifting and contested terrains. In other words, music, more than other forms of representation, highlights the *fluidity* of place, and how this fluidity is a product of history, memory, imagination, and the ways they intersect. What is more, music not only reflects spaces, but also often *reimagines* them as it creates and critiques social actions and institutions. It also illuminates the political and cultural currents that are produced as old spaces disappear and new ones open up.

A range of structural tensions and identity categories impact the production of space. Neoliberal governmentality is complicating these tensions. That is, when government is shaped by market-driven ideologies, underemployed populations are displaced in favor of design-intensive construction projects. The privatization of public resources like water, education, and housing has created more inequality than has ever existed in the United States.[2] The state's reckless policies have primarily impacted people of color. As Sara Ahmed writes, in the contemporary condition simply "being poor, being black, puts your life at risk."[3] Consequently, self-care—which when exercised by people of color has been condemned for being self-indulgent—is necessary for the survival of marginalized communities.

The artists and music we examine below contribute to the dialogue and discourse about who has the right to inhabit city spaces, both public and private. They mobilize their skills to contribute sharp, unguarded, grounded accounts of the living history unfolding in their beloved city. These songs, and others like them, function as rallying cries in what we believe is a moment of crisis in Detroit. Post-bankruptcy, we are witnessing and experiencing the creation of two Detroits: one defined by gentrification in the 7.2 square miles of the city's core and the other consisting of the outer neighborhoods that residents claim government has abandoned. The two Detroits are collapsing and gentrifying;[4] separate and unequal.[5]

STATE OF EMERGENCY

The post-soul[6] hip hop generation carries a heavy neoliberal load. The construction of the Cross Bronx Expressway in New York in the 1960s displaced thousands of people and destroyed entire communities. The superhighway, which was aimed at moving populations and advancing business development, was planned and funded decades earlier; however, when it surfaced in the 1960s neoliberal interests were well served. Thousands of poor residents—most of whom were Black and Latinx— were displaced from their communities. Adults experienced high employment rates, and young people were forced to attend impoverished schools. Affluent Manhattan and New York City suburbs profited while the South Bronx and the poorest populations in other New York boroughs became seemingly invisible. Disinvestment was also coupled with an intense paramilitary police presence which Tricia Rose argues was rooted in "the understanding that black people are a threat to social order."[7] When the state concomitantly abandons populations and disciplines them with police brutality the seeds of resistance are planted.[8] In Byron Hurt's documentary *Hip Hop: Beyond Beats and Rhymes,* James Peterson cements the innate relationship between the political and racial practices in New York and the development of hip hop during its nascent years. He directly ties the construction of the Cross Bronx Expressway, which left an indelible mark on South Bronx youth, to hip hop's history when he bluntly states, "if you want to understand hip hop imagine a bulldozer wiping out your entire neighborhood."[9] The changes underway that so negatively impacted communities of color in the city fueled calls to action, and hip hop was one of the most enduring responses. Its first flight launched from the South Bronx; it is New York's phoenix.

The ostensible urban renewal taking place in New York flooded the country's most challenged cities. President Eisenhower's mid-twentieth century commitment to constructing a national interstate highway system brought sweeping changes to cities like Detroit, Miami, and New Orleans that disproportionately affected poor Black and Brown people. In her study of Jamaican dance hall and New Orleans bounce, Nadia Ellis describes the havoc wreaked on New Orleans when the construction of I-10 bifurcated the Tremé neighborhood and parts of the Seventh Ward. Reflecting on the implication of this destruction and construction, Ellis offers a chilling assessment:

> The federal government's and the city's plans indicated a radical, problematically hygienic vision of space clearing whereby the public housing buildings would be destroyed to re-build more "modern" and "mixed income" residences—which is to say, privately owned and rented, and no longer fully under the aegis of the state.[10]

Echoes are found elsewhere as well. For example, the I-95 interchange in Miami destroyed most of Overtown, a historically African-American neighborhood, turning almost half the Black population into refugees in their own city. New "extreme localities" such as the Liberty State Projects were born as a result; these localities served as incubators for hip hop in Miami, producing, for example, Luther Campbell, Trick Daddy, Trina, and Rick Ross.[11]

In Detroit, Black Bottom was a thriving African American housing community in the 1920s–1950s, and its adjacent district Paradise Valley was a cultural center and a site of commerce for Black populations. However, the long-term success of these communities was thwarted by a series of urban renewal policies dedicated to removing "blight" and upgrading housing and highways in the city.[12] The highways that were created through the Federal Highway Act of 1956 destroyed Hastings Street, which was a main artery connecting the two areas, and bifurcated the Black Bottom neighborhood. The urban planning connected to the construction of I-75 destroyed many of the city's most prominent African American institutions, including jazz and blues clubs, barbershops, grocery stores, and a branch of the YMCA.[13] In what was then still a majority-white city, government officials and planners had the political power to reconstruct the city as they desired, and the results disproportionately impacted the lives and communities of Blacks who are still paying the heavy price of these federal and state strategies. Displacement coupled with the deindustrialization that followed devastated Detroit, and the city has yet to recover from the loss of what were once socially, culturally, and economically thriving Black neighborhoods.

Over the last half century infrastructure such as roads, education, fire, and police services all steadily deteriorated. As in other rust-belt cities that capitalized on single industry modes of production, Detroit's residents who once found work in the auto industry and government agencies—many of whom also benefited from home ownership—faced unemployment or had to take low-paying jobs that do not provide living wages, health insurance, and retirement benefits. By 2000 the city was 81.6 percent Black, and its population had declined to 951,270 compared to its peak of 1,849,568 in 1950.[14] For more than a decade, developers have been flocking to the city and have settled property deals that activists and city residents say can only be described as land grabs.[15] Land grabs, questionable urban renewal policy, and gentrification displacement underscore the issues that flow through the music we engage in the analysis below.

"Locusts"

Invincible/ill Weaver is well known in Detroit as an activist and one of Detroit's best emcees. They defy conventional definitions of identity. Over the years they have developed long-standing relationships with key social justice organizations in the city, including the Boggs Center, Detroit Summer, Allied Media Project, D-REM, We the People of Detroit, Freedom Schools, the 5e Gallery, and many others. They were also one of the first artists to contribute to the Foundation when Piper Carter reached out to the hip hop community. ill pushes against many taken-for-granted categories of identity. They are gender-nonconforming and refuse the binary of man/woman. ill was an early adopter of the gender-neutral pronouns they and them, and sells a range of "THEY" merchandise online. They are known across communities in Detroit and are looked to for leadership, strategies, and organizational support. While ill is located in formations of whiteness, they are actively accountable and work to dismantle the privileges that come with it. Born in Champaign-Urbana, Illinois, to a parent who identified as Israeli, they had to navigate moving back and forth from the United States and what they came to understand as occupied Palestine. They moved to Michigan as a child and learned English from hip hop: rappers, commentators, and other hip hop heads that shaped their youth and imparted a distinct rhythm and cadence to their speech. As an adult, ill has organized against what they regard as an illegal, unjust Israeli occupation and ethnic cleansing Zionist colonial project, often creating connections among oppressed communities globally. This choice came with costs and often corrosive criticism. They understand well what it means to be white by assignment, while resisting the institutional privilege that comes with it.

Over recent years, they have stepped away from individual performances, embracing a deep belief that ethical cultural production should be collaborative. Unlike some white artists who appear to include Black people around them for legitimacy, ill's artistry represents deep collaboration. For example, "Locusts" provides a scathing critique of corporate development and displacement in Detroit and includes Finale, a well-known emcee who commands support from the city's hip hop audience. He, too, has lived through emergency financial management and has seen the Detroit he knows nearly disappear.

"Locusts," which comments on these longstanding practices and their contemporary manifestations, is the final track on Invincible's 2008 album *Shapeshifters*. A collaboration with Finale, it features prominent activists Gwen Mingo and Ron Scott.[16] "Locusts" questions redevelopment processes and practices that have been underway in the city for decades. Since Invincible and Finale penned the words for "Locusts," the situation has become more dire. The 2008 financial and housing crises had a catastrophic impact on Detroit. Between 2000 and 2010 the city lost a quarter of its residents. Of those who remain, approximately 40 percent live below the poverty line[17]. Nonetheless, over 700,000 people continued to call the city home during this time of tremendous upheaval.

The song opens with a sample of Mingo's voice recounting the hundreds of fires—up to five or six hundred—in the late 1990s that devastated Detroit's historic Brush Park neighborhood. Similar to the circumstances in the Bronx in the 1970s, there has been little doubt, both then and now, that arson to provide slumlords with insurance checks accounted for most of these fires. Finale and Invincible/ill Weaver's rhymes cut in and deftly move listeners through historical and contemporary policies that have had distressing effects on the city and its residents. In less than six minutes "Locusts" speaks to the racism and classism that were not only the impetus for Detroit's systematic and intentional destruction beginning in the mid-twentieth century, but that also underlie its more recent redevelopment strategies and policies of urban renewal.

In his opening verse Finale forecasts a bleak future. In a salient verse he raps,

> Every jackhammer cracking the concrete
> That's a lost and forgotten piece of the D
> We'll never see in a book or paper
> Replaced with a temp casino
> Strip mall, liquor store
> Another stadium doubling as a palladium, eateries
> The D speaks to me.[18]

Finale goes on to describe a city—citizens and all—that has been "swept away beneath a pile of debris." In so doing, like Marc Lamont Hill's lonely figure "Nobody," he's describing the subject who is on the one hand abandoned by the state but on the other the object of its surveillance.[19] The subject position "Nobody" has a criminal footprint, but an invisible body in design-intensive downtown city centers whose "revitalization" is attributed to an increase in stadiums, theatres, chic restaurants, coffee shops, and high-end retrofitted lofts aimed at high-purchase-power people. The figure "Nobody" is akin to Ralph Ellison's

"Invisible Man" in the sense that whiteness contains and controls him; it sponsors his education and career. In this scenario, privileged white actors go so far as to claim that the Invisible Man's success is the white man's destiny. This Pygmalion project is supported until people step out of their assigned roles and start thinking and resisting, but once the power of agentic thought is embraced, the invisible are erased from history and removed from eyesight. They are propelled and hailed into the Nobody subject position. To be invisible is to bear an unrecognizable humanity. They may as well be "swept away beneath a pile of debris," which is Finale's metaphor for death and displacement. Invincible then chimes in with the hook in a quick-paced, poetic style:

> By the locusts
> Surrounding, suffocating the city and trying to choke us
> Ravaging the crops, making the situation hopeless
> But we staying focused
> Never let the locusts approach us.

The lyrics in the second verse critique past redlining practices, excessively high insurance rates, as well as urban renewal and people-removal initiatives. Invincible and Finale give us a critique of neoliberalism that is unapologetic and cutting. Renewal is ideological distortion for removal, elimination of people who do not fit the new cookie cutter condo world; Black people's homes were razed, leaving what Finale refers to as buried souls under the concrete. In their view, the D is now a shadow of itself, the auto industry's widow abandoned.

In the 2010s, the concerns expressed in "Locusts" resonate like prophecy. In June 2015, *Voice of Detroit*, a local, independent, online publication, published an article by activist Diane Bukowski titled "Brush Park Historic Area—Can We Trust Those Who Wrecked It to Restore It?" The two images that accompany the article are telling. One is a color photo of the homes of Black Brush Park residents on fire. The other is a computer rendition of the plan for a new Brush Park controlled by Dan Gilbert's Bedrock Real Estate.[20] It consists mostly of the "cookie cutter condominiums" Invincible rapped about nearly a decade earlier. Remember, this is the neighborhood of which Mingo speaks on "Locusts," which fires devastated in the late 1990s. The demolition of historical buildings in the 2000s made it possible for developers to acquire the land at no or little cost. David Harvey frames the rise of neoliberalism in part as a response to the economic threat facing the ruling classes after decades of social democratic gains in the aftermath of

World War II. He argues that "neoliberalism was from the very beginning an endeavor to restore class power to the richest strata in the population" and goes on to document the strategies that US state and financial institutions employed to export neoliberalism across the globe.[21] Redevelopment strategies like the recent tax incentive legislation written into Michigan law to benefit multibillionaire Dan Gilbert are the latest iterations of the institutional frameworks created to maintain upper-class power. Doing so is also dependent on the ongoing displacement of the working class and people of color.

"Locusts" returns to Mingo for its last words. Over a slow, sparsely textured beat and a guitar loop that feels like a lament, she explains: "The ideal city is where the residents have an input in the development and they know, they feel they have an input in the development, and they benefit from the development, and when we have development like that the spirit of the development is good." Mingo couches her words in the language of development. In doing so, she grounds her discourse in an ethic of community care that taps into the spirit that Audre Lorde advances in her insistence that care for the self is an act of political warfare.[22] For Sara Ahmed and other scholars who draw on Lorde's theorizing, welfare is both an ethic and a practice of survival. For Finale and ill, survival means evading, if not blocking, the developers/investors encroaching on the city. This final statement brings the album full circle as it incites the same sense of urgency in listeners with which it opens. Its first track begins with a loop of Invincible chanting "It's a State of Emergency; It's a State of Emergence, see." Invincible/ill places resistance—not letting the Locusts get too close to us—in conjunction with revolution; this is their call to action.

"ON MY DETROIT EVERYTHING"

Deidre "D.S. Sense" Smith is a spoken word poet/emcee who is well-known in Detroit. She performs across crowds, having earned notoriety in both poetry circuits and music scenes; in addition to cafés and clubs, she often performs at public events that draw crossover audiences like Detroit's Dally in the Ally festival and community sponsored events held at galleries, community centers, public parks, and museums. D.S. Sense began performing her spoken word piece "On My Detroit Everything" in 2013. It is a text with a rich tapestry that speaks to post-bankruptcy Detroit and neoliberal governmentality while illustrating how one woman's tenacity cuts up the very fabric of neoliberal logics and gentrification. It also critiques the hip hop industry's hold on artists and articulates with

FIGURE 4. Deidre "D.S. Sense" Smith, On Her Detroit Everything.
Photo: Xanthi Shine.

bravado D.S. Sense's perseverance and that of Detroit in challenging times. D.S. Sense describes the genesis of "On My Detroit Everything" by explaining, "My life mirrored what the city was going through—down but then resurgence, revitalization. Simultaneously me and the city were coming out of our places and stepping into view again. Everything that I am is synonymous with Detroit."[23] And like the city of Detroit she is experiencing the tension between the push and the pull of neoliberal policies and the community's resistance to them. For D.S. Sense, spoken word poetry and her emcee practices are expressions of cultural citizenship in her community; she rallies against the ideology of market-based investment.

"On My Detroit Everything" opens up space for self-articulation in the context of self-in-community. Before she addresses community, she begins with the self and body image.

I know I look cuddly, soft as a down pillow
but did you not consider my skeletal frame is metal
Did you not consider you're soft as a bowl of Jello
My tummy is toast brown, your belly is so yellow
Is magic when I flip my mouth
Is classic like All Stars under Levi-Strauss
Need I announce you want it so I brought that bounce
Be lookin' out for killers 'cause I've got that clout
I air it out, assume I'll go that route
What's she about
Lionheart lie beneath my blouse, but hear me out
I'm sayin' bump it in your Scion
You know those little cars that resemble a box
You're lukewarm, you're resembling hot
You've been warned, you're got the game fucked up, like you're in porn
Lyrics flying from my head like my roof is torn
What's this red and blue pill shit? The truth is orange

The dense rhymes in this first stanza provide a response to the power dynamics that D.S. Sense experiences in her day to day life as a Black woman who is a hip hop emcee, spoken word poet, and Detroiter. Body image may be every woman's struggle but Black women in the United States are subjected to, and work to overcome, unique representational practices and material histories. Colonialism bore modern slavery; insidious theories of scientific racism, social Darwinism and eugenics justified ontological Otherness between the races. The colonial gaze is indeed controlling, but it is not monolithic; each attempt to freeze the frame of Black women as sexual objects and servants inadvertently opened space for their resistance. This legacy finds form in the photography of the nineteenth century and the pornography that colonial whiteness craved. In the present, scholars catalog, critique, and unsettle images of Black women that colonial anthropologists produced in the nineteenth century.[24] In her examination of the ways in which Black women appear in historical and contemporary forms of pornography, Mereille Miller-Young invokes the trope "A Taste for Brown Sugar" to demonstrate that even when Black women have been cast in a male, colonial gaze within pornography, they have always resisted, often in ambiguous ways.[25] Black women have been alter cast as exotic and desirable on the one hand, and maligned as lesser in God's eyes, on the other. D.S. Sense is neither a cuddly Mammy nor an exotic Other for consumption. She is a force, facing those "yellow bellies" with her "toast brown tummy." She claims the strength of steel while accusing her critics who view her as soft as Jello. She invokes the subject position of a "killer" to signify the cutting power of her art; she "airs out the clout" in surprising ways.

Later in the piece she creates a tapestry of actors wherein branding, popular music, Greek mythology, and corporate greed coalesce to fuel her subjectivity (as "raw D").

> I had dreams of putting my city on
> The rose grew from the sludge of the Synagro
> You hos don't hear me though
> Cold, since I was rockin' the rose gold herringbone
> Now fill my cup to the brim
> This is the winner's circle
> Now why you fuckin' with them?
> I unlearn what they teach us
> Extinguish the flame
> I've been enlightened Prometheus
> The God in me, Mary Mary
> It's a God emcee
> You shall get buried
> Thou shall not fuck with raw D or he
> Will face a thousand deaths like he faced J. Vorhees
> Boy please, I breathe this shit

The lines "I had dreams of putting my city on/The rose grew from the sludge of the Synagro" refer to the specific ways corporate abuse has an impact on the city's health. As a young teenager, D.S. Sense and other people in her Detroit neighborhood witnessed an employee of the sewage recycling company Synagro dump waste from an unmarked truck in broad daylight. When her neighbor, Mr. Johnson, questioned the driver about his actions, the driver said that he was told to "dump in an empowerment zone," which is code for low income neighborhoods. In other words, mirroring the mentality of state officials, corporations view land that lacks "development potential" as urban wasteland and the opinions of residents—many of whom are low income and African American—are seen to have little impact on public discourse. Synagro's actions add waste to what is already considered a wasteland. This is ironic given that waste management is a part of the neoliberal discourse engine. Detroit's latest urban renewal plans figure into the problematic. Investment is geared towards the city's downtown and midtown districts with little resources or development taking place on the periphery of this 7.2 square mile core.[26] Challenging policymakers, D.S. Sense uses her poetic voice to amplify the issues, shaming polluters. In doing so, she claims her space and connection to other Black environmental feminists forging their way into ecofeminisism's hitherto whitewashed and exclusive discourse. They conceptualize practices like that of Synagro's as environmental racism.[27] Cacildia Cain explains, "due to the intersections of environmental racism and sexism seen in Flint (Detroit's sister city, 60 miles due North), Black women have been involved in environmental movements in order to survive."[28]

Despite the daily challenges of life in the city that confront residents like D.S. Sense, she refuses to succumb to the difficulties. On the contrary, she tells us that she's been "cold since I was rockin' the rose gold herringbone." In other words, her skills go back to the 1990s, when herringbone necklaces were popular fashion accessories. She hasn't needed the fire that "they" provide for survival; she can make her own way. The vagueness of the term "they" applies to the corporate elites who run the hip hop industry as well as the city.

From mythology she turns to her faith, invoking the gospel duo Mary Mary's song "God Is In Me." This musical citation reaffirms her religious constitution. Her gestures toward fashion, music, and mythology demonstrate the complex ways that social institutions forge identities. Moreover, her experiences, courage, faith, and lyrical skills have enabled a self-valuation as badass, a woman as lyrically dangerous as Jason Vorhees, the antagonist in the Friday the 13th films.

"On My Detroit Everything" and emcee practices like those D.S. Sense embodies contribute to community organizing and, as such, are representative of Black, female-centered political work. We build on Michele Tracy Berger's argument that the actions of Black HIV/AIDS-positive women in Detroit in the 1990s should be viewed as political work.[29] In D.S. Sense's words, "community work is servitude. It is about committing to causes bigger than yourself. I do community service leadership. I use artistic, hip hop expression as my community activism."[30]

Throughout the poem, D.S. Sense repeats the hook:

And you know I'm on my
On my Detroit everything.
I'm on my Detroit everything
I'm on my Detroit everything
So clean
On my Detroit everything

In each iteration she claims pride in her city and, like herself, she sees Detroit at the top of its game, which in turn is tied to her own growth and change. When she performs this poem in public, audiences commonly chant the hook along with her. This song is more than an anthem; in many ways, it is the beginning of a new brand and a new movement that invites everyday people to claim their rights to the city as agentic citizens. When she spits the hook, intensity builds, along with identification and invested participation. The related brand "OMDE" is based on collective economics and grassroots organizing. In "On My Detroit Everything," community service and cultural organizing become a combined effort.

"DETROIT HUSTLES HARDER": RAPPING ANTHEMS IN THA D

In 2007, a local company began printing the phrase "Detroit Hustles Harder" on shirts. Aptemal Clothing co-founder Joseph "JP" O'Grady explains that the expression "came from us growing up in the city, everybody trying to make something from nothing . . . . People here just need to work harder to get by."[31] Within a few years they sold so much "Detroit Hustles Harder" product that running the clothing company became a full-time job.[32] While "the hustle" does not mean the same thing to all people, it has become a rallying term in the city that both Nique Love Rhodes and Mahogany Jones directly reference in their tracks "Blue Collar Logic" and "Detroit Made."

"Blue Collar Logic"

In July 2015, Mahogany Jones released the track "Blue Collar Logic." A New York City native, Mahogany did not see much substance in the local hip hop scene when she first moved to Detroit in 2002. Over time she developed a strong sense of community with local artists, activists, and citizens. "Blue Collar Logic" captures her intense relationship with the city and its people. Concomitantly, the track's instrumentals communicate Detroit's powerful and entrenched relationship with hip hop. Syncopated drums, a subtle bass line, and synthesized effects are all part of its design, but the scratching and other turntablism techniques over the "I'm from Motown" sample are its most prominent features. As the video illustrates, it is Detroit hip hop pioneer DJ Los who cuts the breaks and scratches over the beat, and it is his voice we hear on the recurring and cut up "I'm from Motown" sample. Mahogany's choice to work with Los is not accidental. While her lyrics speak to all of the different landscapes that mark Detroit, as the first artist to record hip hop in the city in the 1980s, his contributions to the track invoke Detroit as a hip hop city with a history. In the first verse, Jones articulates her historical knowledge and rhetorical genius, invoking religious and revolutionary metaphors to illustrate Detroiters' spirit and strength:

Not anemic, got iron mixed with the cement
Concrete flow immovable, believe it
Legendary is the pedigree, we a breed of phoenix
Levitate through ashes, us against the masses
Who else that you know makes aggression fashion
Feel our passion—ain't nothing about us passive.
Matchless, we put a patent on classic
Underground railroad passage progressive
We busy making demands we don't do suggestions
Questions?[33]

Whereas ill and Finale warn against the removal of poor people of color from Detroit, Mahogany is resolute about the immovability of Black populations. Her interpretation suggests that Black people are not only invincible but also a permanent part of Detroit's many scapes of life. As with Nique, ill, and Finale, concrete also plays a major conceptual role in her lyrics. Its mix has a double consciousness. On one level, Black souls are laid to rest below, while above new "cookie cutter condos" emerge. In "Blue Collar Logic," the mixing of iron and cement represents Black Detroiters' strength and longevity. Their right to the city is embodied in Mahogany's anthem.

In the second verse, Mahogany creates two competing calls to action. She invents revolutionaries who are capable of being the solution to urban problems. Mahogany moves between Black working class sites and white-collar design-intensive downtown spaces, claiming each city space as her peoples'. Class is written into her worldview, particularly in the lines, "world is my stage pay me my per diem, who better to feed um, teach um and reach um?," as she reads per diem as working class dues. In her next rhetorical move Mahogany swerves into the language of the hustle. She is keenly aware of the global fascination with Detroit. The latter she attributes to Detroiters' endurance and the history of citizens refusing to quit, thus the line "the 31st of never, never!" The latter conditions are the results of neoliberal state and urban planning tactics to which she refuses to submit. She rejects the idea of the removal of Detroit's population.

Mahogany's explanation about why she wrote the track speaks to the negative publicity the city has received in the mass media for decades

FIGURE 5. Ronald "iRonic" Lee Jr., DJ Los, and Mahogany Jones, "Blue Collar Logic" video. Produced by Sharif Chauncey.

that posits Detroit as an imploding urban wasteland in the aftermath of deindustrialization, a cautionary tale to other cities across the United States and the globe. She explains, "As a native New Yorker, relocating to Detroit was major for me. I never thought another city could speak to me so profoundly—until I moved to Detroit. 'Blue Collar Logic' is my ode to a city that has been, is, and will always be full of great genius, beauty, and innovation. I wrote this song as the spirit of Detroit to remind its residents and the world at large that we are here—we have been here and we are here to stay!"[34] Jones captures the spirit of Detroit's working-class character and its hustle.

"Detroit Made"

Nique Love Rhodes released her track "Detroit Made" on SoundCloud in December 2015.[35] Curious as to why this track at this time, we met up with her at the Café Con Leche in Detroit's New Center district—one of the latest sites of redevelopment—to find out. Nique explained that she had no intention of writing another Detroit anthem on the heels of Mahogany Jones's "Blue Collar Logic" and D.S. Sense's "On My Detroit Everything" but felt compelled to do so after hearing the track's instrumental for the first time. The track is a combination of live music she recorded with her band The NLR Experience, synthesized sounds, and sampled voices. Like "Locusts," "Detroit Made" signifies on neoliberal tactics; however, it repurposes the nature of hustle discourses. Unlike Lester Spence's monolithic view of hustling, where it is always already a neoliberal trap, for many artists successfully hustling is a source of pride. The lyrics Rhodes raps in the first verse are potent:

> I'm cut from that royalty, African blood and Holy spirit flowin' in me
> I'm from Detroit city, where the hustle never dies
> We make the cause right, so you know I got drive
> Watch me pull off, I go off
> I'm staying in my lane
> The only time I swerve, is when I'm about to change the game.

Over the course of our conversation we asked her what it is about "the hustle" that resonates with Detroiters and more specifically with herself and other artists in the city. Nique said, "What it is, is hard work. And you can talk to so many people here and everybody does multiple things and that's that hustle . . . everyone here is hustling and has different hats they wear to one, put themselves in the position to be at the table, and also pay the bills. So that's the concept of hustle."[36] What Nique describes has been the material reality for hundreds of thousands of Detroiters for decades. The redistribution of resources, land grabs, outsourced jobs, outright abandonment, and risk management logics are the neoliberal processes that benefit private companies, who profit off the very conditions Spence believes the state has the responsibility to resolve. When the state behaves like a market the entrepreneurial hustle produces the grind. And yet, the state does not behave simply like a market; its existence creates and sustains the conditions by which market logic can rule. With few opportunities for stable, well-paying jobs, people in the city have had to do whatever it takes to fulfill their basic human needs, working exhausting hours for dwindling returns. This track documents these experiences as they are unfolding in the present day.

While it is easy to get behind the cool cachet of "Detroit Hustles Harder," a range of hip hop scholars are cautious about the need for DIY hustle. Lester Spence, for instance, is highly critical of the entrepreneurial impulse driving independent artists like those in the Foundation. In fact, Spence pinpoints the concept of the grind as the latest iteration of what it means to hustle. The grind to which Nique Love Rhodes refers in her track, and her explanation that "everybody does multiple things," speaks to overproductivity for less pay and benefits. If the state fulfilled its role the hustle would not grind down labor. And yet what Spence dreams about is just that—a nostalgic imagination. Foundation artists like Nique do not glorify the hustle, nor do they miss the fact that the state is neglecting its responsibilities to its citizens. This is exactly why the Foundation provides an alternative worldview, a place where self-care is not only celebrated but actively lived. Artists hustle to survive; it is their welfare and their warfare.

After the first verse Nique chants, "I'm from Detroit City, yeah, yeah" numerous times. The lyrics of the hook are but one layer in a cacophony of sounds that also include a loop of a boy's voice faintly repeating the phrase "oh hell ya, hell ya," and muffled voices that stand in for the people of Detroit. The second and last verse functions like a reunion with the city that emphasizes its underground resistance and history of pushing back against corporations and policies that largely hurt its population. Nique raps,

> Get the message, we the blessing, people benefited from
> Gas tax, kings and queens, renaissance we overcome, yeah
> Even when our water shut off, or times are grey, we make a way
> We Detroit, we okay.

Here the concept of hustle reappears but this time in a more directed version that speaks to citizens pushing back on the city's forceful neoliberal plans for redevelopment and Detroit's own water crisis.

The two are intimately connected. Over the past few years, water bills in Detroit have skyrocketed, making the basic human right to water unaffordable for many. Since 2014 the city's response has been to shut off water access to households that do not keep up with their payments, even as the United Nations has gone on record saying that these actions are a violation of basic human rights.[37] Academic and activist Shea Howell explains that "these water shutoffs are not about unpaid bills. This is about dispossession of the people. These shutoffs are intended to drive people from their homes."[38] Akin to the intentional decimation of Black Bottom and Paradise Valley in the mid-twentieth century and the abundant arson that devastated Brush Park in the 1990s, water shutoffs are the most recent state sanctioned land seizure practice in Detroit. The high cost of water for residents and the city's extreme measures in dealing with unpaid bills are its latest strategies for opening up for capital accumulation domains that were once regarded as "off-limits to the calculus of profitability."[39] Jobs are diminishing, yet taxes are increasing to support privatization models that govern human needs. On the surface taxes seem like a straightforward way to fund public service projects; yet, when governance operates like a market system those projects are not deemed worthy of funding.

Reflecting on the track, Nique explains,

I talk about the history of how you have all of this gentrification, and you have all of these out of towners moving in and they're kind of staking their claim on the city, making it their own really, and you have all these people who have been here doing stuff and who've laid the groundwork for a lot of innovative things that are taking place. That's why I say, you know, 'get the message we the blessing people benefitted from,' because people are benefiting, you know, even if you look at the artist community. There are so many artists who were already putting up murals and things like that and now there are new murals coming in. If it wasn't for the people doing the original murals people wouldn't have thought of doing that.[40]

The song ends with a slightly altered chorus where the "I" has been changed to "we." This purposeful move takes listeners from the individual micro practices of identification to a macro mentality of social resistance. The "we" to whom Nique refers is predominantly Black and pushed to the margins. Resistance and awareness are necessary beginnings in her world of revolution. Like Nique, Adrienne Brown shifts the individual's intentionality to the level of the social.[41] Examining the car as a site of resistance, she reconceptualizes hip hop analytics. Brown contends that lyrics about the car are commonly misread, leading to a misunderstanding of the car's function in hip hop narratives. She argues that material possessions are commonly understood as excess or commodity fetishism, while in actuality "they refuse to map exactly onto the mainstream through privatization."[42] Instead she imagines a "spector of commonwealth and collective value lingering."[43] It is interesting that Brown's sense of aesthetics requires us to move away from lyrical analysis to attend to other musical elements such as meter, timber, beat, and cadence. If scholars make this shift, she believes that the result will create an ontology where new ways of "looking, seeing, and being" surface.[44] Brown's argument is instructive; however, although she argues against lyrical analysis, she returns to texts to correct mis-readings. Her analysis is grounded in the very cultural forms that she hopes hip hop studies will be less shaped by in the future. However, through her engagement of hip hop texts she makes a significant point that is often overlooked. She argues that when artists make pronoun shifts from "I" to "we" they shift from individual to social levels of critique, opening a space for audiences to see themselves in the "we." This principle is at work in Nique's move to the community when she alters the chorus to "*we* from Detroit City."

· · ·

It is challenging to be a revolutionary hustler; for Lester Spence one precludes the possibility of the other. The time it takes to grind, to have one's hands in many-low paying pots, does not set the stage for revolution. Spence contends that the ideology and practice of the hustle that is popularized in slogans like "Detroit Hustles Harder" contribute to the normalization of the conditions that force entrepreneurialism.[45] He cannot see agency in the hustle, nor the identification that comes with the sentiment. Detroiters hustle as a means of survival, not as acts of glorification. They are propelled toward the neoliberal hustle as they push against the abandonment and violence that follows contemporary neoliberal logics and practices of governmentality. For the women of the Foundation, hustling is also tied to a practice of self-care that under racial capitalism—where so many lives do not matter—by necessity extends to community care.

The music and poetry we analyze here reveal both the insidious side of renewal that runs on neoliberal fuel—leading to the hustle and grind—as well as the rights that the poor and disenfranchised are seeking to reclaim. Their inclusion in transformation plans is essential for citizens to experience a "renewed right to urban life."[46] On the contrary, under the racial capitalist and neoliberal conditions that govern Detroit post-bankruptcy, the hegemonic perspective of the state, investors, and the press is one in which the city is a de facto *terra nullius,* a "Nobody's land" eagerly awaiting revival. The anthems of Invincible/ill Weaver and Finale, Nique Love Rhodes, Mahogany Jones, and D.S. Sense sound out the muffled, too often muted voices in Detroit that are symbolically and materially annihilated in the press, in the mayor's reports, and through the governor's financial emergency plans for predominantly Black Michigan cities like Detroit. They make audible the work and community care happening across a variety of platforms and social justice networks in the city. Each artist wades into the contested terrains that make up what has become "two Detroits"—one graced with design-intensive luxuries and professional opportunities and the Other replete with dilapidated buildings, faltering city services, impoverished schools, food deserts, and scarce job prospects.

Collectively, "Locusts," "On My Detroit Everything," "Blue Collar Logic," and "Detroit Made" offer four erudite responses to neoliberal revanchism. On "Locusts," Invincible and Finale offer a remorseful critique of the destruction of the city as they knew it. In "On My Detroit Everything" D.S. Sense incites identification with the city. She calls out "lukewarm" rappers for not only lacking lyrical skill but aligning with the industry's neoliberal business tactics that include the commodification of bodies and the privileging of a discourse that keeps poor black communities in their place. Against this trajectory, D.S. Sense claims the city as if she and Detroit live in the same body. "Blue Collar Logic" is a determinate resistance of removal. Mahogany Jones makes the case that Black Detroit has been here and will continue to be here, whether the state sees and hears them or not. Lastly, Nique Love Rhodes's "Detroit Made" repurposes neoliberal discourse and practices to map the grounds of hustling on her own terms. Each of these artists' tracks evoke agency, self-care, and consciousness about the neoliberal locusts that have invaded the city. Post-bankruptcy, Detroit is contested terrain; hip hop emcees are part of a larger arts movement that is creating dialogue, forging space, and engaging the social imaginary in the ongoing struggle to situate Detroiters at the center of its future.

3

Negotiating Genderqueer Identity Formation

If You've Got a Rack You Ain't Makin a Stack
—Miz Korona

October 7, 2013. We mull over the Foundation's mission statement as we drive down the Lodge freeway on our way to the Cass Commons Building. This location was the last home of the Foundation before it ended its run of hosting weekly open mic nights in the summer of 2014. We ruminate, anticipating what might come of the conversation we are about to have with seven key Foundation members. After a year of consistent engagement with the collective, we've set up a conversation about gender and sexuality for many reasons, one of which haunted us as feminist-identified ethnographers. We kept asking ourselves, "Why is feminism an uncool F-word in this community?"

I rant a bit to Bekka: "Ok, so pedagogy is right up in the mission statement, and so is the aim of reaching youth." Bekka follows with her own insight, "I know. Empowerment is in there too." We are reaching for links to feminism; doing gender politics in its absence is inconceivable to us because of our material, political, and ideological experiences and realities. We are white women academics, public intellectuals who live outside the pressures that Black and Brown populations in Detroit face on the daily. In that habitual grind we have witnessed Detroiters testifying in hip hop tracks and other forms of poetics about the state of the city's conditions, enduring patriarchal structures, and cultural blind spots.

Politically, Detroit is both progressive and patriarchal. It is drenched in a history of white supremacy and Black patriarchal forces and institutions. It birthed the Nation of Islam and served as the site for famous speeches by Martin Luther King, Jr., and Malcolm X. However, with respect to its gender and sexuality politics Detroit has a long way to go, despite the women, men, queer, and gender-nonconforming identified activists that lead its social justice and community building organizations. Some of these institutions, such as D-Town Farm and the Boggs Center, have commanded the attention of actors, media personalities, and activists nationwide. From Jimmy Boggs and Grace Lee Boggs's revolutionary conceptual grounding to Ruth Ellis's work with queer and transgender youth populations, and more recent figures like adrienne maree brown's[1] treatise on emergent social movement strategies and Tawana "Honeycomb" Petty's[2] rethinking of anti-racism organizing efforts, women and gender-nonconforming social actors command Detroit's cultural and political community-building work. The strident efforts of these organizers who engage in community activism and cultural organizing in Detroit face exhausting challenges.

Gay and gender-nonconforming artists within Detroit's hip hop underground face similar, historically entrenched obstacles that women and men face on other fronts. Many of these artists have to make decisions about coming out and the extent to which they choose to conform to gender narratives within the local scene as well as the hip hop industry at large. If they choose not to succumb to gender- and sexuality-related pressures they must endure the consequences, which can include less attention, respect, and financial compensation than artists who conform to binary, hegemonic gender logics—be they DJs, b-girls, or emcees. What is more, they must convince their communities that sexism is an enduring issue. Chimamanda Ngozi Adichie's reflections are instructive; she ruminates, "I feel lonely in my fight against sexism, in a way that I don't feel in my fight against racism. My friends, my family, they get racism, they get it. The people I'm close to who are not black get it. But I find that with sexism you are constantly having to explain, justify, convince, make a case for."[3] This is the daily struggle of Foundation artists. When one adds gender-nonconforming and/or queer to the mix the conditions become even more messy. Lack of recognition results in fewer networking and performance opportunities and in turn, artists in these positions earn less than those who conform to societal and industry standards, notably the men who dominate hip hop. Miz Korona coined the phrase "If you've got a rack, you ain't makin' a stack"[4] to sum up her twenty-year experience as a Detroit emcee. Over the years she has witnessed her male counterparts, some with less skill, receive the fruit of their labor but is yet to reap similar financial rewards. She attributes this outcome in part to her queer identity and resistance to displaying hegemonic femininity. Of late, she identifies herself as masculine-of-center, which means, in part, that her look and performance of self lean toward a more masculine sensibility, and yet she feels as if she is also very feminine. She wears long braids, can pull off a snap back hat, has a sneaker collection that would make Kanye smile, and she spits lyrics like a beast. She is formidable on stage, bearing a large, brightly colored "REVOLUTION" tattoo on her forearm. Yet, masculine-of-center does not foreclose the possibility of femininity.

It is within this context of progress and constraint that gender and sexuality identifications play out in Detroit's hip hop underground. Here, innovative and erudite forms of thought and cultural production emerge. In this gritty mess of material, symbolic, and sonic production the following questions guide the direction of this chapter. First, to what extent do gender politics inform the practices, worldviews, and cultural production of Foundation artists in the hip hop underground? Second, how do their practices and cultural production reflect hip hop feminism and pedagogy, if at all? And finally, what forms of masculinity do men who support the Foundation accept and reject? We feel this last question is deserving of analysis and discussion because the Foundation has always aspired to inclusion and men constitute part of that outreach. From its inception, men who play pivotal roles in Detroit's hip hop scene served as supporters, contributors, and at times, teachers within Foundation spaces and events. This ethic is an example of bell hooks'[5] proclamation that feminism is for everybody and not just the prerogative of women.

Pedagogy is inherent in the Foundation's constitution, not only across the elements, but also in its cultural organizing work. We contend that the arrival and aims of hip hop feminism, hip hop pedagogy, and genderqueer theorizing coincide with the Foundation's emergence, commitments and practices. Long before the #MeToo movement the Foundation was laying down space, opening up consistent places for women and queer artists, academics, and activists to share their love for hip hop's aesthetics, politics, and community commitments. In what follows, we draw on conversations we have had with key actors and supporters of the Foundation, both women and men; after working through moments of gender and sexuality negotiations we trace the relationships between identity formation and processes of cultural production. Along the way we weave cutting-edge literatures that cut across hip hop feminism/pedagogy and contemporary theorizing on masculinity in hip hop culture.

"WHITE WOMEN'S SHIT"

From our standpoint as white women and academic ethnographers, when we began this project the worldviews and philosophies of Foundation artists and their supporters seemed in sync with general feminist aims and goals. After all, here was a diverse group of Black women who consciously chose to band together—many on a weekly basis—for the purpose of forming community and uplifting women in hip hop. For a period of time (2013–2014), in addition to supporting the Tuesday night open mic nights, some women came together on Sunday afternoons for what can be best described as consciousness-raising sessions, where they ruminated on life as Black and Brown women in Detroit. Knowing better than to make assumptions about their relationship to feminism, we organized a group meeting where we asked questions and listened as the conversation about their take on feminism unfolded.

Over a period of years attending events, engaging with Foundation artists' music and videos, and collaborating on "Legendary," we learned that participants in Detroit's hip hop underground embody a wide range of knowledge, opinions, experiences, and practices pertaining to feminism, gender, and sexuality. While we could see these meaningful differences play out in cultural production and interaction, we did not know from where the members' stocks of knowledge originated. In other words, we did not know what combinations of influence—home, school, streets, faith, and popular culture—shaped their understanding and assessment of gender and sexuality. In an effort to create a deeper context of reflection, in 2013 we organized a group meeting where we asked questions, listened, and participated in a conversation about Foundation artists' take on feminism. Nine women, including the two of us, participated in the two-hour session held in the lower level of the Cass Corridor Commons building. With the exception of ourselves, all of the women present were African American. Six of the nine are college graduates; two women have not had any experience with post-secondary education and one was a college freshman at the time. Among the college graduates, three had some direct exposure to feminism in their coursework. We include segments of this conversation to situate the differing interpretations, arguments, and identifications that emerged when the group engaged in a fast-moving, ideologically rich discussion about gender and sexuality politics. In the section that follows we digress from the approach we have taken in other chapters and use pseudonyms in place of members' birth and/or stage names. We settled on this approach because it was not our intention to single out specific individuals for their politics or knowledge base; on the contrary, we wanted participants to feel free to express their opinions and ask questions without feeling compelled to consciously frame their discourse for the public eye. The insights from this session revealed layers of reach and resistance that we did not anticipate. In some ways the conversation matches up with research contending that many Black women lack an interest in feminism because they do not see it as culturally relevant or attending to the breadth of their experiences.[6] In other ways, the conversation offers alternatives to feminism as sites of learning and identification.

We began by asking, "what's up with feminism in hip hop?" From the get go the responses varied widely.[7] Without hesitation Phoenix remarked, "All the cool, hot chicks in New York are feminists," to which most in the group responded with a laugh. As our conversation unfolded, it became impossible for some members to hold back their thoughts, with Sweet Brush—a visual artist who was also a graduate student invested in women's and gender studies—blurting out at the start of our conversation, "Yes you are a feminist; you are a feminist too (pointing at specific individuals). I am a feminist too." Immediately after she made this claim, another woman, Specs, chimed in, saying, "I don't know what feminism is? I just don't. [pause] Women hating on men?" Later, she asked, "Is feminism reverse sexism? Like we in the Foundation are going to do it better than men?" Because of her academic training, Sweet Brush situates her life experiences, opportunities, and privilege within a historical feminist framework, and she encouraged the other women in the room to do the same. Yet, for those who were not invested in it—academically or otherwise—prior to their work with the Foundation, feminism is not a framework they identify with despite their first-hand experience with sex-based discrimination. Sweet Brush went on to explain, "It's like this: for me it means that I'm gonna call a man out if he needs it, but that does not mean I hate you. It just means I am calling you out for things you are doing." In response, Specs said, "You know what my friends say when I do that? 'You're just being a girl.'"

Specs's understanding of feminism reflects what Michael Kaufman and Michael Kimmel call "the guys' guide to feminism."[8] It is self-serving and removed from feminist principles and goals. Specs is unaware because no one in her neighborhood, school system, peer group, or family has invited her to consider another view. When she pushed back, she was told resistance equals weakness. Power is indeed contradictory and productive; it is Specs who questions who gets paid on bills, and yet when open resistance is articulated, it feels like reverse sexism to her. Only discourse drenched in sexist edicts can produce this effect. It operates akin to the ways that talking openly about race is considered an act of racism in "post-racial" America. Clearly, in these instances the word "girl" is used as a putdown to silence women who call men out on sexist, discriminatory behavior. It also works to normalize the superiority of men under patriarchy in the hope that women will not protest their experiences and the inequalities to which they are subject and disrupt the gender hierarchy. Frustrated, Sweet Brush replied, "See that's just a misconception," and with a teacherly tone she went on,

> Let me give you a simple definition. bell hooks says, it's fighting against the objectification of women—an attempt to end sexism. As a hip hop artist your work, if it is empowering you in an attempt to empower other women, if it provides a space for women, to me that would be feminist. I don't necessarily believe that everyone has to identify.

Despite saying that she doesn't believe that everyone has to identify, the fervor with which Sweet Brush insists that everyone present is indeed a feminist, and her turn to bell hooks to explain why, suggest that she does indeed wish that more Black women, especially those affiliated with the Foundation, would claim feminism.

At this juncture, others joined in. Intrepid, who couldn't attend the meeting in person, was on speakerphone. She remarked,

> Do I consider myself a feminist? Not really. So I care basically about the issues related to it. But I feel like I walk in the room, I walk in a triple minority. I walk in as an African American, as a woman, and a lesbian. But for me as far as my identity is concerned the thing that has always been most challenging to me, it's been my race. It's race issues that I care about. They are at the forefront of my mind. Race has been more of a factor than gender for me.

Quiet followed Intrepid's remark, a thoughtful silence. For Intrepid, her intersectional identity is marked by three social categories: race, gender, and sexuality. Intrepid's view that race trumps other identity categories is not unique. Patricia Hill Collins has also identified Black women's proclivity to conceive of race as more immediate than gender in their daily lives.[9] Detroit's context also figures into Intrepid's experience, as it is one of the most racially segregated metro areas in the country. It is this viewpoint that leads Adichie to feel lonely in her fight against sexism.[10]

In another instance, Foundation members explicitly named white, second-wave liberal feminists in their reasons for why they don't identify as feminists, saying, "We are not feeling Betty Freidan and Gloria Steinem. When they fought for sexual freedom, mothers like ours cleaned their houses and looked after their kids."[11] Even those members with exposure to feminism experience its discourse as somewhere between what Joan Morgan has termed "white women's shit,"[12] what Foundation artist DJ Listen says "is not holistic enough,"[13] and what Intrepid thinks is "extra, kind of in your face, protesting, rah, rah."[14] This disconnect between Foundation members and feminism is both noteworthy and to some extent predictable. For some women their knowledge of feminism comes from popular rhetoric that frames feminists as man-hating, and even in instances where this is not the case, it is often still looked at as "white women's shit."

In 2015, we sat down with Tawana "Honeycomb" Petty, who had recently become an active member with the Foundation. She is nationally recognized as a poet, author, and community organizer. When we asked her how race comes into play when Black women think about feminism Honeycomb reflected, "Yeah you'll have Black women that are like, 'yes I'm a feminist,' and they studied it. But just generically, people think of feminism as a white woman thing and the black version of feminism is an Angry Black Woman thing."[15] Echoing Joan Morgan's and Patricia Hill Collins's views, the Angry Black Woman of which Honeycomb speaks is the script of the strong Black woman who can do it all on her own, is never vulnerable, and needs no one but herself and her work ethic to survive. However, as Collins explains, the strong Black woman is a myth.[16] The trope is a response to poverty, racism, and internalized racism. Working from this view Morgan characterizes the strong Black woman as one who is fed up with men, raises her kids alone with fortitude, and has given up on the prospect of finding a desirable Black man.[17] Separation and abandonment from men can figure into the formation of the strong Black woman. That Honeycomb likens the dominant reading of Black feminism in the community to the Angry Black Woman is daunting. Angry is not unexpected; that feminism is connected to the lack of vulnerability is more problematic.

Interpreting why Black women who claim feminism do so despite its negative association with the Angry Black Woman script, she explains,

> There's more power in standing up for the angry Black woman than there is for almost isolating your race. You're basically saying there isn't a man out there that couldn't do anything you could. I got all this shit together. The

only thing I needed him for, if I needed him, is for sperm. Black men think they are losing their power. . . . The irony is a lot of Black women in attempting to take our power back are like, damn right I'm an angry woman.[18]

Honeycomb questions how anger, strength, and feminism become synonymous. Working through men's responses to feminism, she says, "They use the 'feminism' word like ho to make it a negative thing . . . Feminism is a dagger they throw at women."[19] Carving out a new kind of language, creating space that hitherto did not exist and reforming citizenship along the way, Foundation members ideologically embody feminism and yet the name trips some women up; historical and ideological baggage filters their reach and resistance. Invincible/ill Weaver is one of the only gender-nonconforming artists in our community. Along with Piper Carter they champion "gender justice" as a much more palatable and inclusive conception of cultural politics. Others embrace the term feminism, whereas some see it as secondary to racial identity battles. Foundation members' relationships to feminism draw on second-wave white and Black feminism as well as the work of contemporary hip hop scholars and sister organizations like the Crunk Feminist Collective.[20]

HIP HOP FEMINISM

Since Joan Morgan's coining of the phrase, hip hop feminism has made strides remixing and extending concerns that have shaped Black feminist thought for decades. Borrowing a phrase from Missy Elliot's fourth album *Under Construction,* Whitney Peoples details the ways in which hip hop feminism itself is under construction, both *flowing with* as well as signifying *ruptures from* earlier Black feminist thinking.[21] Starting in the mid-1990s, third wave Black feminists felt an urgent need to respond to a Black feminism that they believed was out of touch with "the current realities and needs of young black women" as well as their relationship to hip hop.[22] Whereas second wave feminists were content to critique hip hop's misogyny, third wavers argued for a feminist consciousness that allowed women of the hip hop generation "to examine how representations and images can be simultaneously empowering and problematic."[23] In their comprehensive review essay, "The Stage that Hip Hop Feminism Built," Durham, Cooper, and Morris summarize how hip hop feminism's theorizing and praxis continue to tackle Black sexual politics. In particular, they argue that such efforts focus on challenging the persistence and prevalence of hip-hop "misogynoir;" the compulsory heterosexuality within hip hop music and culture at large; as well as an uncritical acceptance and endorsement of respectability politics.[24]

As we allude to above, hip hop feminists question the normative notions of respectability that have served as the primary ways to understand gender and sexual politics in the public sphere. In the civil rights era, respectability politics was a strategy adopted to contest marginalization. Women growing up in the hip hop era have taken notice that while it may have garnered some Black women respect, it has done so at a price. It means policing appearance, speech, and sexuality, as well as restricting emotion and sexuality. As Maisha Z. Johnson articulates, respectability politics requires Black women to adjust their own behavior to avoid the racist, classist, and sexist stereotypes other people assign them.[25] Foundation artists challenge respectability politics in their music, style, identity politics, and most of all their spirit—that is, their unabashed resistance and intrepid attitudes. With respect to their style, whereas some women challenge respectability politics by donning sexy party dresses Foundation artists more often challenge it in their embrace of combat boots, flannel shirts, cool kicks, and/or dreadlocks.

The efforts, politics, and cultural production of Foundation artists befit hip hop's roots as a resistance movement, but as rap music became commercialized in the 1990s "a stark division in gender roles" became standardized.[26] Without dismissing hip hop culture, hip hop feminism calls into question the hegemonic and heteronormative gender and sexuality norms that the music and culture reproduces, especially on the most visible commercial levels where men are positioned as agentic, subjective lookers and women as passive, objectified Others there to-be-looked-at.[27] Typically, artists who challenge this patriarchal order are marginalized. In response, hip hop feminism posits alternatives to gender/sexuality binaries, heteronormativity, and the version of Black womanhood that respectability politics invokes. It aims to provide "more elastic way of talking about gender relations"[28] in an effort to create more inclusive spaces for women and queer artists in hip hop's public sphere, an ongoing challenge for not only self-declared hip hop feminists but cultural organizers as well.

As our focus group data illustrates, the majority of the women in our study have had little to no exposure to academic feminism. Their identities have been predominantly shaped by their community relations, families, and popular culture. Of course, they engage in ongoing battles with systemic structural inequalities steeped in sexism, racism, classism, and heteronormativity, but without any kind of theoretically articulated feminism as their guide. Both Durham and Rose identify women who distance themselves from feminism, all the while engaging in women-identified, institution-changing work.[29] Women in Detroit's hip hop underground share practices and goals that reflect not only hip hop feminist but also second wave Black feminist underpinnings. To wit, Peoples surmises that the "overall objectives of Black feminism are empowering black women and creating systemic change to allow for social justice, resonating from generation to generation."[30] The Foundation's mission statement bears out this logic:

> This weekly event as a movement focuses on redefining the vital role of women in hip hop. Our mission is to educate and empower the community through sharing love of the arts, inspire change and growth, build leadership, and influence the perceptions and roles of women in hip hop for current and future generations.[31]

To these objectives Gwendolyn Pough adds consciousness-raising work as a form of public pedagogy.[32] Collectively, pedagogy and performance are practitioner siblings birthed from hip hop feminism.

Ruth Nicole Brown has contributed to the growing definition of hip hop feminism and its relationship to pedagogy. As the creator of the Saving Our Lives/Hearing Our Truths [SOLHOT] collective, Brown conceptualizes hip hop feminism as "the practice of engaging young people using the elements of hip-hop culture and feminist methodology for the purpose of transforming oppressive institutions, policies, relationships, and beliefs."[33] Performance is a major element that guides her practices of pedagogy. It is culturally relevant and grounded in hip hop aesthetics; what is more, performance can capture in a moment what can take theory years to accomplish. Spoken word poetry, rap songs, dances, skits, and ciphers open spaces where youth can explore and articulate their feelings, stories, desires, and struggles, all the while guided by peer and adult mentors. Pedagogy is central because it seeks to validate and empower Black girls and women. In all of its aims, youth outreach, performance as pedagogy, creating spaces for women to hone their crafts, and a commitment to multigenerational solidarity, the Foundation carried out a hip hop feminist agenda without claiming its name. Miz Korona is one such artist who advances resistant gender and sexuality politics without claiming the name of any dominant discourse.

"THE MOST SLEPT ON"

Miz Korona is a founding member of the Foundation, and a long-time fixture in Detroit's hip hop underground who is still best known to most for her starring role as the lunch truck rapper Vanessa in the Eminem biopic *8 Mile*. Over the course of her extensive career dating back to the 1990s, she has been the recipient of numerous Detroit Music Awards including "Outstanding Hip Hop Artist" and "Female Rapper of the Year." She has released two full-length albums and spent some time touring in Europe over the course of our fieldwork. In 2018, Miz Korona performed at the prestigious Detroit Institute of Arts [DIA] and is featured in photographer Jenny Ritcher's Detroit hip hop exhibit "De-Cyphered," which premiered at the DIA in 2017.

In 2012 Miz Korona started working on tracks for a new album. Although finances and other setbacks precluded the album's release, the album artwork and a number of completed tracks were later released online as singles. The title, *Sealy Posturepedic: The Most Slept On,* is one we needed her to translate.

> Ok so "Most Slept On" is the title track. . . . That song came about, well the title of the album really came about because people kept telling me I was slept on. 'Man you're the most slept on female emcee. You're the most slept on!' I told [my producer] Chains, man if I hear one more person say I'm the most slept on, I'm going to name my album 'the most slept on'. I get there and this dude was like 'oh shit, that's my most favorite female rapper, Miz Korona. Man, she's so slept on!' I said, God damn it. I told Chains, that's it, we're naming the album Most Slept On . . . . I wanted to make it not so easy. I did research on the highest selling mattress just to make it more interesting, an interesting conversational piece . . . . I did all this googling and such-and-such and here it is, the Sealy Posturepedic is the mattress we sold the most.[34]

To be "the most slept on" is to be the most passed over. Many fans in the community, and Miz Korona herself, do not feel that she has received the accolades she deserves for her emcee skills over the years.

The second half of the album title would also materialize as a track. We now turn to the first verse and chorus of "Most Slept On," followed by Miz Korona's reflections on its incarnation:

> It feels like I'm trapped in the city where the skinny niggaz die
> So in order for me to win I gotta cut a lot of ties
> If men lie and women lie but the numbers don't
> The spot that I'm in must be the reason they uncomfortable
> Number one lyricist of year back to back
> So why in the fuck am I still here?

Rhyming like my life depends on steady shitting in the booth
Like the mic got Depends on it (ugh)
I'm a monster that's what the blogs say
No imposter, sick with the word play
But these herbs stay sleeping on me
Since these weed heads need beds
Welcome to Posturepedic homie,
Don't forget to put the Sealy in front
I'm the truth dog you can disagree if you want
But that'll only justify my claim
It's no accident they trying to shut down my lane

But I'm a move (yeah)
I'm quick wit the reflex
I'm a vet (shit)
All I want is respect
They still treat me like a reject
The most slept
You niggaz ain't woke up outta yo sleep yet?

Miz Korona explains its evolution:

> When I first heard [the beat], I was like, wow this shit is fucking crazy. . . . It felt like some weird, morphing, and in some trance world so I said, damn this beat makes me feel like I'm trapped, trying to get out. So the first line is "trapped in the city where the skinny niggers die." And that's what was happening in my life at the time. I had to cut a lot of ties from holding me back, so to speak, and I thought if I stay around this group of people who were holding me in a box then I won't reach my full potential. They were stuck doing the same things, stuck not doing the same thing, not wanting to leave the hood, not really wanting to do anything to elevate themselves. Every time I looked up, someone kept going to jail or getting shot on my old block. I was like, y'all trapped with the skinny niggers. In order for me to win, I got to cut a lot of ties. The next line is 'if men lie and women lie and but the numbers don't, the spot that I'm in must be the reason they be uncomfortable,' which is true. Then I go on to say, 'the number one lyricist of the year back-to-back,' because I had won the award five years in a row. Yeah, the Detroit awards. So I'm like the number one lyricist of the year back-to-back so 'why the fuck am I still here, rhyming like my life depend on it, steady shit in the booth like the mic got Depends on it?'

Hip hop scholars remind fans, scholars, and pundits that hip hop is an aesthetic as much as it is a site of resistance and/or a tool for social change.[35] Brilliantly, they excavate the edges of rap lyrics, prying open semiotic codes, practices of signifying, homage to ancestors, deliberate inaccessibility, and metaphor. Jasmine Cobb traces the figures in Black history who have shaped emcee delivery and composition styles, like the

Black preacher and the blues singer, among others. When one brings Tricia Rose into the conversation more critical analytics shape hip hop's toolkit. That is, Rose see it operating through the signifying practices of rupture, layering, and flow. One of the many insights that she expands upon in *Black Noise* is her insistence that aesthetics, politics, and repurposed technologies allowed artists to reinvent these practices. In total, they give tracks their texture. For Rose, "vocal rapping privileges flow, layering and ruptures in line." Flow is about "moving easily and powerfully through complex lyrics" and beats and layering refer to the way meaning operates and how things come to signify. Rose gives the example that rappers may deploy layering by using the same word to mean different things; it also explains rhyming patters and the way rap lyrics are written in sixteen-bar verses. Rupture is intervention in style, ideas, ideology, and flow. It is as political as it is aesthetic. The implications of ruptures, layering, and flow, according to Rose, is that "these effects at the level of style and aesthetics suggest affirmative ways in which profound social dislocation and rupture can be managed and perhaps contested in the cultural arena."[36]

A combination of these oral and literary forms is at work in "Most Slept On." These tropes and figures are embedded in her rhyming patterns and wordplay. While playing the dozens is also one of the overt dissing practices that has a long history in African American oral culture, signifying can be more subtle. Henry Louis Gates developed a theory around the concept "signifying," which is a form of linguistic trickery, or "running game" in hip hop's lexicon. As Miz Korona confronts her dis/respectful opponents ("herbs") she works the wordplay in her lyrics: "No imposter sick with the word play/But these herbs stay sleeping on me/Since these weed heads need beds." In these three lines, Miz Korona signifies on always-high potheads who are too sleepy to grasp "dope" talent. She is the truth, "no imposter, sick with the word play." The term sick is often code for talent, but one can also read it like "sic," to signify when a mistake is made. Claiming she is "slept on" is a form of rupture, a social statement about lazy listeners who have tired taste—"they need beds." Words are reversed, interventions are stated, identities are reclaimed. Her tactic here is much like Eminem's move in *8 Mile*. Knowing how Black men in Detroit would treat a "trailer-park white boy," he beats them to it and raps about himself as white trash, busting out of the trailer park. In a similar posture Miz Korona creates the conditions of who is sleeping and who is slept on. Her most aggressive form of signifying appears when she messes with the operations of

FIGURE 6. Miz Korona and DJ Los. Photo: Rebekah Farrugia.

reflection: "Number one lyricist of year back to back/So why in the fuck am I still here?/Rhyming like my life depends on steady shitting in the booth/Like the mic got Depends on it."

In this verse her reversals flow through the form of mic feces. She layers the word "depends"; at once, it is a high stakes measure and a container for leaking feces, urine, and other waste that older, "OG" artists need. ("OG" is short for both "original gangsta" and "old school.") If Korona is slept on, then rappers getting famous are full of shit. On the other hand, Korona is *the* shit and she rhymes to exist. Again, she flips the wordplay in her favor. "Steady" is not just a metaphor for "regular" in the digestive sense; it communicates catalogue and consistent productivity as an artist. The hook brings her flow in line with layering and signifying, metaphor and rhythm: "But I'm a move (yeah)/I'm quick wit the reflex/I'm a vet (shit)/All I want is respect/They still treat me like a reject/The most slept/You niggaz ain't woke up outta yo sleep yet?" She is the embodiment of movement and reflex, like a natural; she is seasoned like a vet, demanding respect. In Korona's framing of experience a veteran commands respect, while OGs are easily slept on, and in the end, those who do not show love and respect are not "woke." This track is not a preemptive diss song. It is a signifying tale about lacking stocks of knowledge in today's hip hop industry. She is not talking about the hyperlocal, per se, but about those players who command the market, the heteronormative ideologies that discipline women, especially women like herself who Miz Korona terms "masculine-of-center."

STEPPING OUT IN "WHO I AM"

In August 2012 we witnessed Miz Korona's first public performance of her track "Who I Am" at a free outdoor event at Detroit's New Center Park. The park is located on the southwest corner of Second Avenue and West Grand Boulevard on the northern edge of the 7.2 square miles of urban renewal. When Miz Korona came out publicly in her track "Who I Am" in 2012, after a fifteen-year career as a known emcee, she accomplished a double intervention: she both ruptured hip hop's compulsory heterosexuality in a city drenched in heteronormativity and also took a stab at society at large. A Black woman coming out faces a triple displacement, even as doors break open. She already battles gender bias as well as overt and institutionalized racism; to question sexuality and claim a queer identity places her in that "triple minority" subject positionality that Intrepid called into question in our focus group interview. Taking on sexuality amplified her battle for legitimacy. And yet, Miz Korona is no self-proclaimed victim. She is proactive and swift with positivity. Miz Korona identifies the homophobia that continues to structure Black queer lives in general, and more specifically structured her own life until she came out and publicly embraced her queer identity. Here we engage the hook and one key verse to situate her journey. The hook is the punchline of her story and is repeated several times in the track:

> So take me for who I am
> Cause I won't change for no woman
> And I won't change for no man
> I can only be who I am.

Despite her embrace of her sexuality in the hook, the deeper turmoil she has confronted that began at home, at church, and in her neighborhood mark the breadth of her struggle:

> Growing up I was confused
> They caught me kissing a girl
> They told me straighten up, it's a cold cold world
> People won't accept that lifestyle that you living
> And from that moment on I got used to pretending
> Living in the fantasy
> Trying to live a normal life

Even though the track includes her sadness, near hopelessness, and reflection on what counts as normal, it was the forces that challenged her that made her stronger—her faith and the eventual acceptance of her family. By the end she claims queerness and is unwilling to change for anyone. While aggressive lines exist in this track, Miz Korona employs what Adam Krims terms the sung style of rap.[37] She is more melodic, closer to a singing voice than in most of her other songs. On the recorded version of the track, Ideeyah sings the hook. The beats are uplifting and gritty; the music and her melodic, bass-heavy voice can evoke clapping, dancing, or reflection.

In Detroit, stepping out as gay comes with costs. One risks the critique of the church, normative state organizations, club owners, foundations, sponsors, agents, and of course, everyday fans. In our view, "Who I Am" is the riskiest song that Korona has produced. When we asked her how the beat came about and how she processed the writing of the lyrics, once again we learned that she begins with the beat: "A producer emailed me some beats [and] that one jumped out at me and the sample is from a Mary J. Blige song. She says 'so take me for who I am,' then I'm like, man, I could flip this and use this beat. Like I didn't even imagine where I was gonna go with it lyric wise."[38] Tricia Rose calls sampling a form of "musical archeology," where "one uses another's voice to say what they want to say."[39] It is intertextual in that Mary J. Blige's song "No Drama" is being used and put to new meaning; she is also being honored for her insight. Imani Perry considers this mode of citation a "shout out" to those artists, ancestors and public figures who deserve honor.[40] To sample is to resituate and Miz Korona does just that as she flips "take me for who I am" and opens up lines of sexuality. When we asked her what it is like for queer artists in Detroit she explained that

> I'm a little leery in certain settings . . . and it's sad that we have to have a separate club for gay and trans and bi people; that we can't go to a quote-un-quote straight bar, listen to music and have fun with our straight friends and family without being bullied, [but I'm] not going back in closet for anybody. I was in for way too long and was told that I wouldn't work in the industry. [I'm] not overtly feminine. That's what's held me back. A lot of people feel that way. This song right here is just me touching on some of those subjects and like I said, I didn't know where it was gonna go. It just felt right . . . and a young kid who was in this situation, anything similar to what I was growing up and being told that how we feel on the inside is a sin, it can probably help them. And I didn't know that that's where it was gonna go.[41]

She explained the roots of different verses in the song by contextualizing her experience.

> I lived, growing up, feeling like the black sheep, feeling like I wasn't gonna be accepted, feeling like, I wanna be normal because everybody around me

is normal, and praying every night that God would make me what is "normal" to the point that I contemplated killing myself a couple times. You know what I mean? I was just like, I don't wanna, I don't want certain members in my family telling me you better straighten up or you're going to hell. Going to friends' houses, 'why are you hanging out with that bull dyke?' I was in elementary school. I didn't know what gay was.[42]

Even as she explains the song's genesis she unpacks unanticipated if not contradictory feelings. "When an artist actually lives what these [queer] kids go through every day because they've been there, it's more relatable. I didn't write it to make anybody feel any type of way. It was a cleansing for me that needed to be done."[43] She acknowledges that queer kids may relate to her song, but she did not write it specifically with others in mind; instead, she claims it as her personal cleansing. Intention and effect can be at odds and accomplish both acts in one gesture.

A wealth of the literature about queer hip hop artists or queering hip hop is about the lives of gay men or transgender artists like Fly Young Red and Big Freedia and the spaces they occupy.[44] In a more inclusive analysis, Rinaldo Walcott broadens the discussion to include questioning the role that capitalism plans and the ways that artists circumvent it.[45] He argues that a genuine queer hip hop should be bound up with anti-capitalist critique and thus resist market forces. Especially pertinent to our work, he goes on to stress that "it is precisely those artists making queer hip hop who for example might not sell product beyond their local, who should be central to our analytical efforts at the site of the representational and indeed the lyrical."[46] Miz Korona charts a course where openly queer hip hop artists can be themselves.

MAKING MEN MIGHTY: MASCULINITY IN HIP HOP

The men who love, support, mentor, and revere women hip hop artists are genderqueer in their own right. That is, they queer the lines of normative masculinity outside of gay subject positions and complicate the key scripts that shape hegemonic and at times heteronormative hip hop masculinity. At the outset of her book *Prophets of the Hood: Politics and Poetics in Hip Hop* Imani Perry points to a simple and yet profound reality about hip hop culture when she states that "to listen to hip hop is to enter a world of complexity and contradiction."[47] Gender identity, whether it is perceived as traditional, non-conformist or "a little queer," is mired in complexity and contradiction. Even the most politically motivated artists cannot escape contradiction. Why or how should they? In our view, contradiction is an inherent condition that shapes human existence. While it exists in every cultural form that humans create, rap artists receive uneven criticism; that is, they receive harsh critique for their perceived misgivings. Michael Eric Dyson has asked, "why should hip hop artists carry more burden, take more heat than others" for contradiction and inflammatory ideas?[48] For example, what fans or critics go after Merle Haggard's straight-laced ideas, those steeped in anti-drug proclamations like "we don't smoke marijuana in Muskogee" and pro-war sentiments such as "We don't burn our draft cards down on Main Street," that he recites in the song "Okie from Muskogee," for his contradictions/untruths? In his daily life Merle was actually a hard-drinking pothead. These contradictions did not shape the discourse surrounding country music in general, or Merle in particular. Hip hop artists do not receive these types of cultural passes. In fact, one could easily draw the conclusion that rap is the most misogynist form of contemporary music if relying solely on public discourse for information. Contradiction is not simply an issue that shows up in the artistic work of emcees; it traverses the entire discourse around hip hop.

We acknowledge the pain and problems that openly misogynist rap can create; we also contend, along with other hip hop scholars, that rappers did not invent sexism.[49] Rap artists reinvent and situate it in the context of street knowledge, ties to the hood[50] and the conditions of manhood that it takes to survive postindustrial urban life.[51] Instead of pointing, we unpack conditions—pushing open ethnographic pockets of knowledge that help explain the practices that lead to both dangerous gender dynamics as well as routes to recovery.

The narratives through which artists in this chapter tell their stories about gender, sexuality, family, and community open paths not often traveled by gender critics. Our ethnographic trajectory ushers in new routes that deviate from the commercial roots of gender inquiry. In the following section, we scrutinize literature that addresses the particular ways that masculinity is theorized in hip hop studies before we advance the notion that men who practice cultural organizing and community-building in Detroit reproduce normative identifications of masculinity on the one hand, while they also create alternative, if not non-conformist, ways of understanding and living gendered lives. In so doing, they disrupt the very grounds of normativity.

It's a Thug Thing

The iconic men who drive hip hop's commercial arena have evoked considerable scholarly and journalistic attention.[52] Across the literature, an emergent range of scripts have been attributed to them, including Thug, Gangsta, Bad Man, Ladies' Man, Pimp, and Hustler. In many ways, Thug functions like a master code, as it can absorb all of the aforementioned types. With the exception of the work of Toby Jenkins,[53] few analytics exist that uplift men for their intelligence, creativity, rhetorical prowess, fatherhood, or leadership—that is, unless one looks to hip hop's underground[54] or to cultural critics and social theorists like Michael Eric Dyson and Herman Gray.[55] Instead, the most ideologically suspect subject positions have become dominant lenses through which Black men are viewed. We argue that these scripts do not capture the complexity or contradictions that many men bear in their daily lives or through their processes and practices of cultural production.

Analyzing the Bad Man trope, which at times he uses interchangeably with Thug, cultural historian Jeffrey Ogbar argues that sexual promiscuity, excess (having money and material power), as well as being able to strike fear in another man are qualities that define a Bad Man, aka Bad Ass N*****.[56] As he critiques Ice Cube's most aggressive, misogynist lyrics, Ogbar addresses contradiction. He reminds us that Ice Cube's manager is a fierce Black woman who commands a stunning set of professional accolades. That being said, Ogbar concludes with the overall assessment that thug life is "ghetto pathology."[57] While swagger and being cool are part of this trope, Ogbar spends less time on the "cool pose" than many masculinity scholars. In his book *Thug Life* Michael P. Jeffries contends that while the thug trope is signified through hard, even violent messages and lifestyles, it also possesses qualities that complicate and contradict notions of thug life, those generated by rap music's notorious icons like Tupac, 50 Cent, Jay-Z, Ice Cube, T. I., Snoop Dogg, 2 Chainz, Rick Ross, and Trinidad James.[58] The cool poise constitutes the dominant performance of masculinity that courses through hip hop culture. This pose captures the embodiment of thug complexity through a number of key binaries: killer/lover; protector/abuser; loyal to mothers/mother shamers. These oppositions cut across the aesthetic styles embodied in icons like 50 Cent, all greased up on the cover of *Source* magazine, tattoos showing and guns hanging off the side of his baggy jeans. At once, thugs are tough and sexy; what is more, in Byron Hurt's documentary *Hip Hop: Beyond Beats and Rhymes,*

Tim'm T. West, an openly queer emcee and member of the Deep Dick-ollective, commented that "it is not just women who are looking at him [50 Cent] with desire."[59] Tim'm's statement exemplifies a genderqueer reading of a dominant, masculine, threatening-looking Black man. Like Byron Hurt, Jeffries' work draws our attention to these types of contradictions, teasing out the violent and vulnerable dimensions of thug life.

Before Jeffries, Imani Perry advanced a similar assessment, noting that complexity and extreme contradictions can exist in a single artist like Tupac.[60] Perry pokes at the odd alignment of acts in Tupac's life. She reminds us that while Tupac was serving time for a rape charge, he wrote the song "Keep Your Head Up," which is a tribute/anthem dedicated to Black women, particularly those living in broke, under-resourced neighborhoods. The perception of misogyny and affirmation are bound together; one act did not underwrite the other. Rather, Tupac left critics and those who revere him a palimpsest of fragments articulated by contradiction, desire, and complexity.

Perry also offers fans, scholars and critics cautionary considerations; that is, she insists that rap is not liberation music, even though hardcore rappers may posit political messages and sensibilities that turn the tough side of "thugness" inside out.[61] Like Perry, Richard Craig posits a circumspect set of assessments of thug complexity in his work that examines the conditions under which women find thugs and their lifestyles desirable.[62] As Joan Morgan admits, the women in Craig's study agree that nobody is hotter or can get a sister more wet than a thug. Even "respectable" groups like Destiny's Child write lyrics about street men, saying, "uhh he's talking right . . . carrying big things if you know what I mean."[63]

Tempering the aggressive, dangerous thug character coursing across hip hop culture, Mark Anthony Neal posits a new trope that queers dominant narratives about Black masculinity. In *Looking For Leroy*, Neal springboards off the 1980s television show *Fame's* character Leroy to examine a space where Black men can "appear gay" and yet display dominant, heterosexual proclivities.[64] Leroy has a strong, sexy Black body. He is a dancer but also bold, buffed and risky; Leroy is the kind of man that young impressionable heterosexual men in the making can find attractive and badass at the same time. Beginning from *Fame*, Neal tracks the construction of Black masculinity and the thug construct across genres. Along the way he identifies productive contradictions that exist within Leroy's path. And like the queer characteristics that Leroy bears in Neal's construction of Black masculinity, vulnerability, resilience, desire, and success are features that the men in Detroit's hip hop underground who support the Foundation display. These men, like Neal, are creating spaces where a complex Black social actor like Leroy can thrive.

Men Musing on Masculinity

The men who support the Foundation are drawn to the artists and the collective itself for an array of reasons. The inclusivity of Foundation spaces was appealing. Valid, Bryce Detroit, and Will See all told us that they enjoyed the vibe, the inclusiveness, and the willingness of the participants to be vulnerable. Implicit for some and explicit for others, the 5e Gallery's history with the Foundation was a pull in itself for men, some of whom were involved with youth development at the gallery. The Foundation's launch from within the gallery came with built in legitimacy and easy access for the men who were always around.

Politics also motivate many of the men who supported the Foundation. The progressive spirit and mission that Piper and the members of the Foundation advanced fit tightly with the goals and practices of many men who identified with the 5e Gallery. Sustainable urban farming, environmental justice, resistance to emergency management, water shutoffs, and advancing the interests of the extreme local propelled both the 5e Gallery and the Foundation.

Gender and sexual fluidity extend to men who supported the Foundation. The women of the Foundation embody a range of genders and sexualities, from the hyper-feminine to masculine-of-center. The men who support them also occupy a range of complex masculinities. Some bear hard bodies, while others are thin, nerdy, and unapologetic about their expression of manhood. Like the women of the Foundation, these men come from multiethnic backgrounds and span the age spectrum from eighteen to forty-five, with a few in their early fifties. Some attended and graduated from college, while others have high school educations. All of them are radically self-educated in the arts, media literacy, and all parts of the music industry.

Perhaps one of the most driving forces that men admire is the talent that flowed through the Foundation. Men have moved from mentors/teachers to, in many cases, collaborators. As DJ Los contends, in the larger community "men do not think women are at their skill level."[65] However, at the Foundation men had to face the reality that women rock the stage; that is, because the Foundation guaranteed women a place to get on the mic or the turntables, canvas, or dance floor, women were not only on the ticket but the featured artists. In other sites in

Detroit's hip hop underground women do not get on shows; sometimes they are even discouraged from participating in open mics. The sheer presence of talented women shaped the men's appreciation for women artists. Along with the unique space of inclusivity, a women-centered stage and subsequent flow of energies, the enactment of the Universal Zulu Nation's core principles—peace, love, unity, and having fun—were employed. Our local ancestor and water warrior Charity Hicks coined the term "Waging Love." Many women in the Foundation, along with the men who support them, live this principle fiercely.

Men who supported Foundation events are diverse; some openly embrace politically minded hip hop, while others aim for a more commercial sound and party-style music. Over the course of our fieldwork we engaged many men at musical events, activist fundraisers, films, and public discussions. In what follows we examine interview data drawn from a number of individual interviews that we conducted with men in Detroit's hip hop underground. We tap into these particular interviews to tease out ideas about gender and sexuality so that we can compare the thoughts emanating within those conversations to the musical messages and images that Detroit artists are producing. That is, we weave dialogue into textual analysis so as to pinpoint how gendered worldviews trickle into and out of musical productions.

DJ Los is renowned in Detroit's hip hop scene. Along with E-Z B, he recorded the first hip hop album by a Detroit artist. Titled *Untouchable,* it was released in 1988 on his father's label World One Records. Over the span of his career he has worked with well-known Detroit artists such as Jay Dilla, Proof, Slum Village, and Supa Emcee. He continues to produce music and to DJ for Detroit's hottest artists, including many with ties to the Foundation such as Miz Korona, Mahogany Jones, and Lady Fire Fly. When we met up with him, he had this to say about why women struggle for legitimacy in Detroit: "Since there are a lot of lesbians in the scene folks shy away from them. They don't get on the bills like they should."[66] When women's talent is measured through the trope of sexual availability it neatly fits into the kind of masculinity that Los agreed is wrapped up in "cool posing" and a "tough-man, women are for sexing" mentality.

Of all the men we engaged, no one offered more conceptually weighty, historically grounded Afro-diasporic views than Bryce Detroit.[67] Bryce is a music producer, emcee, poet, and environmental activist. He created HERU, an organization aimed at a unique style of youth-centered media literacy grounded in principles of community knowledge and sustainability. Like Will See, his musical and activist collaborator, he is present in an array of cultural organizing projects across the city; making music is but one of his many endeavors. Bryce explained to us that as a music producer and manager who specializes in "justice entertainment," he is committed to never sexualizing women or criminalizing Black people to earn a profit. "When we caught ourselves writing songs about sexual gymnastics for women artists we had to step back." This introspective move led Bryce to dwell in the conceptual and lived space of the divine feminine, a concept drawn from "Black African ancestral practice." In his view, the divine feminine attends to recovery, while the divine masculine is more about creativity. Nurturing for the sake of making life better for others is how he views the divine feminine at work. To illustrate his point, he shared an anecdote of a woman who began cleaning up the street around 6 Mile Road and Livernois Road. In an effort to reclaim and beautify her neighborhood she boarded up windows and painted brightly colored murals. She did this because she "did not want our babies to have to see blight when they walk to school." Her efforts are an example of other-oriented healing work that is not inspired by self-gain. For Bryce, reflection and other-centered care is associated with the divine feminine. Unlike western models of binary genders, Afro-diasporic theories do not work from the same assumptions. Feminine and masculine energies and identities can cross. Men can enter the realm of the divine feminine; so too, women can embrace the divine masculine. Bryce's work with the Foundation was connected to his embrace of the divine feminine.

Both Bryce and his colleague Will See referred to Piper Carter, the founder of the Foundation, as a visionary. It is highly significant that Will See credits her with doing work similar to that of the #MeToo movement, but years earlier. During our conversation Bryce recalled his first meeting with Piper when the Foundation was a fledgling organization. "I came to a Tuesday night open mic and only about nine of us were around. Piper said, let's just talk. I have never seen such a vulnerable, loving display of sharing."[68] Piper embodied everything he values in gender activism—openness, honesty, vulnerability, and outreach. Bryce reflected that once he experienced Piper he knew that his organization HERU needed to partner with the 5e Gallery. Once that happened formally in 2011, Bryce became a regular member of the Foundation; he even sat on its board for a brief time before the decision was made that women would constitute the board. It was Bryce who institutionalized the "no clap policy" at the Foundation. He explained, "I told Piper when people lay down crap we won't clap for them. We might not throw them off the stage, but we are just going to sit there

FIGURE 7. Bryce Detroit and Will See performing at the Detroit-Puerto Rico Solidaridad fundraiser. Photo: Rebekah Farrugia.

and not show any love." For Bryce "Justice Entertainment" has standards; call and response love is only awarded when the principles that guide gender standards are uplifted. In Detroit, this philosophy is not a part of the dominant discourse.

Supa Emcee is perhaps the most commercially successful artist that we have come to know in Detroit who has been a long-standing supporter of the Foundation and regularly attended its open mic nights. Like Miz Korona, Supa was also featured as a battle rapper in *8 Mile,* and he is a leading member of the oldest rap group in Detroit's history, the Almighty Dreadnaughts. Supa released his first solo mixtape, *By Any Means Necessary,* in 2005 on his mentor Proof's Iron Fist label. In 2007 he dropped his first solo album, *Hood Hero,* one year after Proof's death. Resituating himself in the game with a new team, Supa released *The Immortal* in 2015 on the local label Titan. Over the course of his career he has toured nationally and been the recipient of a number of Detroit music awards. His music addresses topics that range from authenticity and truth, to racism and displacement, to brotherhood and betrayal. He has been a dominant player in Detroit's hip hop community since the days of the Hip Hop Shop in the 1990s through to the 5e Gallery era and continues to actively produce and perform music.

In 2015 we attended the album release party for *The Immortal.* It was held at the location of the original Hip Hop Shop, which was experiencing a brief renaissance under new management at the time. There we witnessed some of Detroit's hip hop legends celebrating his success including Red Bone, DJ Los, DJ Dez, and members of Slum Village. If one were to judge Supa Emcee straight off his presentation of self it would be easy to place him in a Bad Man world of masculinity. He musters a hard look—always rocks stylish clothes and marks himself with bright colors in the names of his heroes, from sports teams to hip hop legends to his superhero namesake. He can twist slang and standard English into a new lexicon like no other. His flow, cadence, and presence are like that of the Black preacher that William Jelani Cobb conceives as a historical precursor to the contemporary emcee.[69]

We asked Supa Emcee his thoughts on masculinity and what it means to be a man and a hip hop artist in Detroit in 2018. He thoughtfully replied,

> A leader, a father, a husband a protector, a mentor, a guide, the strength, a soldier, a community voice, lover of women, elderly and children. Defender of women, elderly, and children. A big brother, powerful person, the shaper and molder of mind, [a] born star.[70]

Turning to hip hop specifically, we asked him if the culture offers lessons, cautions, or other sentiments that bear on masculinity. He said, "I position myself in the world of hip-hop as a hero, right or wrong; a free speaking lover of the arts. HIP-HOP offers us all life lessons on a record, if you listen and watch smart enough!!!"[71] His conception of womanhood is both normative and progressive, riddled with contradiction. When we asked him to reflect on what holds women back in hip hop he surmised that

> It's because of the way in which they choose to compete in hip hop culture. I believe women in hip hop should compete as themselves in all their femininity instead of interpreting vicariously what men are doing. I love the female emcee and their true expression of womanhood in hip hop.[72]

It is not a stretch to read "all their femininity" as an essentialist claim. His observation that women "interpret vicariously what men are doing" reflects much of what Ogbar concludes in his gender research.[73] Women who perform the hard styles or bold, blunt sexuality that is typically reserved for men garner little respect or accolades. For Supa Emcee, a women's truth is tied to her femininity. For those women not feminine enough, masculine-of-center, or gender-nonconforming, this assumption does not hold up. We wrapped up our conversation musing on what it takes for a woman hip hop artist to blow up in Detroit. In his view it requires, "Love, talent, drive, passion, and focus!! A good team and of course money." Our research illustrates that even with these conditions in place women still face challenges. Whereas Supa views "true femininity" as a natural manifestation, for many of the women in the Foundation this idea forces conformity, particularly when artists' presentation of self challenges ideas about "hegemonic femininity." What is more, part of having a good team often presupposes access to agents, bookings, and sponsors. All artists who do not conform to hegemonic gender logics, but especially trans and queer artists, including those like Miz Korona who may identify as masculine-of-center, have a harder road to travel. Supa Emcee, unlike DJ Los's perception of Detroit's men, does not assume women are not at his skill level; he simply rejects women thinking they have to be like men to be successful and assumes that women who do not present a feminine sensibility are mimicking men as opposed to simply being themselves.

On Our Way to Will

January 25, 2018. We pull up to the lot behind the Cass Commons, happy to have a parking spot. It's often full but no events are scheduled for tonight so it's quiet and empty. A few weeks ago we attended a gathering here for the Detroit-Puerto Rico Solidaridad event—a fundraiser for the purchase of a water filtration system. In 2015 we were also here for a similar event that was raising money to assist with Flint's water crisis after high levels of lead were found in the city's drinking water. Environment-related events are common here since the East Michigan Environmental Action Committee [EMEAC] operates the building's day-to-day administration in this building that is more than one hundred years old and was once a church.

It's 6:50 p.m. We're a few minutes early for our interview with Will See, so we text him to ask at which door we should meet him. He has keys to the building and we are grateful for the opportunity to meet in this quiet and meaningful place where we first interviewed Piper Carter six years ago. Ten minutes later he is at the door along with his six year old son Leroi. For the past three years, until last month, Will was EMEAC's director. He continues to be a cultural organizer in the community, focusing on bridging gaps between activist and artistic communities. For the next hour and fifteen minutes the three of us sit at the edge of a long table conversing about Detroit, Will's art and activism, gender issues, and Detroit's queer art community. He keeps his coat on and his laptop open; the music he produces is just a click away. He takes his time answering many of our questions; his responses are thoughtful and purposeful. We only have time to sample a few of his tracks before we leave.

Will See's conceptions of masculinity are like those of many other men with whom we spoke: complex and contradictory. When we asked what informs his sense of masculinity and what it means, he began by saying, "there are two stories about masculinity." Then he went on to explain:

> I was born in [19]78 and came up in the '80s and '90s. There is a whole resurgence of rappers in their forties coming back. I can't say exactly what it means. Masculinity, you can call it a certain kind of integrity. Not being a punk. You hold yourself to a certain kind of standard and you do not exacerbate your weakness and cry about it. On the other hand, I have a son. We have two dogs; one fifty pounds the other a hundred pounds. Sometimes he cries when he plays [with them]. Some of the kids in his age group, the boys cry a lot.[74]

A little later and without hesitation Will makes the claim that "Detroit is the most radical city in America." Minutes later he's quick to state that "Detroit is a very patriarchal city." To support this latter claim, Will informs us about a Black Lives Matter billboard on the northeast side of the city on which the word "Lives" had been crossed out and changed so that it read "Black Dads Matter." Showing nonverbal signs of disapproval and giving a pensive sigh, he added, "my wife says that I have become more patriarchal since moving to Detroit." Confusion is his conclusion about this claim. Both of these moments bear on his interpretations of two stories of masculinity. In his first story, masculinity is both a marker of integrity as well as a standard and a force that does not call out weakness, certainly not through crying. On the other hand, when we asked him who inspires his work, passion replaced nonverbal perplexity. He remarked, "part of why I became a poet is because I did not feel like I could express certain things, that I could not in hip hop. I felt both a psychological and a performance block."

In "When Brothers Dance," which he often performs as a song, Will See communicates strength and vulnerability, brothers loving brothers, and the kind of masculinity that looks tough on the surface. The two significant role models in Will's life that inspired its creation were his deceased brother Leroy and Blair, one of Detroit's most beloved poets, who has also passed away. Blair was a strong and powerful gay Black man who crushed stereotypes and publicly displayed his vulnerability. Contextualizing his relationship to Blair, Will See states,

> Blair was the Tupac of my life. Blair was my man; that's why I wrote the poem. He sang at my wedding. I did the memorial for him; first time I officiated a memorial service. He was a unique talent—he had a lot of talents: singer, songwriter, poet. He could do a set playing guitar, singing, doing so much. The art scene felt his absence.

Clearly the impulse to suck it up and be a man, to not cry, and to perform the tough guise underlies Will's sense of manhood, yet his art and love for brotherhood interrupts this standard sense of being. Vulnerability is the subject and object of the other side of masculinity's story. And like the double-sided double consciousness that emerges from Will's two imaginations of masculinity, there are two stories and two losses embodied in the text of "When Brothers Dance." The first verse bemoans the loss of his brother; the second pays tribute to Blair. Pain, hope, and freedom pepper Will's testimony. The title borrows from an Ethridge Knight poem from *Belly Song and Other Poems*.[75] In the second verse Will creates an homage to his beloved friend Blair, who died long before the Detroit poetry community was ready to bear the loss. Will See speaks on and loves his queer kindred spirit.

I ain't the only I here whose life you put your mark on
Day time (dear) just got a little darker
Autumn chillier, winter grab another parka
Poetry scene don't have the same spark (gone)

Artist Activist 'fore I knew what Soul Circuit was
International—showed me what a tour circuit was
Big Laughter—never bashful
Aw shit Blair
You were supposed to be on this goddamn hook there
(When Brothers Dance)
we was supposed to be closer
you could have used my A/C come crash on my sofa
It's wild, cat. Detroit Lions Villanova
Joni Mitchell said that good thing till its over

You never know sir, and what you did with the Jackson fam
Flipped him upside down—I ain't talking breakdancing man
Dominique Dawes, remember the time
The American Minds of some goddamn Africans

Anthems man—defined Detroit in the 2K
Now we sit around and wonder just what would you say

In your absence Blair—the writing games floo flay
You ain't just the shit—you the mutherfucking doo-kay

Excuse me—I'm a go 4 over on this here track
Use these bars as libations. Bring D Blair Back
You are Black, queer, and strong. That's a D Blair Fact
Deep Soil, Night Sky, want to be D Blair Black.

A sung style of rap[76] characterizes Will's modality of delivery. The poem is heavy with brother love, both sibling love and the affection men ought to be able to share. Will is reaching for a queer Black figure that forever touched Detroit's arts scene with affection while longing for his return. Along the way, his wordplay cuts into the rich reality of Blair's character: bare facts are D Blair Facts. Lines like "We supposed to be closer . . . you could have crashed on my sofa" reinvent how Black men show care and connection. In the past this style of testimony was rare in hip hop; when Nas released "One Love," a shout out to brothers in prison, his demonstration of a soft side of thug complexity was unique. Recently, it has become increasingly common for commercially successful rappers—such as Kendrick Lamar, J. Cole, and Vince Staples—to display self-reflective vulnerability. "Aw shit Blair, You were supposed to be on this goddamn hook there" is a cold reminder that Blair is gone from this earth but alive in Will's verses and performance. At once, articulation becomes the energy of life and the trace of cultural memory. From "collecting family for funerals" in the D, to saying goodbye to a beloved friend and artistic mentor, Will See puts his vulnerability and heart on his sleeve. In so doing, he creates dope, overdue hip hop poetics, while he busts open the narrow range of emotional intelligence that many critics suggest hip hop culture has to offer men. Despite the commercial success of the aforementioned artists, straight "legitimized" men in the rap game rarely reach out to queer kindred spirits. Whiz Khalifa and Jay-Z are notable exceptions. Most men do not go there in their lyrical stock houses. Insecurity and masculinity are not mutually exclusive; those who are unwilling to recognize this contradictory reality are not prepared for genderqueer practices of manhood in Detroit that embody raw, aggressive styles of performance as well as vulnerability.

Valid: In the Throes of the Cool Pose

Valid is young, white, Serbian, and intrepid. An Eastside native Detroiter who grew up in Dearborn Heights, and a Wayne State graduate, he has as much love and attachment to Detroit as any of the artists we have featured in our work. Valid was a consistent supporter of the Foundation who regularly attended the open mic night and considered the 5e Gallery to be his hip hop home. The following self-articulation from Facebook illustrates his rich musical bio. Valid sees himself as one who has

> risen from Detroit's legendary hip hop scene. Valid came up under the wing of the gritty pioneer, DJ Butter. He continues to blaze the stage while dropping fresh joints and gaining notoriety in studios, at shows, and on FM 98 WJLB, Detroit's radio home for hip hop and R&B. Since dropping his first mixtape, "The Mixtape Reform Package," "The Maria EP" and a joint project, "The Us-12 Experience" with producer Topp, Valid is now completing his debut album, *Beyond Physics.*[77]

In addition to his self-report, he has also released several music videos on YouTube. His music is as complex and contradictory as his relationship to hip hop. We draw on our fieldnotes, interview data, and textual analysis of one of his videos and the contested Facebook discourse that circulated after its release to engage the range of differences that exist within the community of men in Detroit's hip hop underground.

In his discussion of hip hop, race, and masculinity, Jeffrey Ogbar notes that white emcees struggle for legitimacy in different ways than Black and Brown men do.[78] Their battles traverse more than acquiring mad skills. Since Vanilla Ice came on the scene in the 1980s, white rappers have been viewed as suspect, questioned as posers and cultural appropriators even when they are considered true to the game. One need only consider the public battles between Benzino and Eminem. Benzino believes that white folk have no business stepping into hip hop, particularly as emcees. Facing pressure and forging a place for their truth, white emcees often play into the "cool pose." Valid's image is shot moving with swagger, attracting if not commanding the sexual attention of women, leaning on or driving classic cars, sporting gold chains, flipped flat-bill hats, and his look is always completed with fresh sneakers. He does not stoop to the practices of slapping women's butts or throwing money at the camera; however, he does not hold back in displaying his desire and love for Black women who embody hegemonic femininity, hip hop style. Valid and other white emcees like him face another requirement for the acquisition of legitimacy. White emcees require the physical and often sampled presence of Blackness as a form of acceptance. One will often see artists like Bubba Sparxxx, Iggy Azalea, G-Eazy, and even Eminem surrounded by well-established Black emcees like Royce da 5'9", Missy Elliott, Timbaland, Cardi B, and A$AP Rocky, who function as hype men and women alongside these white artists. In most of

Valid's videos, Black men are featured as part of his crew and Black women are his love interests.

And yet, not all of his work is about cool posing, loving ladies, and the display of Detroit style shine. In one moment his lyrics are serious, capturing instances where he praises fallen friends; in the next song, he is all about having fun and party music, imagining women who are "freaks like Trina." Even when high-stakes social politics underwrite his rhymes and the visual images that fuel his videos, he cannot escape the "cool pose." He shares a reality with artists like Lil Dicky. While Lil Dicky does not have a hard body like Valid, he still needs Black artists to give him public props. Something interesting is happening at this moment in hip hop; when a meager, white-looking Jewish kid can imagine himself in "Chris Brown's body," and Chris Brown sings back about the privileges that come with the embodiment of whiteness, racial lines begin to bleed. Lil Dicky also includes Snoop Dogg in animated videos, playing a role with major authority. No matter the form of masculinity that the white emcee bears, the presence of Black artists function like authority figures; Blackness is a necessary condition for validation. Valid fits many registers of hegemonic masculinity even as he attempts to elide them. His masculinity is rugged. His hair is long and thick, often tied up in some kind of man-appropriate ponytail, but not hipster looking, and he sports a well-groomed, thick beard. Valid lives in a commanding, tall, muscular body. When one addresses him he is smooth, affectionate, and open. He embodies all the moves, in gesture and word, that harder rappers perform, despite the nature of his complex rhymes. In 2014, he produced a music video that he perceives to be paying homage to women. However, when one adds the visuals to the lyrics, some of the standard heteronormative tactics and traces of Bad Man masculinity peek out.

When Valid uploaded the music video for his track "New Nasty" to YouTube, some women took to social media, Facebook in particular, to express their discontent. Their comments ranged from disappointment to outright accusations of sexism. The video includes many images of sexy, scantily-clad Black women whom he physically caresses and moves with to the extent that desire is like a character all unto itself. Below Valid explains his frustration with the criticism he received on Facebook for how he chose to represent women in the video:

LET ME CLEAR THE AIR REAL QUICK: my song (the original and remix) titled 'New NASTY' is not what you may think the title entails. And in my remix i mention all the women of hiphop in my verse as a salute to them and i caught word that couple ppl did not find it flattering to those ladies and i'm ASSUMING it's because of the title 'New Nasty' and i can't front its been bothering me all day. I think that is kind of unfair because when you actually LISTEN to the lyrics of the song my 'New Nasty' is my perfect lady that i look at as a queen and in both versions i mention marrying this female figure im spittin' about. My 'New Nasty' is never described in either version as being my new 'h*e' or 'freak B**tch'. 'New Nasty' is just kind of a fun nick name me and her may have for each other, that's the concept of the song. Sure, it may have SOME sexual connotation, and i do say 'she freakier than Trina' but hey that's what grown folks do behind closed doors and i see nothing derogatory or disrespectful about that at all, its just another way of saying 'New Lover'. Now if some one wants to say 'NASTY' is the wrong choice of word because it has a negative connotation, to those i say this is HIPHOP . . . where the word 'THUG' as Pac would say is different than the traditional definition, Pac said 'And yes, I am gonna say that I'm a thug, that's because I came from the gutter and I'm still here. I'm not saying I'm a thug because I wanna rob you or rape people and things.' in HIPHOP we say 'dam, you a ILL mc' or 'dam that beat is so SICK' neither do the words ILL/SICK have a positive connotation, and no one wants to be ill or sick . . . but in Hip-Hop these words have been flipped to mean something POSITIVE and some kind of endearment. this idea in Hip-hop from taking a word w/ a negative connotation and flipping it to mean something positive is NOTHING NEW AT ALL. . . . WITH THAT BEING SAID. . . . miss me w/ this political correct BS, and listen to the damn song and let the concept hit ya before you assume things.[79]

Clearly, intention and audience interpretation do not match up. Valid is responding to the lyrics and the title of the song while the complaints women levied were connected to the imagery in the video; the engagement does not meet. He sees his gestures in wordplay as an open, adult display of love for women, predominantly Black women. He thinks his display of love captures what Ogbar contends is one of the most positive consequences of Black women's presence in hip hop's commercial game—that is giving praise to their beauty and sexuality.[80] But Valid is caught between intention and effect. Even if we grant that the lyrics do not carry problematic connotations, the video imagery complicates the critique. When imagery is layered onto verbal and written messages issues of control emerge, as does the particular positioning of the women in the narrative. Valid does not address the level of image in his retort. Words carry a heavy weight for him, perhaps because it is his primary mode of production, but others become authors when word meets image. Still, the images in "New Nasty" conform to the most dominant ways men and women connect in rap videos: chase and catch.

While Valid has received some pressure with respect to gender representation, he has a sizeable fan base in Detroit that includes women.

Miz Korona tells a running tale about Valid: "That guy is everywhere. If there is a show in the D Valid will be there."[81] Valid's extended family came up in Detroit as merchant-class immigrants who worked their way to whiteness and achieved social mobility.[82] At the turn of the twentieth century Serbians were lumped into the all-in-one size Eastern European ethic stereotype of "The Hunkie."[83] Class location varies across the men we engage. Whereas Will See and Bryce Detroit came up in middle-class Black neighborhoods and graduated from high-level public and private universities, working-class alliance binds Valid to his most intimate peers, like his long-time mentor Supa Emcee. The bonds that he shares with other kindred artists, particularly those who are featured in his work, are equally important. What is more, some of his collaborators are well-known Black men and women on the scene. There is nothing strategic about their bonds. Nonetheless, if these conditions were not in place, the critique he received for "New Nasty" would look different; that is, it would not come exclusively from women. Like Lil Dicky, Valid is validated by the company he keeps.

Valid receives welcome in the hip hop scenes that fans of the Foundation and 5e Gallery and artists value in Detroit. He has been featured on 107.5's freestyle battles, winning more than once. He is invited to perform at parties like Piper Carter's fortieth birthday bash and other events that DJs Sicari, Dez, and Los have hosted. He came to support both Miz Korona and Mahogany Jones when they performed at the DIA, and he was one of the most regular performer/patrons that the 5e Gallery ever knew. He is complex, one of the most alternative self-identified Thugs we have yet to meet in our course of study, who continues to bend our preconceived ideas about gender and hip hop in Detroit.

. . .

Our conversations with Foundation members illustrate the wide range of perspectives they embody with respect to gender identity formation. While only a few members identify with and openly advance feminist allegiance, all of them live the values that hip hop feminists share. The Foundation forged its mission through pedagogy, performance, sustained conversation, and community intervention. Its members support fluid conceptions of gender and sexuality, openly disrupting misogyny and heteronormativity. They assert a practice of citizenship that begins in community and cultural practices. Foundation artists also reject the politics of respectability that coursed through the logics of second wave feminism, even in some forms of Black feminist politics. Prominent hip hop feminists and gender scholars assert that second wave respectability politics limited the sexual agency of Black women.[84] The hip hop generation and the women-identified artists, fans, and practitioners who form it tear down the politics of respectability through speech, fashion, music, outreach and of course, performance. And yet, despite their openly political work they are not alone in their reluctance to claim feminism. Hip hop gender scholar Kyra Gaunt also distances herself from the category. She explains,

> Sometimes I don't like to call myself a feminist . . . I prefer to call myself a hip hop scholar with a specialty in gender studies, or I tell folk I specialize in teaching hip hop from the perspective of race, gender, and the body. As Audre Lorde once wrote, 'I am not only one piece of myself.'[85]

Like Gaunt, Foundation members echo what Mark Anthony Neal claims about artists like Queen Latifah: that is, they create strong women identified messages and images, but do not turn to feminism as a platform for action.[86]

The supportive men with whom we have had significant interactions also live complex forms of masculinity and sexuality. None of the men we have come to know are gay, but they work with and promote many of Detroit's queer emcees and DJs. At times they perform the cool pose and dominant modalities of masculinity. Supa Emcee, for example, claims that as a man he "conquers." Valid claims a revisionist reading of what counts as a thug, all the while conforming to conditions of whiteness. Bryce Detroit and Will See wage war on traditional tactics of gender identity. Our conversations and the cultural production that we analyze reveal the complex, slippery ways men and women negotiate gender, sexuality, and survival in a deeply competitive environment. Detroit's hip hip scene resembles the commercial market in that men dominate; however, there exist more cracks and fissures where gender and sexuality continue to form.

4

Vulnerable Mavericks
Wreck Rap's Conventions

Gender has certainly received a lot of play in hip hop studies, journalism, and documentary film; but by and large, the categories through which both men and women have been examined up to this point have been narrow, leading to a worldview governed by a restricted set of practices and tropes. Also, much of the formative scholarship that has addressed the intersections of Black feminist politics and hip hop cultural production has focused on the production and reception of women in the commercial hip hop arena. When one studies women who make hip hop in the underground a different, complex set of practices, ideas, and identities emerge.

In this chapter, we examine the ways that Foundation artists wreck the sexist practices that circulate in hip hop culture. We borrow the concept of "wreck" from Gwendolyn D. Pough, who uses it to define "moments when black women's discourses disrupt dominant masculine discourses, break into the public sphere, and in some way impact or influence the U.S. imaginary . . . . "[1] This term operates much like Tricia Rose's view of a rupture, which she conceptualizes as a displacement into dominant discourses.[2] Displacements can take the form of musical intervention, gender-based critiques, or political commentary. We intervene into the ways women have been categorized as hip hop producers by wrecking the current scripts and offering an alternative concept that advances Black female subjectivity. Redefining the cast of characters that dominate the ways women in hip hop have been understood and represented, we offer the Vulnerable Maverick as a new cautious category.

This construct is purposefully contradictory; it captures the strength and openness that shape women's civic and artistic lives. The artists' beats, rhymes, and processes of production offer an alternative framework for understanding how women create spaces for themselves in hip hop culture. The subject positions examined in this ethnographic study traverse earlier understandings of archetypes like the Mammy, the Matriarch, and the Jezebel,[3] and even more progressive categories like the Fly Girl, Queen Mother, and Sista with Attitude.[4] The topics these emcees address and the identities they forge serve as productive, complex, intersectional routes that reveal the deep layers of subjectivity that women making hip hop live. The experiential particularities that constitute their individual and collective consciousness include elements such as their faith, their lived experiences as Black women, and as Detroiters. Embodiment is a force that undergirds their aesthetic and political drive. It shapes their "flyness" as well as their commitment to addressing physical and sexual abuse in their lyrics. It is the ground where cool beats and clever rhymes meet social critique.

Tapping into women-centered art, we focus on our conversations with four emcees, two producers, and a sampling of their work: Nique Love Rhodes's album *Against All Odds: The Epic* (2013), Mahogany Jones's album *Pure* (2014), Insite the Riot's EP *Girl Meets Beat* (2015), and a number of singles Miz Korona released between 2016 and 2017. The music we analyze here is a contemporary extension of the work of politically motivated emcees from hip hop's early years in the 1980s and 1990s, as well as classic women blues and jazz artists. These artists combat the dominant, hegemonic two-dimensional representation of African American women that is epitomized in commercial hip hop and popular culture at large. Unapologetically, their work demonstrates the multidimensional characters of women artists/social actors. Moreover, the music, imagery, and counter-narratives that these women create are significant because they defy and traverse the existing stereotypes, scripts, and controlling images of women in hip hop that dominate commercial and academic spaces. Additionally, while it is becoming increasingly common and acceptable for men to give voice to their emotional selves, their faith, and vulnerabilities in the commercial hip hop arena, this space does not afford the same possibilities or profitability to women rappers. The analysis that follows examines these complex narratives and gives insight into the artists' lived experiences as well as the issues that motivate their work. Collectively, they explore themes of inner strength, love, beauty, domestic violence, spirituality, and other matters relevant to their experiences as Black women connected to Detroit and its hip hop underground. Ultimately, our analysis reveals how disruption throws new formations and imaginations of power relations into motions.

We take up feminist cultural critic Aisha Durham's call to make visible alternative visions of hip hop and encourage consumption of more diverse representations.[5] We believe that the most productive and fruitful approach to this analysis is to resist choosing between a focus on aesthetics or social relationships and to instead begin from the position that aesthetics are socially grounded; in other words, forms of media and popular culture are both cultural product and social process. Our analysis combines musical critique, field notes, and interviews with artists and producers to compose a multidimensional representation of African American women that is virtually nonexistent in contemporary commercial hip hop and popular culture at large.

CONTROLLING IMAGES AND SEXUAL SCRIPTS

Numerous scholars have commented on the problematic and sexist state of contemporary hip hop culture.[6] The majority of research on women and hip hop examines the representation of women in male-centered and controlled images, music, and culture. The commercial industry constructs and justifies particular social arrangements that embody a hegemonic masculinist social order in which women are represented as passive objects and men as agentic subjects. In 2008, Tricia Rose declared hip hop to be "in a terrible crisis" because it "has increasingly become a playground for caricatures of black gangsta, pimps, and hoes."[7] Shifting the focus to Black girls' and women's relationships to hip hop, in *Pimps Up, Ho's Down* T. Denean Sharpley-Whiting explores the genre's increasing alliance with the sex industry and the ways it traffics, publicly celebrates, and normalizes images and behaviors of sexual violence, sexism, and anti-lesbianism, among others.[8] Adams and Fuller argue that the commonly deployed terms "bitch" and "ho" in misogynistic rap are the modern-day equivalents of the Sapphire and Jezebel scripts of the past.[9] They argue that these images provide a rationale for the history of sexual assaults on African American women. With some exceptions, the lyrics and images of women in commercial hip hop uphold these representations.

When they are acknowledged, examples of agentic female emcees continue to be women whose popularity peaked in the 1980s and 1990s, with the most commonly referenced artists including Queen Latifah, MC Lyte, Salt-N-Pepa, Roxane Shanté, Lil' Kim, Foxy Brown, Lauryn Hill, and Missy Elliott.[10] Writing on these early representations, Cheryl Keyes identifies four distinct categories of women rappers: Queen Mother, Sista with Attitude, Lesbian, and Fly Girl. The Queen Mothers comprise Afrocentric icons such as Queen Latifah, Sister Souljah, and Yo-Yo. Women like Lil' Kim and Foxy Brown who value attitude as a means of empowerment define the Sista with Attitude script, which Rabaka extends to include women rappers and neo-soul sisters who share classic blues women's "myriad expressions of *black and blues womanhood.*"[11] In this sense "attitude" refers to "their critical posture or oppositional stance toward the established order."[12] Imani Perry complicates the category with the addition of the phrase "bad women." Bad women disrupt the dominant space that men occupy in hip hop and "at times even offer a feminist critique."[13] The Lesbian category includes the likes of Queen Pen who plays with image and fixed gender roles; sometimes she's femme and other times she appropriates the cool pose typically associated with male hip hop culture. Lastly, Fly Girls such as Salt-N-Pepa are sexy and fashionable but also independent and agentic; they are erotic subjects rather than objectified women. Mark Anthony Neal and Joan Morgan have expressed their appreciation for the erotic power and contradictory positions that Fly Girls exude.[14]

The pervasiveness of hip hop narratives in popular culture have directly influenced the evolution of foundational images of Black women like the Jezebel, Mammy, Welfare Mother, and Matriarch into, as Dionne P. Stephens and Layli D. Phillips break down, the Diva, Gold Digger, Freak, Dyke, Gangster Bitch, Sister Savior, Earth Mother, and Baby Mama.[15] The Earth Mother is defined as someone who "celebrates the diversity of body sizes, natural hair texture, and skin colors" but whose "consciousness takes her out of the sexual context that exists within Hip Hop culture."[16] Lauryn Hill is the quintessential example here. In couching these representations as almost exclusively damaging, Stevens and Phillips fail to illuminate the nuances of the dynamic, powerful, complex, and at times contradictory representations of women emcees; much is lost when hip hop culture as a whole is reduced to a sexual context which in itself is viewed as negative.

These controlling images and sexual scripts are the main frames of the commercial industry, seeping into the ears and eyes of those fans who consume hip hop exclusively from commercial outlets. Scholarly work that critiques these representations is valuable and necessary but it is not sufficient, as it leaves unexplored the productivity of a diverse range of women engaging in the cultural production of hip hop. The work that women in Detroit's underground produce reflects and intervenes into the scripts that hip hop scholars have critiqued and coined. The women of the Foundation offer alternative subjectivities and more productive routes for forging identities and spaces from which to circumvent, dismantle, and develop the state of the industry. Their work captures the ethics underneath the steadfast feminist axiom "the personal is political." It begins from the personal, the ground from which social and political forces are confronted, wrecked, and reimagined. The power to overcome begins with reexamining sexual abuse, addiction, racial reasoning, and nihilism. As a result, alternative women-identified spiritualties and worldviews emerge in the music and cultural production of Foundation artists. The Vulnerable Maverick is the lens through which we rethink women's subjectivity in their roles as cultural citizens and producers. In this pairing, vulnerability and strength share the stage. It is a response and contrast to the controlling image known as the strong Black woman, which forecloses the possibility of vulnerability; women who are cast in this controlling image are portrayed as alone in the world, surviving with fortitude all by themselves, often without the help of or desire for men. The Vulnerable Maverick however, is an attempt to detail more accurately the complexities of these women—both of their music and their personhoods, coding and stretching hip hop's idioms on their terms.

SPIRITUALITY, EMPOWERMENT, AND BLACK WOMANHOOD

Insite the Riot is an artist, community builder, and urban development practitioner. Her EP *Girl Meets Beat* brings both her personal experiences and political message to the fore. While her music has always been politically motivated, these tracks are more personal than in her previous work. Commenting on the writing process, Insite states, "On this album . . . I wanted to look behind the curtain a little bit. 'Cause I had people tell me, 'I love your message, but I don't know who you are.'"[17] The weaving of the personal and political is most apparent on "Winner," as she moves from recounting her childhood experiences to explaining the meaning behind her name.[18] The track opens with a sample from Detroit-based R&B singer Anita Baker's track "Sometimes." Its opening lyric, "Everybody wants to be a winner and take their place at the top" is looped twice. As Baker's vocal lines kick in, so do sparse, syncopated drumbeats. The second time around a synthesizer adds an additional layer to the original track, giving it a funky edge before we hear from Insite. On top of these musical elements, in what Krims describes as a "speech effusive" emceeing style characterized by enunciation and delivery that is closer to spoken language,[19] Insite raps about her childhood in post-industrial Detroit and overcoming significant life challenges that especially affect people of color in urban areas in the United States. Citing a historical sample of African Americans who fought for freedom and shaped her consciousness, the chorus in particular emphasizes the track's message. Encouragement, determination, and self-love are primary themes that course through the song. Fueled with hope, Insite endeavors to uplift listeners. She raps,

> For Dred Scott, for Harriet
> Overcome obstacles, face more barriers
> My mission I accept and I choose
> Either way you go we all win, draw or lose
> Lick off your wounds

Insite grew up in Detroit in the 1980s and 1990s at the peak of industrial decline, which meant excessive job loss, increased poverty, and flight from the city whose population hemorrhaged during these decades. Writing in 1993, Jerry Herron summarized the state of Detroit at the time as "the one place that everybody else can agree on by agreeing they no longer want any part of it."[20] In addition to the challenges that living in Detroit poses for many of its residents, Insite lost her mother at age fifteen and raised her younger brother. She also attended college on a basketball scholarship and earned a master's degree in public policy.

While quick and dense rhymes dominate the verses, towards the end of the song Insite breaks away from rapping to clarify her identity:

> I go by the name of Insite the Riot and I encourage everybody within earshot of my voice to incite your own riot. And what do I mean by that? I mean to incite the revolution in your thinking. To recognize that anything you wanna be is possible. To recognize that anything you wanna have is possible. Don't let nobody else tell you different. So in a nutshell I'm telling you to do three things: One, know yourself, love yourself, and three, let your light shine, shine, shine.

The strength and perseverance that dominates Insite's music encourages audiences to elevate their consciousness in order to empower themselves and incite positive change in the world. For Insite, empowerment begins with the self before it affects the social.

Mahogany Jones' album *Pure: Volume I* also addresses empowerment; however, she often examines it through the lens of Christianity. In her words,

> I was inspired to record *Pure* by God at the height of wanting to distance my gender from my art, and seeing that I only wanted to do that because of the discrimination I consistently came up against—and what better way to use my art, than to use my heart to do something to create a change for myself and prayerfully other women, whether emcee or astronaut.[21]

As for the themes it privileges she lists:

> Forgiveness, women giving themselves permission to take up space, women recapturing agency over their bodies and not being conditioned to make choices to be overly sexual, domestic violence, sexual assault, colorism—it's not just a black thing.

For Mahogany in particular, Christianity is a significant part of her identity that she brings to bear in her music even though she does not identify as a Christian rapper.

> I don't ever want to be like, 'you need Jesus!' even though I think people do need Jesus. The reason I make my music is because I grew up in church and I grew up in a cult really. So when I was eighteen, I was done with Christianity. Done. Done and done, like done. And I just came back to it, and when I came back to it, it was one of those moments. I want to make music and media that never felt like they fit into church . . . . which is why it's also difficult to label myself as a Christian rapper. For a while when females wanted Christian rappers my name would come up. Then this thing sort of happened where my content wasn't explicitly Jesus, Jesus, Jesus, and the Christians were like, 'yeah, about that.'

The "yeah, about that" sentiment that the congregation members stated imposed judgment on her decision not to mobilize exclusively Christian content and themes in her music.

Further along she added,

> Christian hip hop and Christianity is extremely patriarchal to the point where at times it feels like it hates women. Christian hip hop is just super condescending, super dark ages when it comes to the role of women. It's subtle. It's like when women in Christian hip hop get billed for concerts, it's like the token black girl or the token white person. It's the token girl. 'Oh you're here for the girls' . . . . Christian hip hop unfortunately is a reflection of Christianity or American Christianity in this very patriarchy and very misogynistic environment.

FIGURE 8. Mahogany Jones, Insite the Riot, and Nique Love Rhodes. Photo: Rebekah Farrugia.

Mahogany opens the double-sided hinge of identification. Her spirituality is a powerful calling, but even in those sacred spaces closest to home and heart, the pull of patriarchy is deeply felt and expected. She can claim Christianity, but it only claims her on terms that contradict her well-being as a woman and an artist. Instead of being pigeonholed, she renounces its label and in doing so defies the script it seeks to uphold.

Nique Love Rhodes is a self-proclaimed "everyday revolutionary" who has been rapping on stages since she was thirteen years old. Growing up attending a black church in Detroit made a particularly strong impression on her:

> It was a non-denominational church and they would let me perform on Sundays. People would give me good feedback. And you know in Detroit, every good musician came from the church. Most musicians will probably play at church somewhere. The musicians were like, you should do stuff like this, and gave me a musical background in it. If it wasn't for my mom getting me into church and giving me a notebook, I would be a completely different person. I lived off Joy Road and it wasn't a good neighborhood. I would come home from school and my dad would be on drugs, and there would be drug dealers at the corner of the neighborhood, but it was that spirituality [that got me through].[22]

As she explains it, the church was Nique's condition for possibility, the space that gave her a stage and a community that offered safety, even—

or rather especially—when her neighborhood did not. The experience of church is existentially different for each artist, but all of them feel deeply shaped by Christianity.

It is significant that empowerment, revolution, and spirituality are intertwined for all of these artists, albeit in diverse ways and to different extents. Jones's music rarely addresses these concepts one at a time. The track "Skin Deep" from her album *Pure* features Insite the Riot and Ozara Ode.[23] It questions the privileging of light skin, highlights the experiences of girls and women living in Black bodies, and emphasizes the need for Black girls and women to love themselves unconditionally. Musically, it is somber from the start. Jazzy saxophone and piano melodies overlay a light and slow percussive beat throughout. In a speech-effusive rhyming style that in this case is characterized by an especially crisp delivery, Mahogany Jones raps:

> They say I'm so black in the evening I'm invisible
> Must live life in the night
> The only visuals of me that I see are individuals
> Who are slaves
> Who are maids
> Who are criminals
> Only worthy of wages minimal
> Blatant in they programming messages subliminal
> For every black princess there's a black president
> There's only been one for the years we been residents
> Too far right on the spectrum of the color wheel
> To get equal rights so our true beauty we conceal
> Cause Black and ugly have always been synonymous
> Not to mention what this does to my confidence
> Black girls rock but really what's more common is
> We're put under rocks and made to be anonymous
> Rarely celebrated
> Why is it a great occasion
> When someone on the cover of Vogue's not a caucasian
> *(Chorus, sung by Ozara Ode)*
> They say, beauty is only skin deep
> Play it for the little brown girls on repeat
> They say, beauty is only skin deep
> Play it for the little brown girls on repeat
> They say, beauty is only skin deep
> Play it for the little brown girls on repeat

The track's instrumentation and tempo, as well as Ozara Ode's vocals, invoke the music of famous 1930s jazz musicians such as Billie Holiday and Ella Fitzgerald. The juxtaposition and layering of this jazzy sound and Jones's and Insite the Riot's rhymes create a multigenerational opening that signifies a new sensibility. The music and lyrics call on us to reflect on the history of whiteness and colonization and call into question its prolongation while illustrating the impacts of its continuation, especially on girls and women of color who continue to be exoticized as well as seen and treated as less than white women.

Mahogany explains the genesis of the track:

> "Skin Deep" is essential because it's important for people to take in different shades, shapes, configurations of what beauty is. "Skin Deep" exposes how us dark women struggle with colorism and how lighter complexioned women struggle as well with being pegged a certain way. So either you're dark and you're a Mammy and undesirable or you are fair-skinned and the object of every man's sexual fantasy. Both are unfair, not balanced, and "Skin Deep's" role is to expose it and remember no matter where you are on the color wheel you are fearfully and wonderfully made by God—you are not less than.[24]

Discussing the track, Insite the Riot explains that it expresses her beliefs that "vulnerability is a strength, self-confidence is a necessity, and recognizing our own beauty is vital."[25]

Speaking about his contributions to the track's production, Ronald "iRonic" Lee Jr. contends,

> Being a son, a brother, husband and father, I saw the importance of this project. When Mahogany came up with the idea I was on board from the start. Once I had the vision it was easy to find the right production and artists to assist with the process. These issues are frequently experienced and seldom dealt with or even expressed artistically.[26]

The relationship between producer and emcee is mutually enriching; iRonic Lee knows Mahogany's life, faith, personality, style and most of all, the urgency underlying her rhymes. He provides musical layering that meshes with her cadence and flow. Together, they create fresh texture, where colorism and institutionalized racism brush up against perseverance and the joy of self-love in melodic rhythms, a jazzy hook, and a soft and steady voice.

Mahogany Jones has been working with iRonic since before she moved from New York to Detroit in the early 2000s. They met at a gig on the east coast where both his wife E.P. Da Energy Provider and Mahogany were invited to perform. Impressed with his production work on E.P.'s tracks, Mahogany and iRonic began a hip hop partnership that continues to this day. In July 2018 we met with iRonic to learn more about his work with Mahogany. We linked up across the street from the Cass Corridor Commons at the Cass Café, a longtime restaurant that features the work of local artists on its walls and partners with the Allied Media Conference every June. iRonic took his time theorizing why his production work has been a good fit with Mahogany's emcee work for all these years.

> Mahogany, she kinda walks a thin line between soft and rugged but she walks it well 'cause she has a very captivating personality. She's very feminine. She's very feminine in what she does but at any given moment she's very assertive and direct and can be conceived as aggressive. So it's funny because as a producer that's kinda how I approach my music. It's like a match with us. The ruggedness of Detroit, being a native Detroiter, that ruggedness but you add that soul history, that soulfulness. I try to incorporate that in my music. And that's one thing she gravitated to, the soulfulness of my music. The soulfulness of my sound.[27]

Speaking about *Pure,* iRonic confirmed Mahogany's statement that "she didn't want to do it initially. I was like no we have to do it. This is what's needed." We also learned that Mahogany and iRonic wanted female producers to contribute tracks to the project but they were unsuccessful in their search. It is significant that iRonic is not only willing to work on projects like *Pure*—that tackle difficult, women-centered themes about women's agency, domestic violence, assault, and colorism—but that he encouraged Mahogany to pursue the project. Producers have a lot of power over tracks and it is not far-fetched to conceive that their direction and control could extend beyond a track's instrumentals to its lyrics. Given the dearth of women producers in Detroit, working with men is often inevitable; Mahogany and iRonic Lee's partnership signals the impact that producers can have when they support women emcees whose rhymes speak to women's everyday life struggles.

Jones' track "Never Again" features R&B singer Gwenation. It is about one woman's courage to break free from patterns of domestic violence. In contrast to "Skin Deep," "Never Again" features driving guitar and synthesizer sounds punctuated by digital strings and brass instrumentation. Digital mallet percussion beats drive the track; a string stab echoing a Middle Eastern flavor provides an additional layer of sound. Tape hiss gives the track an analog sensibility. This timbral quality is fitting given that the lyrics also take us back in time. A subtle echo effect marks several of the lines and signifies the reverberation of childhood memories in the mind of the narrative persona. As identity is conjunctural, so too is Mahogany Jones's narrative structure. Jones raps:

When I think back
Dig into my knapsack
of childhood memories when mama used to rock ice packs
Eyes blue black lips drip bloody red
Used to think up in my head all the ways to kill him dead
Instead I just cried aloud
Try to drown out all the sounds
Especially the ones where mama's body thumped to the ground
Didn't make another round
That one was a straight K-O
Mad because I figured that my mom was wise enough to know
This is not what love is like
Mama say that lovers fight
Mama won't you fight to win
Kiss me on the head good night
Tell me with the strangest grin
Everything'll be all right
Everything was all wrong
We shoulda been long gone
How you figure lettin' somebody beat on you is being strong?
She was right though
I didn't comprehend
Cause when you think that you're in love the rules tend to bend
Reality and fantasy all begin just to blend
Easier to play pretend
Friends start to recommend I leave him
He tells me that he loves me, I believe him
How can I leave him?
How can I leave him?
Tells me if I try that he'll kill me—I believe him.

As the track moves into the chorus—sung by Gwenation—the drum beat changes, the sound is fuller, and more upbeat:

Never again
Never will you play with my mind
Never will you waste my time
Never again
Never will you break my soul
Never will you take control
Never again

"Never Again" gives voice to the complex context in which abuse plays out, not only between victims and abusers but also the latent affects it has on the children who witness it. It reveals the multifaceted conditions that entrap women but we also see the layers of resistance that lead women to overcome these conditions. In commercial hip hop women are rarely afforded the opportunity to explore such a dynamic and dialectical articulation of abuse and recovery. Whereas men are extended the luxury of being complex and contradictory, women's voices and concerns continue to be represented as two-dimensional, if not silenced altogether.

Spirituality, love, and empowerment are also resonant themes on Nique Love Rhodes's album *Against All Odds*. She embodies what Krims identifies as a "sung style" of rapping characterized by "rhythmic repletion, on beat accents and pauses."[28] Nique is especially personal on the track "5.20.88" (her birthday) and effectively uses herself as living proof that hard times can be overcome. Musically, the qualities of the beat are striking. The song begins with digitally produced piano and horns. These melodies are followed by a repeated sample of Nique's voice saying/singing "5.20.88"; at times scratching effects manipulate her voice. In our conversations Nique shared that when she hears this track's beat it evokes nostalgia. When we hear it coupled with her delivery and lyrics we feel our pulses rising; our ears are poised to listen and our bodies want to move.

Dion Burroughs, the producer behind the beat, explained that when he works with artists he talks with them at the onset to get a sense of their preferences and rapping style. In his view, Nique "sounded very militant and the type that wants to inspire so I guess that's why I figured I'd make some type of anthem music where she could do that."[29] The soundtrack is upbeat, funky, and fast, while the lyrics tap into the play of appearances and everyday struggles. Nique makes herself vulnerable from the start as she unveils that despite impressions that she's "been through nothing," her family faced many challenges while she was growing up that she overcame with the grace of God. In the second verse audiences learn that enduring her past is what gave Nique thick skin and the ability to rise above significant obstacles.

> It was the 20th of May in the year 88
> Anthony became a father
> My mother was Katie Ann
> They truly did love and raise your girl well
> But from 7 to 17 life became like hell
> Dad got addicted to drugs then later he bailed
> Which in turn left mom all alone
> Struggling to raise me as a single parent on her own
> And on top of that pain
> I felt like an outcast, a misfit
> 'Cause I always had my own swag
> And different from everybody 'round me

So 7 to 17 I hated the real me
But now I'm loving myself and learning how to live free
5.20.88

Getting below the surface of appearance takes listeners into her father's drug addiction, her feelings of abandonment, as well as the pain of watching her mother live the struggles of single motherhood. The lyrics are direct and poignant; the weight comes through the bass line and her flow. One can feel the raw emotion shining through each beat, bar, and rhyme. It contains the seeds of contradictory effects. On the one hand the music makes a body bounce; and yet, the lyrics take listeners up and down a spectrum of struggle, strength, and success.

VOCALIZING VULNERABILITY

While the rappers in our study commonly adopt critical stances, there are additional layers to their rhymes that complicate their identities. In fact, they demonstrate complexity that goes beyond the description of "Sista with Attitude" that Keyes and Rabaka mobilize. Going back to Insite the Riot's comment about her verse on "Skin Deep" and the other conversations we've had with these artists, it is significant that part of presenting a strong self includes sharing moments of doubt and vulnerability. These are expressions that commercially successful women in hip hop like Nicki Minaj and Cardi B rarely advance because the conventions of the commercial industry do not invite them to share.[30] It is striking that male rappers such as Kendrick Lamar and J. Cole, on the other hand, are praised for exposing their insecurities. But Nique Love Rhodes's autobiographical track "5.20.88" is impactful because she discloses the hardships she faced growing up with a drug-addicted father and struggling single black mother.

Like Nique, Insite also goes to that place where the personal becomes political. Commenting on her decision to get personal on "It's Over"— a track about failed romantic relationships—Insite shared,

> What was communicated to me and channeled to me is that my best art will come out when you're vulnerable. All of that stuff has always come out. I write poetry and stuff and that's the stuff I don't usually share, but I recognize that people can connect to that in a way they may not be able to with other things.[31]

The first verse and refrain most acutely capture the vulnerability that Insite discloses on the track. It begins dramatically with horns playing melodic, sustained high notes that dominate the song's texture. Drums and bass provide the backdrop. A sample of a woman's voice singing "it's over baby, over. It's over baby," in an R&B style adds another layer of musical meaning. The horns cut out as Insite begins to rap,

Can smell the plasma on my sleeve from when my heart bleeds
You interpret what I'm feelin' like the art piece
But since art speaks I hope your spirit has ears
Bloodied emotions, see I'm tryin' to fight back tears
I am a light sphere, darkness clashes with my fashion
And in the past I have confused love with an orgasm
Thus I've endured patterns of weavin' my own web
Then act deceptively surprised by the spider's legs
The question still begs, but I answer not
I see my skillet, know the color of your kettle pot
Planting seeds in the soil of a barren lot
Allergic to my solitude, and anaphylactic shock
Needle marks from the epipen
Hey, if life must give me lemons I pray that they be organic then
With an agave blend, vitamixer spin
If this is a production of life's lessons I must channel in

The song's hook captures the idea that when relationships end both peo-ple experience the indelible mark of growth and pain. In subtle meta-phors Insite likens bad relationships to a sick body, epileptic and allergic to repeated mistakes. "It's Over" not only demonstrate openness but also the maturity, growth, and wisdom that can come with self-reflection; it also articulates darkness and how it can be overcome. It takes strength to reflect on failed relationships and to use these experiences as opportuni-ties to learn about ourselves in the process as we move forward. When we asked Insite what motivated her to share these experiences publicly she explained, "I wanted to look behind the curtain a little bit; I wanted to have fun. I wanted to just touch on some things that folks can relate to . . . folks can relate to having a tough time in relationships."[32]

Insite is not alone as she pulls the curtain back and makes visible the challenges and rewards that come with not only managing relation-ships, but also life as a Black woman and hip hop emcee in post-bankruptcy Detroit. All four of the artists whose work we analyze here offer lessons about relationship building. Whether they address abuse, misogyny, struggle, racism, drug abuse, or poverty, all of their messages lead listeners down a path of relationality. They convey the notion that the self is part of the social. Their music is as dialectical as their ideas about selves in societies.

Miz Korona operates as dialectically as Nique, Mahogany, and Insite; however, her style is much more hard-edged than the artists we have engaged thus far and her delivery is best characterized as a speech-effusive style similar to that of Insite the Riot. In her early career she battled and often beat male rappers. Recalling these days she remarks, "Back then, I snuck into clubs to see what's up. Then I jumped in."[33] Lyrically, Korona is a force—aggressive and open, commanding and soft; however, she is more likely than other women connected to the Foundation to have her music censored because she doesn't shy away from profanity. No matter the content, all of her rhymes are undercut by edgy beats. Sonically the music is as epic-sounding as her compelling voice. Compared to many women, including those we discuss here, Miz Korona's vocal register is low and her voice naturally bass-heavy. This quality gives her a distinctive edge that lends itself to gritty, pulsating soundscapes that suit the Detroit context that is the subject of so many of her songs.

Her track "Set Fire," released in November 2017, exemplifies Korona's complexity.[34] In her words, this song speaks to "my internal struggle that I inherited from my mother. Even though she was fighting health issues, she still had fire for me, to see me successful and to see other people be successful. She is the one that taught me to push harder even through struggle."[35] "Set Fire" articulates this story of struggle that includes an unwavering mother-daughter bond, healthy dreaming, and perseverance. Like many rappers we have spoken with who first hear a beat then craft lyrics to go with it, this ode to her "momma" was inspired by a beat that her good friend Conflict produced. Within a day or two of hearing the track Miz Korona learned that her mother had to be re-admitted to the hospital. Her mother's health weighed heavy on her as did her work and life issues at the time. In many ways, this particular track reflects Miz Korona's typical writing process, wherein beats inspire her words. As she explains it, "I like to get inside the pockets of the beat and feel it. It takes me places."[36]

In the first verse of "Set Fire" Miz Korona discloses her struggles as an emcee and her love for her mother:

This feel like waking up to a check full of commas
On that Mary J shit no more drama
I'm here to kill the game so I spit like a llama
I ain't never giving up
gotta do it for my momma
And I promise we'll make it outta debt one day
Into that house on the hill and jet set runway

I know seeing the world probably ain't as important
As you seeing success for ya daughter
So I feel I oughta do like Kobe
And go hard in the paint ever since the surgery
I know your heart beating faint
But don't complain much
I know it's painful to watch your child struggle
Still going through the same stuff
I went through when I was just a rookie
And you got the nerve to say that I am
One tough cookie, naw
I'm not as strong as the woman that made me
A real-life diamond, priceless grade D.

At the end of each verse she invokes spoken word to command a different form of listening. After the first verse she declares, "Yeah, you know you're my heart momma. You gotta stay strong. Keep that heartbeat."

Twice, once in each verse, Miz Korona spits wordplays that reference the dual power of Mary J. Blige, both the drama she stirs up and calls out as well as her monetary success. She dreams of financial security but refuses the drama and excess that often follows a rapper's fame. The mother-daughter theme that cuts through her narrative creates seeds of resonance for any parent-child relationship. The lament and musing on her mother's health as well as her strength and unbreakable support come through the lower, more gritty registers of Korona's voice. The contrast between the sentiment flowing from lyrics evokes a "Killing Me Softly" emotion and yet it is articulated through a "boom bap" voice, particularly when Miz Korona takes stock of the pain felt when a parent watches her child struggle. Both the lyrics and her mode of delivery reveal the layers of Korona's complexity; she is hurting for her mother while she pulls strength from her spirit, all the while eloquently rapping about delicate issues through a strong, if not dominant voice.

In the second verse, Miz Korona shifts the narrative back to her own obstacles and crossings. She expresses gratitude for the support she receives locally and vexation for the industry's indifference to her. She also discloses the loneliness of everyday artistry, particularly when messages come at her calling her worth into question; despite the negativity she embraces a keep your head up attitude. The reality is that underground artists live in flux. Some shows turn out huge audiences, while other times, only a handful of people show up. On top of haters in the world banking on failure, women who present as masculine-of-center face even more obstacles in their paths to success. Nonetheless, she has no plans to change her course or style. Rather, she keeps on keepin' on. From here, she returns to the spoken word style and concludes with this last affirming thought: "Don't ever let nobody tell you what you can't do. You gotta stay strong. Stand firm. Just 'cause they think you ain't make it when you should've don't mean you ain't got a chance, yeah. So set fire to 'em."

The beat to "Set Fire" is much more subdued that those found on most of Miz Korona's earlier work. Throughout the track, a sparse high hat and bluesy guitar riffs underlay her vocals. In the second verse she is outspoken about how much she has struggled as a career artist. Her metaphors cut through material markers, power claims, and prowess. She is a "problem" for industry sharks, haters, or "wack" rappers who try to take her on. And yet, despite the accolades bestowed on her in the local community, she has struggled to achieve notoriety and success on a national, commercial scale. In fact, she has a stronger following in France and Germany—where there is a strong love for both hip hop and the city of Detroit—than in the United States. The verse ends with her reflecting on how lonely an emcee's journey can be. On first glance, these two admissions seem contradictory, but while she has a loyal Detroit fan base, she has faced resistance from some of the major players in the city's hip hop underground. Time and again she has been told that she is "the most slept on" rapper. In other words, she is someone who should have "blew up" by now but has not. "Set Fire" is her public reflection on her career and letting go of the "haters" in her life.

In an interview with the *Detroit Free Press,* Miz Korona reflects on all of the constraints she has faced and what keeps her motivated, saying,

> It can be very draining, being that it's such a male-dominated field and you have people who close so many doors on you if you don't fit the image or mold that they feel women should. When I was younger, men who I worked with made passes at me until they found out my sexual orientation. And the fact that I'm now openly lesbian really closed a lot of doors. Like: 'How can we market you? You're not sexy enough. We need you to dress sexier or cut your hair or be more feminine or not rap so aggressively.' Why should I be meek? A shell of a person is what I'd be if I strip everything that's me to be able to have a record deal.[37]

In this same interview, she also details the disciplinary tactics the industry imposes on women. Being sexy, performing hegemonic femininity, and taming a strong voice are the unwritten costs of record deals. The stakes of success are high when women like her defy industry image makers. Yet, while there are men in Detroit's hip hop scene that dismiss her because of her sexuality and strong persona, on the whole her lyrical skills are admired in the underground contexts we have witnessed.

As we write this Miz Korona is a forty-year-old openly gay Black woman. At this point in her life, "making it" refers to having an enduring work ethic, a passion for life, and lifting up others. Financial support is always a condition, and yet relational and spiritual qualities shape Miz Korona's values and commitments. She cannot be boxed into any single script. She is neither invincible nor without flaw or vulnerability, and yet, her commitment to resist is unwavering. To capture "Vulnerable Mavericks" is to illustrate the fluidity of identities, unbound by hegemonic sexuality and industry standards of embodiment and voice.

MUSICAL SOLUTIONARIES

Classic women blues artists laid the grounds for these daring emcees to push boundaries. They merged the spiritual and sexual, personal and political, public and private.[38] Unlike their foremothers, the Foundation artists we examine here do not necessarily couple sexuality and spirituality. Their ideas about sexuality are tied to their sense of self-respect and resistance to industry norms that continue to objectify women. At one point or another all of them have expressed their disappointment with the hypersexualized, two-dimensional images that dominate the representation of Black women in commercial as well as many underground hip hop spaces. While Foundation artists' rhymes address sexual themes, they consciously choose to represent their bodies in ways that do not call attention to their parts but rather keep the focus on their whole beings. The introspective, spiritually, and politically motivated music that they create presents alternative ways of being. At times, they are explicitly critical of the narrow range of Black womanhood presented in popular culture, and in other instances, they focus on issues such as the environment, race relations, racialized bodies, poverty, and abuse, all the while challenging industry and popular culture norms that communicate who Black women are and who they should be.

Ruminating on the rampant homophobia, materialism, and misogyny that dominate the commercial hip hop industry, Ruth Nicole Brown considers "what the world would be like if there were more life-affirming images for me and my girls to run into and to play out on a daily basis."[39] We do not have to wonder. Foundation artists traverse the limited, controlling images—frozen frames—and sexual scripts that shape the literature focused on women in hip hop. A frame does not move; if anything, it freezes one's agency. Through their music, these artists offer alternative subject positions and depth that invites the study of subjectivity rather than image and tired scripts. They disrupt the field of what is known, even forging beyond the Queen Mother, Sista with Attitude, and the Fly Girl. The women of the Foundation are committed to producing life-affirming messages and images that enable current and future generations to reimagine hip hop and women's roles within it. They rhyme with the bold, sensitive, reflexive style of Vulnerable Mavericks. We offer up this term not as yet another script but as an analytic that captures the fluidity, contractions, and complexity that constitute their relationship to Black womanhood. Mahogany Jones, Insite The Riot, Nique Love Rhodes, and Miz Korona bring spirituality and vulnerability to the table as forces of political power in and through cadences that groove bodies and grow brain power. They gift hip hop heads with funky beats and brilliant poetics, all the while producing culture that defies what is known. In the spirit of privileging artists' voices, we turn to Mahogany Jones as we conclude,

> The whole purpose of the *Pure* project was to evoke conversation, because I feel like in order to get people to shift their paradigm you have to engage the way they think about things. You have to generate conversation. There have to be certain things that spark it more than entertainment things. I think of *Pure* as a movement for which one day I'll be the curator.[40]

In their own ways, each of these artists collectively contributes to movement building. They create complex narratives that allow audiences to "pull back the curtain" and understand who they are. Along the way, as they tap into their intuition, experiences, and introspective reflections, they illuminate the ways that hip hop can be used to construct dialogue rather than dystopia, community rather than commodification. Their work opens up a new kind of musical movement where women are cultural revolutionaries and creative solutionaries.[41]

5

"Legendary," Environmental Justice, and Collaborative Cultural Production

See the headlines
We are disenfranchised
but when we got lemons
what we do?
Make that lemon pie!
And that's why
I walk with my head high
cuz it's twice as hard as a chick
but I get by and stay fly.

—Nique Love Rhodes, "Legendary"

This chapter employs an interdisciplinary framework that invokes research from eco-musicology, popular music studies, urban geography, and urban planning—intersections that have only recently begun to receive attention in musicological studies.[1] Commenting on the importance of musicological attention to environmental concerns, Aaron S. Allen explains, "musicologists can provide insight on how composers, musicians, and others react to and communicate about environmental problems in their works, performances, and communal music making; and we can consider how listeners and audiences react and respond to such experiences."[2] Building on Allen's insights, we situate the process of making the track and video for "Legendary," as well as its analysis, within ecomusicology in an effort to understand how hip hop can be a strategic tool for building environmental awareness and advocating for change. Most importantly, it is significant that it is Black women who are employing hip hop in Detroit to communicate local environmental concerns to the community and the state.

We weave theoretical currents from the emergent literatures shaping ecomusicology and the relationships between urban geography and music in both the production process and analysis below. This theoretical background helps us contextualize the processes of production that led to the making of the track and music video for "Legendary."[3] The artists broadcast their interpretations of city-space, environment, and musical life throughout the production processes. As researchers and collaborators on the video, we mobilized hip hop's aesthetics as a working methodology. That is to say, we embodied improvisational aesthetics from hip hop's organic traditions of freestyling, battling, and cyphering. Our methodological work is grounded in "ways of doing and being in the sonic, kinesthetic, linguistic, and visual practices and expression of hip hop."[4] Camera work, sound adjustments, movements within scenes, clothing choices, site selections, and choreography emerged organically throughout the production process. This is not to say that improvisation is random; rather, a history of hip hop culture and skills underscores emergent practices. It takes an assemblage of stockpiles of knowledge and skill sets to invoke an improvisational aesthetic. As such, we offer a framework for people who do hip hop collaborative work.

The sonic stanza that we invoke above from Nique Love Rhodes is part of a larger verse from "Legendary." Members of the Foundation worked collectively to produce the track and video with the aim of foregrounding a women-centered depiction of Detroit and gesturing towards solutions for overcoming contemporary environmental and social conditions consuming the city and its citizens. "Legendary" captures the ways strong women recast racial injustice, environmental ruin, and social abandonment. These issues are not unusual in Detroit; rather, they are all too familiar.[5] However, the process of collaboration that went into the production of "Legendary" is atypical.

BROADENING THE BOUNDARIES OF ECOMUSICOLOGY

In the 1980s, musicologists began to call attention to the discipline's tendency to confine its area of study to the realm of aesthetics and meaning. Scholars such as Susan McClary and Lawrence Kramer launched a paradigmatic shift in the field as they drew on cultural and literary theory to articulate connections between music, politics, and identity.[6] The western art world's tendency to purposefully treat music as a museum piece disconnected from context or politics was being called out as a political move in itself.[7] Building on this interdisciplinary cultural approach, ecomusicologists are bringing environmental factors to the fore. Thus far, ecomusicological studies have most commonly focused on the relationships between people and natural environments, such as popular song's ability to reflect and affect contemporary attitudes toward rivers, the environmental impacts of massive mountaintop removal mining, and the ecological imprint of large-scale events such as the excessive carbon footprint of U2's 360° tour.[8] To date, little attention has been paid to the musical compositions of women and people of color in any genre.

Few studies draw connections between music and the environment from the perspective of women. Denise Von Glahn's *Music and the Skillful Listener: American Women Composers and the Natural World* gives voice to nine middle class women who compose art music in an effort to explore the ways that they "have understood nature and expressed those understandings in their music."[9] She offers some insightful conclusions pertaining to the composers' broad conceptions of nature and their overwhelming emphasis on collaboration "as a principal mode of behavior informing everything else."[10] In justifying her limited focus on middle class white women who produce art music, Von Glahn mentions the compositions of African American composer Margaret Bonds (1913–72) but specifies that no systematic study has been undertaken that considers the experiences that African American women have with nature. In an effort to extend this productive conversation beyond the confines of the aesthetics of art music, we highlight the cultural production of Foundation artists as it pertains to environmental sustainability issues specific to Detroit.

Despite a growing recognition that hip hop is a cultural form that offers rich environmental critique, it remains an understudied genre in musicology and has only received marginal attention from ecomusicologists.[11] As far back as 1993, writing a year after the Los Angeles insurrection, Philip Bolhman observed, "rap music has yet to stir much of a response from the disciplines of musical scholarship" despite having "become one of the most convincing ways of encountering history."[12] Two decades later Mark Pedelty concurs, "with its linguistic depth and topical range, hip-hop is particularly well equipped to deal with environmental matters."[13] Openly political hip hop embodies a sense of urgency and activism that is compatible with Aaron S. Allen's position that "ecomusicological approaches have the possibility to offer new *social critiques* about the intersections of music, culture, and nature—and, in general, about the world around us."[14] Similarly, Alexander Rehding states that what binds ecomusicology is a sense of urgency, praxis, and activism.[15] Detroiters are feeling an acute sense of urgency, if not emergency, about the material, economic, political, and social conditions in which they are living. These battles were perhaps most apparent in the emergency financial management struggle as well as Detroit's Future City vision for urban renewal.

MUSIC, PLACE, AND DETROIT'S ETHOS

In the 1970s, observing that the soundscape of the world was changing, R. Murray Schafer called for researchers from several independent areas of sonic studies to begin conversing with one another in an effort to further our understanding of the relationship between people and the sounds of their environments.[16] Concurrently, in *Noise: The Political Economy of Music,* Jacques Attali called for the imagination of "radically new theoretical forms, in order to speak to new realities" and claimed that music was one such form. To this end, he urged scholars "not only to theorize *about* music, but to theorize *through* music."[17] Since these crystallizing moments in soundscape studies, sound has received greater recognition as a methodology for social research.[18] In the 1990s Susan J. Smith took up the ongoing social research bias towards the visual and urged scholars, particularly geographers, to pay more attention to the significance of sound in their interpretations of the cultural landscape. Building on Schafer and Attali, Smith argued that "sound, especially in the form of music, has a social and political significance which, if it could be heard, might influence, change or enrich the interpretation of particular scenes." Quoting John Shepherd, she adds, "music can illuminate the nature of our relationships to each other and to the environment."[19]

In the twenty-five years that have elapsed since Smith's call to action, scholars across disciplines have delved deeper into the study of music's relationship to politics and place to the extent that increasing attention is being paid to how acoustic space functions in public space.[20] A recent example of this attentiveness is Marina Peterson's ethnographic study *Sound, Space, and the City: Civic Performance in Downtown Los Angeles,* which explores "the meanings and makings of the civic" through the conception and production of free summer concert series. In Peterson's words,

Civic performance offers a locus for understanding intersections of broader concerns facing urban residents and scholars, including social relations and diversity, public space and civic life, privatization and suburbanization, and economic and cultural globalization.[21]

She goes on to note that around the world similar projects are underway in an effort to imagine neighborhoods, activities, and developments. City-sponsored events designed to appeal to a diverse crowd provide the basis of her project. Examining these events, Peterson illuminates the city's efforts to redefine spaces and increase civic engagement. Los Angeles' commitments to using music to engage the public speak to the goals and issues that the women of the Foundation not only face but openly engage.

Even though it is not a universal goal of hip hop artists to redefine spaces, it is common for emcees to call into question and/or reference places in their tracks for one purpose or another. Artists concerned with civic engagement and social justice issues purposefully do so to bring visibility to the poor conditions and locations in which Black, Latinx and other communities of color live. Artists heavily reference geographical place because it plays an important role in the development of diverse rap styles and differences in local hip hop cultures, even within the United States.[22] In the introduction to *The 'Hood Comes First: Race Space, and Place in Rap and Hip-Hop,* Murray Forman notes that "rap's lyrical constructions commonly display a pronounced emphasis on place and locality."[23] Rappers often explicitly reference particular streets, boulevards, neighborhoods, and telephone area codes because of the tethering of socio-spatial information to locality, what Forman refers to as the "extreme local."[24] John Connell and Chris Gibson make a similar point:

> Geographical space is not an 'empty stage' on which aesthetic, economic and cultural battles are contested. Rather, music and space are actively and dialectically related. Music shapes spaces and spaces shape music. In various ways sounds have been used to create spaces and suggest and stimulate patterns of human behavior in particular locations.[25]

This observation is not specific to hip hop, but it is useful in explaining why hip hop continues to be preoccupied with geographical space. Hip hop music originated on the streets of the South Bronx because of and in response to the poor material and economic conditions of its Black and Brown residents. Thus, from the beginning, hip hop culture recognized and was born out of this dialectic between geography and music.

ON THE MARGINS OF URBAN DESIGN

While zoning laws may not seem like obvious objects of study to grasp environmental conditions and the state of Detroit, they too shape what can be done on purchased land. It was not until 1940, after twenty-two years of effort, that the Detroit Common Council approved a zoning ordinance. It took nine more years, until 1951, for the city to put a master plan in place.[26] The city was an industrial leader long before 1940. What is more, environmental protection policy did not exist in Detroit until the mid-1970s. Up until this time companies could build anywhere they deemed productive, despite the proximity of homes, farmland, cemeteries, or water supplies.

These debates continue in Detroit and their effects are as ideological as they are material. They reflect the challenge of managing environmental welfare in the city. To understand the politics of environmental protection and sustainability one has to look under the hood of current urban renewal plans to see the spoils. The 2012 Detroit Future City [DFC] Strategic Framework Report outlines a fifty-year vision for the city's development. A set of strategies and actions to transform vacant land in ways that would increase its value and productivity were included as part of the plan.[27] At the time of our work on "Legendary," law professor Peter Hammer had posited a fierce critique of the stakes that were tied to Detroit's then current trajectory of urban planning. Analyzing the DFC report, Hammer argued that the language and vision of the committee's blueprint for Detroit was misleading. In a public lecture he stated, "The Detroit Future Plan looks green friendly; however, critical scrutiny reveals that the plan's language is duplicitous."[28] Charity Hicks, the policy analyst for the East Michigan Environmental Action Council [EMEAC], articulates the community's perspective:

> Detroit neighborhood associations, citizens' groups and community-based organizations were not consulted nearly enough, if at all. We have outsiders making decisions for Detroiters, again. Land grabs are rampant. Our voices are not there. Foundations put Detroit Future City together and it is their interests that are being served in this plan.[29]

While DFC claims to be doing speculative planning, Hicks voices the concerns of the community who see their work as another insidious force contributing to the destabilization of Black populations and their environments.

Hammer and Hicks were certainly not the only critics of the plan. In 2013, the Detroit Chapter of the Sierra Club published a report on the state of the environment. These authors also questioned the DFC's vision, claiming that it misleads residents. They posited, "the basic plan to channel resources toward certain target areas of the city while neglecting others remains intact and fundamentally contradicts the principles of environmental justice."[30] Along the lines of Hammer's assessment, the Sierra Club report warned readers to fear the language of urban renewal. The authors worried that the DFC's work was masking the city's plan to neglect nearly two-thirds of the landmass that constitutes the city of Detroit. In 2017, the DFC released a five-year strategic plan; as of 2019, its social, cultural, political, and environmental implications remain to be seen.

Resisting the city's practices of urban renewal, Detroiters have engineered fascinating, hopeful remedies for these changing realities. The local population is fighting a range of racially marked boundary disputes that bear on urban ecology. These boundary battles are tied directly to food justice. While other cities may struggle with industry or housing encroaching into farmland, Detroit is facing the opposite circumstance. While there is a lack of grocery stores that sell affordable, healthy food in Detroit, there is an abundance of fertile land ideal for local farming.[31] In turn, people employ do-it-yourself strategies for growing their own food and raising animals such as chickens and sheep within the city's limits. Anyone who ventures into the Cass Corridor, Highland Park, or Detroit's Eastside is privy to these movements. Investors claim that livestock in residential and business areas will harm profit and disturb citizens. While locals push for urban farms, the right to raise livestock, and alternative transportation, urban planners are imagining cool cities designed to create business centered around leisure activities, such as hipster restaurants, chic music venues, museums, boutiques, public art, and landscapes so crafted that they appear artificial. The press is not reporting on these tensions; rather, the debates are taking place in neighborhood association gatherings and city council meetings.

Urban planning in Detroit is parallel to what Adam Krims theorizes as "design intensity." According to Krims, "the term refers to the tendency in advanced societies for products and services to owe much of their value to aspects of design and informational content, and informational aspects of products and services to develop rapidly."[32] From this perspective, today's design is based in new information technologies. In post-Fordist cities, new technologies are central, as the service industry and highly computer-based leisure practices have replaced manufacturing modes of production. Tech startups sprawl out and nestle into cool cities. Krims turns to Silicon Valley in the San Francisco Bay area and

Microsoft and Intel in Seattle to demonstrate the intricate ways culture is built around industry and vice versa. Design intensity explains the trend toward concentrated cultural regeneration, in the form of industries built around leisure practices like concerts, clubs, fine dining, arts, and theater districts. The planning is highly privatized; that is, corporate conglomerates have tremendous influence designing space—the centers and routes of business—inasmuch as they have a stake in their product design.[33] Business Centered Districts are designed to host a constellation of leisure, consumption, and tourism industries. Young, single, educated, well-paid professionals are encouraged to participate through cultural and financial investments.

If these are the markers of the design intensity of contemporary cities, the questions then become, who benefits from design intensity and what role does music play in urban design? For Krims, city planners play a role but corporate conglomerates have the most influence, in terms of not only access but also sponsorship. He uses post-Fordist neoliberalism to explain the shift from government-sponsored to privatized, corporate-controlled urban planning. It is no accident that elite musical sites like opera houses and symphonies are located in downtown cityscapes, nestled among expensive restaurants, sports stadiums, and other culturally privileged places. These places are highly policed and regulated. They are designed for professionals who have upwardly mobile careers and lifestyles. Detroit's residents are predominately Black, and while many of them work in the city's service industry, at the day's end most travel to the outer regions of the city and often face dilapidated conditions. Working-class people of color often feel out of place in Detroit's design-intensive sites. In response, these Detroiters are creating a rich culture of alternative and underground sites where creative energy flows back and forth.

IMAGINING AND EXPLORING "LEGENDARY"

In 2013 we collaborated on a track and video with Foundation artists for the Ecomusicology Listening Room session at the annual American Musicological Association conference in Pittsburgh, Pennsylvania. The call for submissions was discussed with Foundation members to the extent that those involved agreed that the final product—a music video—should address the multilayered dimensions of marginalization that Detroiters experience. We wanted to address both the place of women in Detroit's hip hop underground and their interpretation of the areas in the city that have been demolished or abandoned. Over the course of our research we learned that the ubiquity of abandoned spaces has lasting effects on the city's human, cultural, and political environment.

Once we agreed to ask the artists if they had any interest in creating a song and video to speak to the call we emailed Piper. She reached out to women in the Foundation to solicit interest. Nique Love Rhodes and Mahogany Jones expressed interest in the project. At our first meeting, we did not break down the call or interpret it. We hoped the ambiguity would lead to creativity. This strategy worked. With only the primer of the conference call inviting music and video projects that address the relationship between music, image, and place, Mahogany and Nique went to work. Mahogany approached Ronald "iRonic" Lee Jr., her long-time producer, and asked him for beats. She shared with him the same call from which we all worked. He gave her several instrumentals which she sent along to Nique. Independently, both artists selected the same beat as the one they liked best. They told us that "it felt like Detroit." That is, the beat produced a certain kind of feeling that evoked Detroit. Once they settled on a beat they started writing verses. Again, they produced independent verses without discussing their writing process. Once they emailed their verses to one another they wrote the hook together. Only after the beat was selected, verses written, and the hook finalized did the artists share the track in the making with us.

While Mahogany and Nique continued to refine their rhymes, the two of us and Piper began to brainstorm the video's concept and production process. This session originated the plan for making "Legendary," and was another site that led to micro-production methods. We sat on couches at the 5e Gallery one Sunday afternoon with notebooks and pencils in hand, storyboarding the aesthetics and sites where we would shoot the video. With no budget our resources and time were limited. We knew that we were going to use the Gallery as a home base; it would be the site of costume changes, conversations about scene changes, and audio adjustments. We chose shooting locations within a few miles of the building. Our goal was to select spots that both reflected the larger narrative of Nique and Mahogany's verses and were aesthetically compelling. Another micro method was in play. We had to agree on the aesthetics of place, sound possibilities, and movement. We wanted one scene to communicate abandonment so we chose a closed community center; its pool looked like a cesspool more than a place where children once played. This park was less than a mile from the 5e, across the street from Wayne State University. At the corner of Martin Luther King Jr. Boulevard and Cass Avenue there is a large, bright multicultural mural that reads "LIVE." Given its uplifting aesthetics and message we thought it was ideal. Piper suggested another mural of a beautiful, young Black girl and two children laughing and swaying on a homemade tire swing around the corner on 2nd Street. The yard in which we shot this mural was private property. Chickens rummaged around as Piper captured the women rapping their verses. Contrasting abandonment with growth, we decided on a local urban farm for our third location. We went west, just beyond the lodge freeway, and shot Spirit Farm. Piper shot the video while we took on the role of production assistants, managing audio, providing feedback on wardrobe changes, and diffusing tensions when we had timing issues. In the editing process, Piper interspersed historical and contemporary footage of people resisting redlining practices, emergency management, and air quality. Along our path of production we asked, how does music video storytelling broaden the scope of debates centered on environmental health?

We also shot driving scenes in Nique's Jeep Patriot to use as transitions between locations. The juxtaposition of sustainable urban farms and large, oil-reliant vehicles reflects the contradictions of living in a city where buses are the only form of mass transit and riders commonly wait hours for service. The Motor City's stake in people's heavy reliance on automobiles is not just a rhetorical jingle; with Krims in mind, we interpret the city's transportation infrastructure as a design-intensive construct which leaves out those who quite literally cannot afford to buy into the system. The issues that "Legendary" raises are especially important for Black women because the concerns of people of color are often overshadowed in environmental and social justice debates. As Rose Gray points out in her review of "red, black & GREEN: a blues (rbGb)"—a hybrid theater piece that explores significant roadblocks to Black environmentalism—"environmentalism is often considered a privileged, white concern."[34] "Legendary" demonstrates Black women's political agency and publicizes their commentary about the conditions in which they live. While the video does not showcase literal imagery of smokestacks polluting the air, declining water tables, or other explicit signifiers of environmental catastrophe, it does illustrate the effects of abandoned land, desolated neighborhoods, and concrete eyesores. In Detroit, Black women have taken the lead on environmental action and they are often in leadership positions at social justice organizations, working tirelessly for change.

In our time with the Foundation we witnessed the impacts of well-known figures in the city like Water Warriors Lila Cabill (Mama Lila) and Charity Mahouna Hicks, especially their imaginations of the Wage Love ethic of care. Both women were founding members of the People's Water Board, a grassroots organization that advocates for access, protection, and conservation of water. Seeing water as the essence of life, the Board succeeded in resisting city-sponsored water shutoffs. Their efforts reached the United Nations, which declared water a human right and took a formal position against shutoffs. Cabill and Hicks were deeply involved with struggles unfolding in Detroit around not only water but also air, land, and education. Cabill was the president of the Rosa and Raymond Parks Institute while Hicks directed EMEAC. Hicks died prematurely from injuries sustained after being struck by a hit-and-run driver in New York City while she was on her way to speak about Detroit's water crisis at the United Nations. When Cabill died in 2019, she was an elderly woman with a commanding political following. Both activists have been deeply missed as they crossed into ancesterhood.

These women moved people into action, educated with a fierce kind of love, and spread the word about environmental issues from Black women's standpoints as they invested in community organizing. They earned the title "Mama" because of their deep commitment to community, their respect for elders, and their relentless loyalty to African culture. Through their labor and now Mama Piper's,[35] we illuminate the aesthetic and political work coursing through hip hop artistic production, underscored by cultural organizing principles. The women making hip hop in this project work within Detroit's underground; their music, imagery, and affect reimagine environmental ruptures, urban beauty, and the possibilities for sustainability.

Familiar with the layout of the Cass Corridor and its adjacent neighborhoods, Piper scouted shoot locations in advance. While planning is not improvisation, the day of the shoot required multiple forms of moment-by-moment invention. Nique and Mahogany both arrived at the 5e Gallery early sporting suitcases full of outfits and shoes. Between different location shoots we went back to the gallery for consultations about fashion choices and wardrobe changes; color had to function like connective tissue that articulated verses to visuals, volume to veracity. Our retreats to the gallery were akin to going "back to the lab again."[36] Working as production assistants in charge of audio while Piper shot the video, we had to react in motion as the emcees meandered through space dropping their verses—staying out of the camera's view but close enough so that the emcees could hear the instrumental being blasted from a consumer grade iPod dock with speakers.

FIGURE 9. Bekka and Kellie during "Legendary" video shoot.
Photo: Piper Carter.

Spaces and conditions in the city organically fit with "Legendary"'s beats and rhymes. At the abandoned community center, Mahogany and Nique jumped off the ledge of the half-empty pool, materializing the refrain's call to action when they rap: "Doves cry/But we gonna jump up off the ledge and fly/Cuz real legends never die." This unplanned move captures the very spirit of freestyling. We learned that practices that materialize "on the fly" create a flavor of literacy that is not expected. Improvisation becomes a layer of hip hop texture once it is transformed into micro-methods.

We completed the project by the conference deadline and were pleased to have been selected. All of us—Nique, Mahogany, Piper, Bekka, and Kellie—caravanned to Pittsburgh. Travelling with them was an education in itself. It was in car rides to Pittsburgh, Columbus, and flights to New York that we learned the ins and outs of rap music, how to rap on beat, and why rap follows a sixteen-bar verse. When we were brainstorming the video's production Nique had just purchased her new Jeep. When she told us about her new whip Rebekah was confused and asked, "What's a whip?!" Nique laughed as she explained that a whip is a car. Our hip hop lexicon grew.

At the conference, we set up our video in the Listening Room and the artists rapped over it during our panel presentation. We contributed the scholarly portion of our presentation, and all five of us took questions from the audience after the other presenters completed their presentations.

This was a rare moment at a musicology conference where Black women had the opportunity to share their artistic interpretation of their city using gritty beats and rhymes. In an interview that Listening Room organizer Mark Pedelty conducted with us at the conference, Mahogany described the track's beat as "blue collar, grinding . . . [with] this pulse in it that feels hopeful." Nique added, "there's a certain spirit in instrumental tracks that pulls out certain things. This is revolutionary and we're revolutionaries so we're gonna tell you how we feel." The beats and larger messages within "Legendary" hearken back to a time in hip hop when the vocal command of women was more openly political.

The first verse, written and performed by Mahogany Jones, is ripe with historical references to racial injustice:

> Socialized to be confined
> Show me how to redesign
> Constructs created and traps bated for my demise?
> I despise
> The lies I spy with my mind's eye
> Like, why crimes so high but graduates so low?
> Why my taxes so high response time is slow?
> Don't care about my welfare
> Don't care about my healthcare
> Don't care about my whereabouts as long as I'm St. Elsewhere
> Where? Why? When? How?
> Did we get to the place where we are now?
> Years of bein' pushed to the edge
> Mess around we gonna jump up off the ledge
> The ledge of reason
> Odds of getting even increase in summer seasons
> In '67 we rioted
> When we weren't invited in
> We were kept divided when we applied for loans
> Denied to move into homes we could own unless we cloned
> A certain tone of skin akin to those zip codes
> Bulldozed more than our businesses
> Flattened all of our images
> Of Paradise in Valleys we live trapped in division when
> Rules and regulations are racially motivated
> To insure certain populations stay uneducated.

The words "the constructs created" can be linked to what George Lipsitz calls "possessive investment in whiteness."[37] He tracks the materiality of white privilege in the form of housing policies and unequal access to loans that kept whites and Blacks divided in urban centers and suburban white-flight expansion. Many of Detroit's housing developments from the 1920s through the 1960s had covenants attached to them stipulating that only white residents could purchase property or rent.[38] The history of whiteness has reproduced itself in contemporary Detroit. This verse also speaks to contemporary life where taxes are high but social services, police, and emergency medical "response time is slow." The structures have not radically changed from the 1940s, when housing developments were legally zoned to separate whites from Blacks and the police were perceived as a threat to Black populations rather than a source of safety. The feeling that no one cares about "my whereabouts as long as I'm St. Elsewhere" conveys the sentiments of abandonment. These lines communicate the invisibility that Detroiters feel. Too often their voices and real living conditions are lost on populations that govern them.

Mahogany also catalogs the uninvited rebellion of 1967. In her words, it took a bloody uprising to change the course of history in Detroit and still the city has not recovered; the improvements that followed did not come from liberal reform. Much of the progressive change has emerged from local communities and activist organizations including the Foundation, Detroit Summer, and the Boggs Center. The Paradise Valley that she references was an entertainment zone—home to jazz and blues clubs, salons, soul food restaurants, and churches—in the Black Bottom district. The neighborhood was home to the city's African American entrepreneurial class.[39] This thriving Black community was decimated in 1964 so that a freeway could be built in its place. Mahogany bemoans this destruction and calls into question the iconic imagery that was also lost.

The hook provides a sense of optimism: "Doves cry/But we gonna jump up off the ledge and fly/Cuz real legends never die." In our interview with Mark Pedelty, Mahogany commented on the importance of perseverance amidst the industrial decline in Detroit. "Yes it hurts, yes we cry. But real legends never die. Legends live on. Our city lives on. Women, we do great things. We live on with the work that we do whether celebrated or not celebrated." When the Foundation responded to questions on the AMS panel, she elaborated, "Detroit is like a bad marriage. In the course of the relationship the wife becomes sick. Instead of helping, the husband simply leaves." Mahogany brings home the point that the regeneration and investment that is happening is missing the local population of Black and Brown Detroiters.

In the second verse, Nique Love Rhodes sees unusual hope coming from unloved places:

Black girl, broken city, pretty woman, beauty in the gritty
Detroit being, see the juxtapose in the flow
When you from this town, you see many things grow
From the concrete, when it ain't supposed to happen
And I'm talking real life, I ain't talking 'bout rapping
See the headlines, we are disenfranchised
But when we got lemons, What we do? Make that lemon pie
And that's why I walk with my head high
Cuz it's twice as hard as a chick, but I get by and stay fly
People study the ruins, got the whole world watching
Seeing what we are doing, and how we build
How we lay the foundation
It comes naturally to birth self motivation
It's our DNA to give birth to pure greatness
Even when marginalized, you can't strip strength that comes from pride
Like you can't take black out of beauty, or real out of who we
Are cuz the soul goes far, and the spirit never dies
So when you see Detroit women, please recognize, recognize

Located within her own subjectivity, Nique likens a woman's beauty to the grittiness of the neglected city. Beauty is connected to Blackness, womanhood, and strength, even when it appears otherwise. She asks listeners to think about unanticipated growth, life coming from underneath "the concrete where it ain't supposed to happen." This is a metaphor for the hustle of Detroiters. She speaks spirit in the ability to improvise with those "lemons that make lemon pie."

Nique also makes clear that people in Detroit know that others around the globe have their eyes on Detroit. It is a model for urban farming and the repurposing of technology and space for alternative ways to create new working environments. Work and race are indelibly linked. Three out of four Detroiters work outside the city limits. It has been an ongoing struggle for Black residents to find work in the city. Responding, Rhodes emphasizes the positivity of repurposed Black identity. Without pause she brings race to the fore in a proud, hopeful style. "You can't take black out of beauty" is one truism. The idea that disenfranchised populations are motivated by "pride, spirit, and soul" opens a way to rethink what is possible in the city and it does so, significantly, from the perspective of Black women. Her verse exemplifies an intersectional theory of identity formation.[40] Nique's statements provide crossroads. They have the ambiguity that allows for forks in the road, as well as a forged sense of urban identity and community. The multidimensional identity claims that emerge in the lyrics of "Legen-

FIGURE 10. Shooting "Legendary." Photo: Rebekah Farrugia.

dary" led us to conceptualize the geographical locations that would match the sentiments addressed within the song.

Given Detroit's role in the track and video, Pedelty asked the artists how the work might have been similar or different if it was about another city. The artists firmly answered that the track and video are unique to Detroit, but draw connections to other places. Nique explained,

> I think this is the beauty of music that people can find their story in something that's totally unrelated. So maybe if somebody saw this video and said 'oh this is a great video about Detroit,' but they can still find the commonality, like, 'I grew up in a marginalized community on the south side of Chicago. Let me research why it is that way.'[41]

The specificity of the lyrics and images along with their indisputable references to Detroit is a purposeful political move employed to explain the current state of the city and the complex relationships that residents have to it. The video also seeks to motivate individuals and whole communities to rise above current conditions and, in Nique's words, "make something out of nothing." Such calls to action are vital to improving local conditions—environmentally, culturally, socially, and psychologically—because leaving is not a simple or easy option for many. In their research on the role of local politics in the restructuring of local economies in the United States, Kevin Cox and Andrew Mair observe that there is a material basis for people to be locally dependent.[42] With only one in four residents employed in the city, housing that is either inaccessible or unaffordable, and schools that are failing the public, the resources and job allocation available to Detroiters can neither provide sustenance nor create conditions for new ways of imagining work. When welfare support, unemployment payments, and delinquency climb, as they do in Detroit, dependency remains a structural problem.

Additionally, in a context where urban spaces are gendered male, this video serves as an example of how music can be used to challenge gendered power dynamics in a manner similar to how women blues singers of the 1920s and 1930s explicitly addressed the contradictions of feminism, sexuality, and power in their music. The work of the Foundation builds on the socially conscious discourse of the classic blues, which articulates a cultural and political struggle over sexual relations,[43] to also include commentary on public space and environmental sustainability. Connell and Gibson argue that much of the media created within hip hop reflects a "symbolic reclamation of the city."[44] The list of names of groups, albums, songs, and films they include as examples all refer to the cultural productions of men. Aware of men's domination of geographical and musical space, they comment, "geographical space is inherently embroiled in gender politics. Space carries within its form the dominant ideologies and politics that, in respect to gender and sexuality in the realm of music, remain overtly conservative, patriarchal and heterosexual."[45]

Women have been all but shut out from engaging in this dialogue and commentary on social location and identity in hip hop. It is significant that a group of women conceptualized, wrote the rhymes for, and shot the video for "Legendary." The women-centered nature of this production openly resists the gender dynamics that are present not only in hip hop culture but also in broader conversations related to space and environmental sustainability. It is interventionist that women are telling a political story entrenched in the politics of space and place. What is more, the video illustrates women in multiple subject positions: as protesters, mothers, farmers, and artists. We are not aware of any literature that highlights the ways that Black women occupy these locations simultaneously. These are not the depictions that one finds in commercial hip hop. It is not commonplace to see and hear women contesting political and physical ruins. Breaking away from the hypersexualization of women is productive on its own terms. The narrative encourages positive responses to hopeless conditions. The dominant subjectivity produced by this music is unlike that of male-centered rap music.

The politics of representation are at stake in "Legendary." Pushing the limits of discourse, Krims sees representation as one force among many that affect cultural regeneration. Krims captures the scope and temporality of urban representations through the concept of "urban ethos."[46] The urban ethos is not a representation per se but a distribution of representations that operates as a discourse. Using hip hop to interpret contemporary post-Fordist conditions, Krims sees the urban ethos as a web, constituted through institutional actors creating blogs, music, music videos, Internet content, and television programs, among other media texts. When all of these outlets expose the same sensibility about urban space the ethos becomes identifiable; in other words, the distribution of representations has done its work.

"Legendary" is constituted in a reconfigured urban ethos distinct from Krims's conception. For Krims, gender relations are polarized in urban space. In the hood, he uses rapper 50 Cent as the example of violent hegemonic masculinity. The hood is one side of the polarity and is more male. The city, however, as signified by the amorphous sounds of Petula Clark's "Downtown," feels softer and safer. Race is unmarked and the sounds of downtown space are imbued with more female sensibilities. "Legendary" does not construct either/or binaries with respect to gender identity and urban space. Instead, it depicts the effects of physical and social abandonment, the traces of racism that have divided neighborhoods, and police blocking protestors with nightsticks and shields.

Overwhelmingly, male-dominated commercial hip hop combats racism and police brutality through an eye-for-an-eye mentality where violence begets violence. These are the practices that Krims addresses in his claim that the hood is male. The artists who produced "Legendary" complicate Krims's binary. Their lyrics and imagery are interpretations of both the history and the contemporary issues that Detroiters face. However, contrary to Krims's view, women do not simply embody the sanitized aesthetic of downtown spaces. Here, we see women all over the city taking on roles in the public sphere that are often relegated to men.

The artists are rapping from a woman's perspective that nevertheless intersects with race, city, and place. The rapid images demonstrate the dilapidated brokenness that Detroiters face, but they also point to hopeful, creative, and spirited movements citizens are launching despite having meager resources. Krims does not imagine gendered space outside of the polarizing effects of design intensity, but "Legendary" redesigns what city and place mean when women have vocal and visual command.

RECLAIMING AGENCY

"Legendary" and the process of its production tell a story about collaboration, alienation, and the reimagining of space in a place that until recently, was primarily defined by racism, deindustrialization, and displacement. Recent ecomusicological studies have observed the powerful role that music plays in challenging and reimagining contemporary environmental, social, and political conditions. Pedelty clearly addresses the symbiotic relationship between music and the environment. On the one hand, he stresses that people, places, and technologies generate songs; on the other, "music helps us define who we are and mediates our imagination of place."[47] In other words, music can serve as a vehicle for understanding our sense of self and opening up possibilities for the kinds of communities in which we want to live. For the most part, mass media representations of Detroit replicate narratives of dilapidation and disparity; rarely do they acknowledge the work of vital revolutionary citizens, DIY organizations, and underground art and culture. Yet, in reality these collectives are responsible for generating provocative ideas about the repurposing of space and technology, creating and maintaining an urban farming movement, and forcing urban planners, politicians, and corporate-sponsored foundations to take neighborhood associations seriously. What we offer in "Legendary" opens space for conscious, collaborative, interventionist work that poses new questions for ecomusicological inquiry.[48]

Through rhymes, videography, choreography, location scouting, swift wardrobe changes, and extemporaneous production we bring to life micro methods in the making—a kind of improvisational literacy for music video storytelling. In the making of "Legendary" we produced a collective flow. Hip hop educators, particularly English education specialists, have contributed a working lexicon for doing hip hop as a mode of study.[49] Similar to how producers and emcees describe returning to the studio as "going back to the lab," hip hop education scholars put this concept into practice in their research and pedagogy. Following their lead, we offer a lab of our own as music video storytelling is a production well-spring.

In "Legendary," Black women draw attention to issues and experiences inextricably linked to racism and marginalization through vivid imagery of dilapidation and loss. However, unlike the messages most commonly represented in commercial hip hop, the Foundation offers solutions to these societal ills. The track provides viewers with a different understanding of the city, one that is gendered female and encourages positive solutions rooted in creativity, strength, and solidarity. This work disrupts the polarity that Krims proposes, of the hood as male and the city as female.

The writings of Grace Lee Boggs in part motivated us to seek out and create musical texts with politically motivated hip hop artists. In *The Next American Revolution*, she calls for visionary organizing, which in her words begins by "creating images and stories of the future that help us imagine and create alternatives to the existing system."[50] Hip hop culture was born out of the struggles and experiences of people of color in the South Bronx four decades ago. For Detroiters, struggle related to deindustrialization, racism, and more recently state-sponsored revitalization have continued to intensify over these years. Hip hop continues to be a vehicle to speak back to and reimagine urban life and cultural citizenship.

Our goals with the production of "Legendary," as well as the documentation of the process and our reflections on it, have been twofold. On the one hand, this work demonstrates the role that music can play in reimagining space and place. On the other, following Boggs, it encourages the vision of new, more participatory place-based concepts of citizenship and democracy. In *Leadership and the New Science*, Margaret Wheatley makes the profound statement that "in this exquisitely connected world, it's never a question of 'critical mass.' It's always about *critical connections*."[51] Many artists and community builders in Detroit, including organizers like Grace Lee Boggs and adrienne maree brown, have put this philosophical approach to movement building into practice. The academic and artistic connections presented here were vital to the vision and production of "Legendary" and the musical and environmental movements that such musical texts inspire.

6

Hip Hop Activism in Action

Hip hop's fifth element, Knowledge, is deeply entrenched in the local work of Detroit's cultural organizers. The Piper Carters, ill Weavers, and Will Sees of today's Detroit lead through the lens of cultural diplomacy.[1] That is, they weave their politics through cultural practices. When Piper first conceived of creating a women-centered hip hop collective, the proliferation of Knowledge was central to her efforts. Whether it was the social actors at the table in meetings or the women on stage at open mic nights, Piper used every opportunity to connect hip hop to a broader context in an effort to encourage community-minded thinking about the practices at stake in the lives of Detroiters. The cultural organizers and artists that birthed the Foundation embody a philosophical orientation reminiscent of the communities of color that organically birthed hip hop in New York in the 1970s. They share the experiences of displacement, disenfranchisement, underemployment, toxic environmental conditions, and food deserts that challenge African American, Latinx, and other communities of color across the United States and globally.

This chapter examines the complex intersections of hip hop culture, activism, and community work in Detroit to highlight the *intersecting*— as opposed to parallel—activity of women of color working within popular culture *and* grassroots organizations. At present, there is a dearth of, and pressing need for, scholarship that documents such efforts.[2] The events we detail—Dilla Youth Day, Denim Day, and the Foundation's collaborations with the Allied Media Conference—cut across categories of youth, sexual assault/healing, and media activism. They are engineered by creative thinkers who unknowingly exercise adrienne maree brown's theory of emergent strategy.[3] brown positions contradiction and imagination in a holistic interdependent relationship wherein interpersonal relationships birth imagination, hope, and possibilities. She also considers openness and transformation of self as precursors to the possibility of changing others. brown draws heavily on Grace Lee Boggs's direct mentorship as well as the Afrofuturist writings of Octavia Butler. She urges her readers to join her in realizing answers to questions about how we can cultivate the muscle of radical imagination needed to dream together beyond fear, and stresses that collective and collaborative relationships are essential for shaping systemic change.

For half a century human rights activist and philosopher Grace Lee Boggs was a leader in Detroit striving for racial and economic justice, but she never worked alone. Jimmy Boggs—her political confidant, friend, and life partner—influenced her deeply. Together they produced a philosophy of organic, emergent cultural movement organizing.[4] This line of thinking birthed multiple generations of Detroit revolutionaries, including those in Detroit's hip hop underground. Her success and recognition became more widely known nationally in the last two decades of her life. When she died at the age of 100 in 2017, Danny Glover spoke at her funeral and President Obama sent a personal note to her family. In 1992, Grace co-founded Detroit Summer, a youth program committed to "planting community gardens to re-connect young people with the Earth and with the community; painting public murals to reclaim public space; and intergenerational and peer dialogues to share our fears, hopes, and dreams."[5] Her writings, actions, and philosophies have motivated numerous Detroiters to continue movement-building in her footsteps. Mainstream conceptions of social movement work often rely on structural and organizational perspectives that favor the centralization of power and routine movement actions. In *The Next American Revolution* Boggs and Scott Kurashige stress that everyday organizing, protesting, and demanding new policies are not transformative enough actions because "they do not change the cultural images or the symbols that play such a pivotal role in molding us into who we are."[6] The work of the Foundation offers an alternate cultural landscape, as well as reimagined symbols sacred to Detroiters.

In our efforts, we employ literature from hip hop pedagogy, hip hop based education [HHBE], and scholarship on music and healing to frame events that the Foundation or its artists planned and executed.

When the artists connect community building to their music and art, a new form of activist identity emerges. We capture their reflections and conclude with some thoughts on how these efforts advance intersecting relations between social justice practices and art movements.

DILLA YOUTH DAY

The affiliations between the hip hop underground and Detroit's extensive activist history are dense yet subtle. Even for Piper Carter, it took attending a Chicago Freedom School workshop for her to view her hip hop and community work as activism and in turn, to self-identify as an activist. Since then her motivation has been ongoing. Piper continues to produce events that strengthen and deepen the connections between art and activism, two spheres of production that are often seen as separate realms of activity. In 2012, Piper produced the first ever Dilla Youth Day in honor of legendary Detroit hip hop producer James DeWitt Yancey, better known as J Dilla. Dilla emerged onto the underground hip hop scene in Detroit in the mid-1990s as one-third of the group Slum Village. At Dilla Youth Day in 2015, Amp Fiddler was the first to take the stage for the evening's performances. He is a man of many talents, with a history that includes record producing and playing keyboards with George Clinton's Parliament and Funkadelic in the 1980s and 1990s. On this night he shared with a packed theater the story of how Dilla and his buddies used to come over to his house and experiment with making music. Fiddler thought Dilla was "exceptional." One day while on tour, he shared some of Dilla's music with A Tribe Called Quest's Q-Tip. Dilla was then invited to work with the group and other popular hip hop acts at the time like De La Soul, Busta Rhymes, and The Roots. He moved to Los Angeles but in 2006, at age 33, he died from complications related to thrombotic thrombocytopenic purpura, a rare blood disease. Fiddler ended his talk with a message of how important it is to give back to the community.

Dilla was a pathbreaking producer and remains widely recognized for his unique and influential sounds to this day. Artists from Nas to Pharrell laud him as one of hip hop's most talented producers and in 2019, Pharrell's i am OTHER company and Arizona State University teamed up with MTV and Save the Music to launch an electronic music production grant named after Dilla. Grammy-winning musician and Save the Music ambassador Robert Glasper insists that "Dilla is the only hip-hop producer that literally changed the way musicians play music. You can always hear musicians trying to emulate him."[7] In the spirit of his do-it-yourself approach to music-making, Dilla Youth Day, which takes place every February, provides educational workshops related to hip hop's core five elements: emceeing, b-boying, beat making, graffiti in the form of graphic design and screen printing, as well as Knowledge sessions that cover issues related to leadership skills, community building, and cultural citizenship. Piper Carter has been its lead organizer since she first produced the event in 2012.

Piper's motivation and inspiration for organizing the first Dilla Youth Day came from an event she organized in 2011. It featured a panel discussion about J Dilla's music and legacy that included Amp Fiddler, Nick Speed, and DJ Head. After the talk, the Urban Stringz Youth Orchestra, led by cellist Cecelia Sharpe, performed renditions of tracks by Lady Gaga, Taylor Swift, and other pop artists. Piper explained how what happened next motivated her to found Dilla Youth Day:

> After they did their squeaky performance I was like 'Let's freestyle.' And one of the kids was like, 'What's that?' And I was like, 'What?!' And the kid didn't know what freestyling was. I was like, you've got to be kidding me! And so then I explained to them, you know it's when you just play, and the kid was like "Naw, I never did no shit like that.' And so all the kids were looking like, you're gonna do it?! And I was like, guys do you understand that the tradition of Black music which is rooted in jazz is the part of improvisation and that is Black music and that is part of the root of where hip hop even comes from? Nah, I was like wow! So we kinda talked about that a little bit and I was like, listen you guys gotta freestyle, and they were shook.[8]

Piper then asked Nick Speed and Amp Fiddler if they would freestyle with the kids. As Piper recounts,

> They did it and it ended up being pretty awesome. I mean it's not an amazing performance but it's an awesome experience. From there it clicked. This is for the kids. They don't even fucking know some simple shit like that . . . I was like that's our duty . . . that year I had started working with youth and I was in the schools doing maker spaces and technology and all that stuff and I was like, I wanna bring all that together for Dilla Youth Day.

Piper organized the first Dilla Youth Day the following year in February 2012 at the Carr building. In 2013 and 2014 it was housed at the Cass Corridor Commons Building, which at the time was the home of the 5e Gallery. Since 2015, it has been held at the Charles H. Wright Museum of African American History. At the Wright, the lower level features workshops and drop-in work stations and the rotunda on the upper level is a meeting space where the elements come together: DJs play music, b-boys and b-girls dance, emcees freestyle, and Black art is for sale. There are also information tables set up around the perimeter of the space with pamphlets about community organizing and upcoming experiences for people of all ages. The event has consistently attracted attendees from all over the city—the Eastside, Westside, North End and Southwest, as well as the suburbs.

Dilla Youth Day is one example of the DIY hustle and maker space practices that abound in Detroit. The day-long event is devoted to teaching youth hip hop's first five elements, its history, the joy it brings, and its skill sets. Dilla Day creates a space where cultural organizing and hip hop pedagogy coalesce; the volunteers, producers, participants, and audiences that make the event possible demonstrate hip hop in action and cultural citizenship in the making. The philosophy underscoring Dilla Day embodies cooperative economics, an entrepreneurial spirit, multigenerational education, creativity, and improvisation—the street skills of hip hop. Acclaimed hip hop DJ and scholar Emery Petchauer argues that emergent work in HHBE that "focuses on aesthetic forms, ways of doing or cultural logic produced by hip hop culture" is an important and necessary platform to understand the culture's forms and the ways they "produce organic ideas, epistemologies, and dilemmas that can inform teaching and learning."[9] Putting theory into practice, under the moniker DJ Illiterate, Petchauer has served as a mentor at Dilla Day, teaching youth how to make beats with other acclaimed local producers. Scholar and cultural activist Ruth Nicole Brown's SOLHOT [Saving Our Lives Hearing Our Truths] collective works from a similar framework of hip hop pedagogy, which she imagines as "the practice of engaging young people using the elements of hip-hop culture and feminist methodology for the purpose of transforming oppressive institutions, policies, relationships, and beliefs."[10] Brown's feminism is grounded in Black Girl Studies and hip hop feminism; advocating for the interests and quality of life of Black girls and women, she stitches hip hop into feminist-motivated practices for reaching youth. Like the scholarship/community work of Brown and Petchauer, Piper Carter's Dilla Youth Day is also an act of hip hop pedagogy, educating young people through cultural practice. Our embedded field note illustrates the myriad of pedagogical practices operating at Dilla Day.

ON THE WAY TO DILLA DAY

Bekka: February 8, 2015, Detroit. Kellie is under the weather so I drive down I-75 to the Charles Wright Museum alone. It is a cold, grey day, like all the days in February but I press on. This is my third Dilla Youth Day since Piper launched the event in 2012. It is the first year the event is at the Wright so I'm not sure what to expect. Programming is scheduled from 1–9 p.m. with an hour break at 5 p.m. There are workshops in the afternoon and performances in the evening so I show up around 3 p.m. I pull open the heavy glass door to the building and follow the thumping beats to the basement. I'm immediately taken aback by the size of the crowd. Hundreds of people of all ages, mostly African American and I'm guessing city proper residents, are wandering around in every direction. I'm taken aback by how many children are here, including infants and toddlers. I hear Consuela's voice on the mic as I turn into the hallway. She is in the center of the carpeted, pavilion-style area leading a Puerto Rican dance that eventually turns into a b-boying workshop. Young children who look to be between the ages of three and eight are having a great time showing off their skills to one another in the cypher.

Afterwards, an eleven-year-old Asian-American girl introduces herself as the CEO of her own business before a video plays that explains her entrepreneurial project and spirit. I learn that she began her own candle-making business at age five. The vibe is uplifting, the sense of creativity infectious. Workshops are going on in most of the other rooms and there's a craft station for younger children. Adults are teaching youth how to make beats and do spoken word poetry. There are leadership workshops for girls and young women with titles like "Keep Calm and Lead," screen printing, and b-boying happening all around. Whole Foods and some local businesses have donated food and beverages.

I recognize a face here and there but mostly I'm on my own. This is the second largest African American museum in the nation and at this moment everything just feels right. It's the perfect place to host Dilla Youth Day. I think to myself, Piper has done an exceptional job organizing this massive event nearly single-handedly. Despite my interest and intent, by virtue of being a white thirty-something suburban woman I am to a large extent still an outsider here, but I take pictures at Piper's request, which shores up my sense of belonging. The events downstairs start to wrap up at around five. At 5:40 p.m. I head upstairs to the General Motors theater. The youth performances are scheduled to begin at six and the theater is already half full. I know from the Wright's website that its capacity is 317. DJ Linda Carter is on the stage. There are people of all ages standing up dancing in front of their seats. As I look around the room I notice that of the 150 people present I am one of very few white people. As on so many other occasions I am disappointed and start thinking about how different metro Detroit would be and what a better place it could be for everyone if there was more cross-cultural communication, especially between white suburbanites and Black and Latinx Detroiters.

Just after six the lights are dimmed and Piper introduced Amp Fiddler to the stage. He takes his time telling Dilla's story. He ends his presentation with a message about how important it is to give back to the community.

6:10 p.m.: The theater is close to capacity. Nearly every seat in the room is filled. Internationally renowned poet, activist, and Detroit native jessica Care moore's seven year old son King takes the stage to recite some poetry. For the next two plus hours a host of young rappers, dancers, and a group of musicians from Cecelia Sharpe's Urban Stringz organization perform. The audience frequently erupts into applause and participates when called upon.

Our field notes reveal that Dilla Day is lived hip hop based education. It draws on every principle of hip hop pedagogy: it is multigenerational, improvisational, about acquiring skills for life, and it offers culturally relevant learning. Youth see themselves as makers, as CEOs, and artists. Across a range of workshops, dance practice, kids making t-shirts and learning to make their own instruments, we see multiple forms of literacy in action. The performances at the day's end bring all the learning into a pleasure of applied performance. The crowd is as elated as the energy of the performers.

In 2015, Dilla Youth Day attendees were encouraged to fill out a survey that Piper created to obtain feedback from the community. Participants' favorite elements from the day's events included learning how to make beats, mixing class, being around well-known older hip hop heads in the community, the DJ 101 station, celebrating Dilla's memory while bathing in music and hip hop, learning about native, Puerto Rican, and African music and dance, seeing the Detroit community come together, and seeing the youth enjoying themselves through music and expression. Many people stated that they'd like to see events like Dilla Day happen more often. Detroiters long for these events because they are so few resources in the city for youth. The community has to step in and provide. The joy that comes from seeing children in action, actively learning, using maker spaces, and then performing what they

FIGURE 11. Piper Carter and Vonda Davenport at Dilla Youth Day.
Photo: Rebekah Farrugia.

learned for a 200 plus audience is intoxicating. Museums and community centers are the places where youth and elders have the most contact outside of family life. The cultural vacuum that exists in a city with such a rich history of art and music is ironic. This absence makes Dilla Youth Day essential.

Foundation member Consuela Lopez organized the Puerto Rican dance session at Dilla Youth Day in 2015. Consuela has a multiracial background that includes Puerto Rican and Cuban ancestry, and she is a devoted cultural and civic advocate who is a community pillar in Detroit. At the time of our writing, she was the director of community and economic development at an advocacy nonprofit agency in Southwest Detroit. In her role she works side-by-side with local, state, and federal law enforcement to assist citizen patrollers in enhancing public safety for the neighborhoods of Southwest Detroit. As the co-director and founder of BombaRica, a performing arts and cultural education group, she has facilitated trainings on Latino identity, culture, and the illustrious history of arts in activism in Southwest Detroit. In our conversations Consuela shared that growing up "it was just music all the time. House music, it didn't matter. I listened to all types of music—country, everything." Her father was a surgeon and her mother was an artist, community leader, and Black Panther. In her words, "My first case of activism was watching my parents. . . . Our house was the house for kids to learn and do stuff. So that activist part is because of them."[11] By her twenties she was already recognized as a mentor in the community and she studied Afro-Latino Studies in graduate school.

When we interviewed her Consuela had recently become involved with the Foundation. Having found a kindred spirit in Piper and believing that there was an active need for a collective like the Foundation in Detroit she began attending meetings and events on a regular basis. Given her extensive community engagement record and her dedication to cultivating leadership skills in the city's youth population, Consuela committed to leading conversational sessions and dance workshops at Dilla Youth Day on more than one occasion. Whether it is through her teachings of cultural heritage, working with law enforcement, or facilitated identity trainings, Consuela's efforts and engagement throughout the community exemplify brown's ideation of alternative imaginations in action.[12] With culture at the center, Piper, Consuela, and all those who help produce Dilla Youth Day are building complexity and growing the future. The event is a space where all things Detroit come together: cultural organizing, commitment to youth, community outreach, and cooperative economics all fold into history in the making.

Dilla Day provides youth training, cultural history, interpersonal connection, and performance. Hundreds of children and adults attend. It draws a diverse array of people from every corner of the Black community as well as supporting organizations, artists, academics, and public officials. Youth leave with historical toolkits and contemporary skill sets that can spark career interests and have the potential to be life changing. Dilla Youth Day embodies the principles of hip hop based education and demonstrates feminist hip hop pedagogy in action. This advocacy and ethic of care is also connected to Mahogany Jones's annual Denim Day event.

DENIM DAY

In 1992, a young woman in Rome was raped by her driving school teacher. The man defended himself claiming that her jeans were too tight, too enticing. The judge bought his argument and he was acquitted. This case riled women around the world to take sexual assault and its prosecution even more seriously. Like the Los Angeles Commission on Assault Against Women that created a national Denim Day in 2011, Mahogany Jones also decided to take action against inaction. Upon learning that 11,000 untested rape kits were sitting in Detroit's police archives, she organized an event to raise awareness and funds to pay for

FIGURE 12. Denim Day Flyer 2014.
Created by Jayne Maire Smith.

their testing. An annual event from 2014 until 2018, Denim Day Detroit brought together criminal justice actors, artists, affected populations, and the general public. Along with informational talks and testimony, poetry, music, song, and dance were part of the night's activity. Art was in every breath that Mahogany took on Denim Day. She employed her emcee skills as host and incorporated call and response, bearing witness, and giving testimony into the evening's powerful program. In addition to the aesthetic and political work that this event accomplished, Mahogany also mobilized practices of self-care to bring community healing into public conversation wherein community work effects political work. Denim Day is constituted in self-care; it feels like a warm swathe that the entire audience bundles up in together.

We attended several of these events over the course of our study. At the 2018 Denim Day we learned that the high-profile stories about the untested rape kits and the efforts of community organizers like Mahogany put enough pressure on the state that funding was funneled for the testing of all 11,000 kits. At this same event a woman testified that the first kit the city tested led to the prosecution of the man who had attacked her nineteen years earlier. Her story was as gripping as the spoken-word poetry and singing performances that also voiced violence, pain, and healing. Our Denim Day fieldnotes capture the audience's presence as well as the orchestration of activism, policymaking, and performative resistance.

Bekka: May 6, 2015, Denim Day, Detroit. It's a warm May evening and the traffic is light and parking ample. We feed the meter and walk the block or so to the event that is being held on campus at the Center for Crea-

tive Studies in Midtown. We arrive at 6:30. As we walk in we are asked
to sign in, handed a program, and welcomed to take a gift bag from the
table. Inside the brown paper bag are a few flyers for local Black owned
businesses and a piece of candy. There is a donation jar on the table.
Performances and talks are going on in the next room. As we walk in
we see Intellect, one of our favorite local poets, emcees, and singers, on
the stage singing and playing guitar. For the past two years she has been
a member of the Foundation. A glance at the program shows that she's
the first performer of the night, which means that we haven't missed
much.

We don't see Mahogany right away but we recognize a number of the
other faces in this room of eighty or so predominantly Black women.
D.S. Sense is selling her On My Detroit Everything t-shirts at the table to
our right and Piper Carter is handling photography. There are also slid-
ers, sodas, and chips for sale. After Intellect finishes her song Consuela
Lopez takes the stage and shares that she is a survivor. That one of the
strongest and most vocal community activists and youth advocates in the
city is a sexual assault survivor throws me for a loop. Mahogany and
Jaci Caprice take the stage next and do a rendition of Mo's track
"Respect" off of her *Pure* album. Mahogany then announces that all of
the money raised this evening will go to paying to process more of the
untested rape kits. It costs $490 to process one rape kit and so far this
evening over $300 has been raised. Less than 1000 kits are left to be
processed, thanks to the generous contributions of community members,
corporations, and the efforts of law enforcement personnel/offices. From
the resource panel I learn that from those kits 188 serial rapists have
been identified, including fifteen who have been convicted. I also learn
that it will cost millions of dollars to prosecute the perpetrators. It is
almost 9 p.m. when we leave. A self-defense demonstration is about to
begin. Like many days and nights when I find myself attending hip hop
or organizing events in the city I learn more than I expected to, like the
importance of speaking to children in age appropriate ways about sexual
assault, starting as soon as they can talk. As we leave my heart is heavy
for all the victims but also hopeful thanks to the survivors who spoke out
and shared their stories of abuse and their healing processes.

The therapeutic uses of music have been studied and applied for centu-
ries, with the earliest known reference to music therapy appearing in an
article for *Columbian Magazine* in 1789.[13] However, it is only in the
last two decades that attention has been paid to the therapeutic uses of

rap and hip hop.[14] The research thus far has primarily been concerned with what happens in clinical and classroom settings. Listening to hip hop has been lauded as a useful coping mechanism in psychotherapy sessions with young African American men and at-risk youth.[15] Don Elligan also advocates for adults to listen to rap music with youth as a means of opening up dialogue.[16] Listening, however, is not the only communication practice at work in musical healing. Hip hop based cultural production has also been advocated as a means for Native Americans to heal from historical traumas and resisting genocide.[17]

At Denim Day, participants and audience members snapped their fingers, nodded their heads, and interjected with "mm hmms" when they heard narratives that moved them, and their faces told their own stories as they listened to others. Their nonverbal communication punctuated music, testimony, dance, and song and in effect, served as a powerful form of catharsis. These cosigning acts confirmed the truth-value of storytellers' narratives and encouraged them to continue.[18] In some cases, the circle was completed when audience members also felt compelled to testify.

It is well documented that listening to and producing rap can function as a site of emotional release, counter-nihilism, and counter-destructiveness.[19] Yet, little has been written about what hip hop music and culture have to offer in the way of fostering personal and community healing among sexual assault survivors, particularly women. Cases of sexual assault are traumatic experiences that often leave survivors feeling shamed and isolated. In laying out the therapeutic benefits of engagement with the creative arts, Archibald and Dewar turn to Judith Herman, a clinical psychiatrist who views connection with others as vital to the healing process:

> The core experiences of psychological trauma are disempowerment and disconnection from others. Recovery, therefore, is based upon the empowerment of the survivor and the creation of new connections. Recovery can take place only within the context of relationships; it cannot occur in isolation.[20]

Events like Detroit's annual Denim Day that Foundation members organize, perform at, and otherwise contribute to are essential to building connections, community, and in turn, healing. They provide safe spaces for community members to witness and testify through the performative power of healing; this space of engagement creates new connections that are essential for recovery. At Denim Day it is also common for women in the crowd to ask questions about how to help individuals in their family and friend circles who they know are being victimized. To best answer such inquiries, Mahogany Jones takes the event one step further and invites officers from the Detroit Police Department's Special Victims Unit to share their knowledge and offer advice for the benefit of survivors and other members of the community. By 2018 all of the rape kits in police archives were tested and in some cases they have led to long overdue prosecutions. Denim Day provides hope, a space for survivors to bear witness, to testify against sexual trespasses, and the sanctity of performance. The healing powers of music, community, and public support cannot be underestimated, whether they come in the form of poetics, policy, or plain speech.

We are aware that healing comes in many forms. The healing we speak of here neither presumes nor suggests a completed medical, psychological, or ideological recovery; rather, it refers to the process by which women in attendance found varying levels of support, empathy, insight and relief for their wounds. The conferences and workshops that the Foundation coordinated at multiple annual Allied Media Conferences open another form of healing. In these spaces, agentic women in hip hop inspired other women to claim their vulnerability, their talent, and their power. In so doing, they gathered a community of raucous revolutionaries and launched an alliance of healing. Hip hop producers, emcees, scholars, b-girls, and graffiti writers all came together on various stages to celebrate all of hip hop's elements, female voices, and African American literacies.[21]

WOMEN AND HIP HOP AT THE ALLIED MEDIA CONFERENCE

The Foundation accomplished another kind of community work and cultural literacy that advanced the networking and organizing skills of Detroit artists making hip hop. In 2012 Piper, Bekka, Kellie, Mahogany, Nique, and Insite traveled to Columbus, Ohio for the Hip Hop Literacies conference that Elaine Richardson (Dr. E) organizes at Ohio State University. Like most hip hop practitioners, Dr. E's organizing is articulated to her scholarship. Using critical discourse analysis, black literacies, and hip hop aesthetics, she reaches toward Black girls and women. Dr. E takes the concept of "literate witnessing" and applies it to Black girls' subjectivity and the processes by which they reflect on their everyday experiences.[22] She writes,

> These acts occur in relation to shared experiences, testimonials, or perspectives and are incited by participation in purposeful communal reading, writ-

ing, speaking, and listening that attests to truth, strong emotions, hardship, or negating behavior as a part of affirmation, healing, and self-recovery.[23]

We saw these principles in action at the Hip Hop Literacies conference. We met Ruth Nicole Brown's SOLHOT crew for the first time. We were witness to their testimonials about seeing calls for help on bathroom walls written by women who had been sexually harassed. We met Afro-futurist visual artists and learned how they are paving their way into hip hop aesthetics, and we experienced Chris Embry's keynote address about hip hop science that was nothing like a chalk and talk presentation. He embodied hip hop, demanded responses to his audience calls, invoked classic hip hop rap verses, and employed street wit. The conference left us full, inspired, and ready to work.

Piper caught the conference bug, making connections with academics, artists, and students. Yo Yo headlined the performance segment that closed the conference. Her presence also stimulated our group. Our drive home was all about how "we need our own conference; one that we create." And so a mission was imagined and put into action. It unfolded in micro steps. The first step required procuring funding and networking. The Allied Media Conference was a fitting site given Piper's background working with the Allied Media Project and its built-in activist network. It also gave us a platform to stretch media literacy into activist action. In our own discipline, media studies scholars have lamented the lack of literacy aimed at social justice work. Douglas Kellner and Jeff Share argue that when scholars advance media competencies to help communities gain power the stakes change dramatically.[24] That is, "literacies evolve and shift in response to social and cultural change and the interests of elites who control hegemonic institutions."[25] The Allied Media Project and the Foundation's work is inherently political; when organizations aim to uplift marginalized communities they fight an inevitable battle against corporate power. The field note below illustrates the community power of co-creation.

Kellie: June 20, 2015, Allied Media Conference, Detroit. I smell the old wooded walls holding up the inside of Wayne State's Cultural Art Center and I hear the buzzing of voices bouncing off them. Running late, I hear sounds of sessions already in motion. The Women in Hip Hop session is by far the loudest group. I can hear Mahogany Jones's voice echoing all the way down the long hallway. I enter the room and see Piper recording the session. She captures everybody. Mahogany,

Insite, and Nique are talking about what and who inspired their artistry and what collectives like the Foundation bring to the city of Detroit. After some discussion the three emcees tell the packed room of forty or so women that all of us are going to do hip hop today—female-centered flow, Mo adds. I know what is coming and my stomach feels tight. My shoulders tense up and I make no eye contact. There it is. Nique announces, "we are going to do a cypher, all of us together. Who can make a beat? Beat boxers in the room?" A younger woman, masculine-of-center, begins a classic style hip hop beat. Mahogany snaps her fingers and begins a line, adds another, and then Insite jumps in and drops a connected set of rhymes. Nique gets back in there for a minute.

The audience looks collectively horrified. It is our turn. Piper zooms in on the next woman nearest to Nique; this middle-aged white woman says a line in a shaky voice. A younger Black woman follows her; she too is nervous sounding, like her voice dropped an octave. I am almost last to go. I can't imagine what I will say. Panic sets in. Nothing is coming, nothing at all. Two women before me say something about Black Lives Matter, connecting it to Black Girl Magic. It is my turn and I shudder to think what I will sound like, with three dope emcess leading us, my friends and mentors. Something about 'enough chatter white haters, Black lives matter' comes out of my mouth. Our cypher began light and ended heavy—a common outcome in many local improvisational moments. Piper uplifts the crowd by offering her own line about collective creating. I feel relieved, excited, and vulnerable. This is what a cypher does to novice participants. And it fits right into the context of the Allied Media Conference. This conference, like no other we have ever attended, evokes passion, vulnerability, hope, and imagination. It is a younger version of Dr. E's Hip Hop Literacies conference, but its audience and agenda go far beyond hip hop; its participants are young, activist, queer practitioners. Few academics rock its panels.

In 1999, the first Midwest Zine Conference was held in Bowling Green, Ohio. The annual event quickly grew in size and scope. As its reach became more widespread its objectives broadened and a name change was deemed necessary to capture its political spirit. In 2003 it became the Allied Media Conference [AMC]. Detroit became the home of the Allied Media Project [AMP] and AMC in 2007. Over the past decade the event has continued to grow exponentially. It draws close to 2500 people annually and offers presentations and workshops on a diverse range of topics from b-boying to blogging to building radio transmitters and wireless mesh networks.[26] Early on in our fieldwork we met with two AMP directors, Jenny Lee and Diana Nucero. Jenny explained that the move to Detroit was logical because it "felt like the most exciting things around independent media were happening here."[27] The AMP's commitment to supporting art, media, and technology projects working for social change correlates with Detroit's longstanding art-activist connections and the ideas of emergent strategy that Boggs and brown promote.

Piper Carter had a relationship with the AMP prior to the Foundation's organizing contributions to the conference. The 5e Gallery was one of thirteen organizations that made up the Detroit Digital Justice Coalition [DDJC]. The DDJC was founded in 2009 to pursue an opportunity for national funding through the Broadband Technology Opportunities Program [BTOP] to close the digital divide in Detroit. In 2010 the DDJC was awarded two grants to support improvements to public computer centers at DDJC member organizations and to support the launch of digital media training programs and a youth media network.[28] As a result, the 5e Gallery received funding for equipment like computers, speakers, mixers, and other tools to teach youth media literacy and other culturally relevant skill sets.

Raising matching funds was a condition of the Knight Foundation grant that Piper was awarded to host a women and hip hop conference in 2016, so she partnered with the AMC. The objectives of the conference included giving visibility to the cultural production of women in hip hop, hosting skills, knowledge training, and exploring ways to promote what women making hip hop contribute to cultural organizing and fantastic performances.

The Foundation had complete autonomy creating our panels, workshops, and performances. The two of us pitched the idea of hosting a panel featuring Ruth Nicole Brown and Aisha Durham Smith, two accomplished hip hop scholars who produce complementary scholarship. Piper and Mahogany garnered the participation of key producers and DJs—including Detroit legend Stacey Hotwaxx Hale—as well as poets, promoters, and b-girl crews. Our weekend-long efforts culminated with a concert that featured Foundation emcees, local b-girl crew Venus Flyy, Flint artist Mama Sol, and Grammy Award winner Rapsody as the headliner. Hundreds of people attended.

Kellie also led a workshop on how race, class, and gender normativity affects hip hop practitioners. Most of the women participating were African American and very open to a deep conversation and so it went down—open, vulnerable, light, heavy, and strategic. This platform was like a Foundation stage, only this time conversation took the place of poetry, beats, dance, and rapping. The discussion that Kellie led was in sync and spirit with the session we organized featuring Brown and Durham. On their panel they talked about bridging hip hop scholarship/ academics with hip hop activists and performers. They discussed their work analyzing hip hop's impact on youth culture and Black girls' lives. Ruth Nicole Brown's work with SOLHOT is connected to Piper's; they both draw on hip hop history and pedagogy and they live performance as a way of knowing. Piper, Ruth, and Aisha all employed Elaine Richardson's ideas about African American literacies, those "vernacular survival arts and cultural productions that carve out free spaces in oppressive locations, such as the streets, the workplace, the school, or the airwaves."[29] While Ruth was speaking on the panel she spotted Shea Howell in the front row of the audience. Shea is a forty-year activist in Detroit, a long-time supporter of Detroit Summer, and board member of the Boggs Center. Tears ran down Ruth's face when she noticed Shea. Ruth then shared that she met Shea and Grace Lee Boggs when she worked with Detroit Summer during her studies at the University of Michigan. Two degrees of separation exist between hip hop scholars and activists, and yet it takes a conference like the AMC, and what the Foundation accomplished within that alliance, to forge identities and remake histories; this is a space where old friends meet again. In these gathering spaces worldviews change and identities burgeon. In each event we showcase, activism and hip hop are co-constructive and coexistent. Activist identity formation is complex in social justice collectives. It is also fluid at the individual level of experience.

NEGOTIATING ACTIVIST IDENTITIES

The events that the Foundation organizes signal its commitment to activist work. Understanding its members' individual ruminations on emergent forms of activism is also instructive. Tracing individuals' diverse understandings of activism and the experiences that link their hip hop sensibilities to community work has much to teach us regarding the varied layers of cultural work that community members engage in and their far-reaching impacts. The cultural production of many of the emcees, DJs, producers, visual artists, b-girls, and organizers whose paths we crossed is rooted in a multidimensional social justice framework.

Overwhelmingly, the artists in our study claim that their experiences as Detroiters have a profound effect on their cultural production. This connection motivated us to inquire about our participants' relationships to activism. Here we explore how they define activism and to what extent they see themselves as activists and/or socially conscious artists before moving on to describing particular events they produce, support, or are otherwise involved with. Some women, such as Consuela Lopez and Tawana "Honeycomb" Petty, made their way to the Foundation through their activist work, while for others, like Miz Korona, hip hop has been the catalyst to their community concerns if not outright community building work. For many, the lines between their involvement with the Foundation, hip hop, and their greater communities are blurry. What we have learned is that in many respects there is little ideologically that separates where many of these artists situate themselves with respect to music, culture, and community. In Detroit, one's actions in one realm bleed into and impact others. In the face of so much struggle for access to basic human rights like water, housing, and healthy food, community ties in Detroit run deep. Compound that with the intimate relationships that the Foundation nurtured—both within and beyond the collective itself—and movement participation is de facto for many.

The women in our study are conscious of the "ideal activist" and there is a tendency to frame one's self and actions in relation to this paradigmatic figure. When we first approached Piper with an interview request in 2011, she rightfully inquired what we wanted to talk about. It was at a Foundation open mic night, so we assumed that our interests were self-evident. At the time we had no knowledge of Piper's extensive work in the community. Upon returning to Detroit in 2009 Piper became deeply grounded in the city's activist communities. Since then, her reach has been extensive and includes involvement with Detroit Future,[30] the East Michigan Environmental Action Council, and Detroit Independent Freedom Schools, in addition to launching the Foundation. In our initial interview with her in 2012, Piper articulated her route into and relationship to activism for us. In response to the question of whether she considers herself an activist Piper thoughtfully replied:

> I didn't until I went to Chicago Freedom School [in 2011]. Detroit Future Youth sent us there for this training. It wasn't until then that I was sitting there and we were learning. I was like, "oh shit. I've always been an activist." When they started breaking down what oppression is, we had this five-day workshop about youth and how to train youth for activism because that's what Detroit Youth does. They had an identity workshop . . . it was

the best experience I've ever had in my life. Everyone needs to have this. We need to bring this back here. It wasn't until we got educated about activism that I had words. I hadn't used words like anti-oppression and identity. It wasn't until then when they broke down the science of it. I had always been an activist, [I] just didn't know it.[31]

Similar to the experiences of the Oakland, California youth that Andreana Clay documents, Piper's impression of herself and her cultural production, social media activity, and organizing efforts was filtered through the "social construction of the idealized cultural image" of activism that circulates in popular and academic discourse about resistance.[32] Clay surmises, "ultimately, the message is that being an activist is a full-time career, not accessible to anyone unless they are giving 100 percent of their time to the cause."[33] These definitions played a central role in the ways that the Oakland youth in Clay's study negotiated their relationship to activism; in our work, static representations of activism seem to have impacted individual conceptions of activism and the degree to which our participants self-identify as activists to lesser but at times still noteworthy degrees. Piper, for instance, is an extremely engaged community member, and though she now self-identifies as a cultural organizer, this is not how she saw herself before attending an identity workshop and some years of reflection, despite her extensive community building efforts.

In her music Miz Korona raps about the state of Detroit and its people. She addresses themes of drug abuse, high risk behaviors, family, identity, social action, love, industry standards, normativity, and being rendered invisible. Early on in our friendship we asked Miz Korona if she saw herself as an activist or a socially conscious artist, to which she replied:

> I don't consider myself an activist. I'm active, I'm involved in it to some degree but when I look at people like Invincible [they're] really there in the trenches. So [they] can say that and really stand firm in it when I just do it part time. No I'm not. I just know about what's going on in the community.[34]

ill serves as Miz Korona's yardstick for measuring her activism because of their extensive community building experience as an organizer with Detroit Summer and Detroit Future Youth network. ill has also facilitated numerous community media projects and workshops in addition to and often in collaboration with their hip hop related art.[35] Since Miz Korona's comments they have gained even more recognition for their work as part of Complex Movements. Boggs's philosophies of community organizing inspires this collective's exploration of the relationship between complex science and social justice movements.

In 2015, we revisited the subject of activism with Miz Korona. In our conversation we learned that her understanding of activism had broadened considerably over the past few years. Miz Korona now sees activism as more than protesting in the streets; she recognizes it in the practices of everyday life. She reflected,

> It wasn't even a couple months after the Trayvon Martin thing happened. My sister was driving on the freeway heading home . . . and you know how it says road work ahead on the little digital thing? Somebody had changed the sign and it said, Trayvon is a nigger. I told her to stop and take a picture. She took a picture and I posted it on my Twitter and Instagram and it went viral. All these fucking people from these media outlets were asking me if they can have permission to post this picture, asking my opinion. I'm like, yeah, because I felt like . . . and that trickled and it made more people post it. And then the news ended up going out there; it was just crazy. But if I hadn't told her to stop and do it, and one other person who probably did not have six thousand followers posted that shit, then it might have gone unseen for a long time and they wouldn't have fixed it and apologized. You know what I mean? So sometimes I use my platform to do what's right, I guess in a political way. Instead of just like, oh shit like damn. Because some people use it wrong. I post sneakers all the time and I get people who are like on the forefront who are like, 'Don't you know what Jordan does? He doesn't do shit for the black people and he doesn't look out for us.' And I'm like, I don't give a fuck; I like his shoes. You know what I'm saying? People come at me like, 'Oh, I thought you were better than that. You were my favorite artist and you post that' . . . . It's my money. If I want to flush this shit down the toilet. You know what I'm saying? . . . I'm not perfect. I just talk about what's in my heart so I don't wanna be categorized as one thing or another thing. I'm just an artist. I just talk about what it's in my heart.[36]

Miz Korona works through her thoughts about activism as she reflects on her own actions as well as the socially constructed cultural images of activism. Mass-mediated representations and popular rhetoric continue to project limited views of activism but they now also include social media activity. This broader understanding may lead artists like Miz Korona to reframe their everyday practices as activist work, but social media spaces like Twitter and Instagram also invite the policing of boundaries around identity categories and the kinds of actions that may or may not qualify someone as an activist. Intimately aware of the policing that social media invites and the pitfalls that claiming the activist label invite, Miz Korona's choice not to identify as an activist but to claim some of her actions as activism is strategic. Doing so makes room for the contradictions that constitute her complex identity and those of most people.

Nique Love Rhodes also shared her thoughts with us about activism. Speaking about her album *Against All Odds* she explained,

> It's cultural activism in the sense that I feel like it's universal. Everybody, whether you are very aware of social issues . . . most people can agree that we need to show love to each other more, you know. More people can definitely say we need more peace in the world. We need more love than hate. And so it's universal in the sense that I [was able to] make it connect to everybody, whether my grandmother's listening to it or my four-year-old cousin.[37]

During this meeting we listened to a number of her tracks. About "Love Heals All," she said,

> The beat, the drum, it's what I love, drum heavy, which is why I have two drummers. The drum beat is what drove me. Sounds like a march or something, then the piano is very melodic and there's an echo chant in the background still gives it that hard feel, which is why I wanted to make a song about, like I'm gonna try in this four-minute song to touch on every possible social issue that I hate. So like, [in] the first verse I talk about the religious divide, I say to my Muslim people, Jews, and all Christians, get back to God, cure religious divisions. Then I talk about the relation between men and women. Then in the second verse I'm talking about racial division. Many people think racism don't exist because we have a Black president. I touch on that. I talk about gang war. People are concerned about whatever crew they're in. I tie that to racism, the color of your skin . . . . I always like to put kind of like a resolution piece in my music and so in this, the resolution is like after I talk about all this stuff. It's like there's hope, there's still redemption, you know. Let's get back to love, let's get to our healing.

Embracing anthemic instrumentals, Nique takes on heavy sociopolitical issues like religious and racial division, as well as love and redemption. For her, music is the site where universal ideas about cultural activism circulate. She does not shy away from controversy and yet she insists that her music always has to have a sense of resolution.

By 2015, most of the women who had been affiliated with the Foundation at some point between 2009 and 2014 saw some facet, if not the entirety, of their artistic efforts as contributing to social justice causes and community building. In 2015, a year after she released her album *Pure,* we asked Mahogany Jones if she thought of her art as cultural activism, to which she replied, "Oh yes, definitely. I think that we are saturated in a culture that, it's the same old spiel, we're drenched in objectification and misogyny." Discussing *Pure,* she explained,

I think it's talking about forgiveness. I think it's talking about women giving themselves permission to take up space. It's definitely talking about just women recapturing agency over their bodies and not being conditioned to make choices to be like openly sexual because that's how we're conditioned. If that's your choice, that's your choice but you also can make another choice. It's definitely about domestic violence, sexual assault, and yeah.[38]

Later in our conversation she added,

I want listeners to take away . . . you know that media has intention. Media has an intention, it's not just random. Really understand what you're consuming. I wish we would consume media the same way that we now read labels to consume our food. We take time, we read the label. Where was it produced? How was it made? Are there GMOs in it? The way we wear our clothes: did slaves make these clothes? Are these slave diamonds? We have to do the same with media. It's shaping the lens through which we live our lives.

Our findings illustrate the complex and diverse relationships that women of the Foundation have to activism. In our conversations Nique and Mahogany claimed descriptors like cultural activism and socially conscious art for their cultural production. They consciously create work that addresses social issues such as misogyny, racism, sexism, poverty, and gang war. For artists like Tawana "Honeycomb" Petty and Consuela Lopez, it was through their community work that they befriended Piper and were motivated to contribute to and support the Foundation as both artists and organizers. Mentioning the Foundation's goals she identifies with, Tawana stated,

I really want us to be able to nurture young women into a space of pure self-love and comfort in addressing the rape culture as it exists in everything today. . . . At its very core, if women come out of there feeling good in their skin, and then combatting self-hatred and not allowing this mainstream to dissect them and destroy them and taking back their power, I think the Foundation will have done some incredible work. It's a huge heap right now.[39]

For others, like Miz Korona and Piper, it took time for them to see their work as contributing to activist goals. In all, the women of the Foundation have strong community ties and a shared sense of identity—dynamics that are crucial to participation in social movement activism.[40]

. . .

This chapter unravels the intricate and intentional web that exists between art and activism in the Foundation's work. Focusing on three key events—Dilla Youth Day, Denim Day, and the Women and Hip

Hop conference within the AMC—we illustrate the complex and conjunctural relationships artists forge between music and community building. Music and politics do not function in separate spheres in the work of the Foundation; rather, they are intricately co-constructive. What is more, community work constitutes political work.[41] Dilla Youth Day brings the politics of knowledge production back into hip hop, as well as offering skills building and multigenerational sharing of cultural performances; culture orchestrates Denim Day as much as lobbying and policymaking form the essential threads of its fabric. With Mahogany leading the way as emcee, testimony and song are always on the program right next to panels about public health and sexual safety. Self-care for women and their well-being is the bottom line goal of Denim Day. It is as spiritual as it is political. So too did the women in hip hop sessions within the AMC provide sites where hip hop practitioners networked, created, consoled, and made plans for a progressive future. Women who produce every element of hip hop, as well as promoters, bloggers, journalists, academics, and organizers came together. In all, these events illustrate the Foundation's relationship to activism and how its many cultural forms are situated in community work. The artists themselves and the events that we examine are connected to what Reiland Rabaka deems a hip hop movement: always multiracial, multigenerational, and with a range of sociopolitical aims embedded in the music.[42] The work of the Foundation opens up spatial politics while it simultaneously reclaims time for women's organizing work to get its due respect.

To grow one's soul is tied to cultivating a community soul. Growing souls means imagining new relationships, with unusual suspects like the police and anti-sex trafficking advocates alongside hip hop artists and rape survivors; it also means providing activities and safe spaces for children who have few public parks, movie theatres, sports outlets and free recreational/leisure opportunities. Dilla Youth Day opens space for new imaginations of teaching and learning, performance and play, and historical knowledge. The Foundation fills sinkholes in a city that does not invest in the populations that have been here for generations.

We showcase how and through what examples Foundation artists negotiate activism in their daily lives and in the music/art they produce. Miz Korona, for example, balances responding to outward hate speech on social media against getting checked for wearing the Jordans she loves, even when the maker does not meet the community's political standards. Piper, on the other hand, did not recognize she was doing activist work until she attended a Chicago Freedom School workshop and learned the language of oppression, displacement, and what intersectional identities mean in everyday life. Others in our study see cultural activism as a universal element within Black music. Collectively, the artists/organizers provide a rich palette of experience that demonstrates the complexity and fluidity of activist identifications.

At once, the Foundation's work is aesthetic, political, and community-based. It is born out of performance and yet produces a new kind of cultural citizenship that reimagines activism as cultural organizing; in so doing, Foundation members rethink taken-for-granted images and symbols as well as policies and practices that mold people and slow their mobility. They reclaim public space and search for strategies to build a sustainable Detroit for its local, often ignored, population. This chapter brings into focus how this philosophy plays out in hip hop community-based performance and organizing.

Conclusion

Women, Hip Hop, and Cultural Organizing

Kellie: July 19, 2014. New Center Park, Detroit. On a warm and sunny July evening, my partner and I drive my visiting niblings[1] to New Center Park for a taste of Detroit's local hip hop scene. The evening's bill includes spoken word poetry, rap, and politics. That last practice—the politics—is not unexpected and yet its presentation produces amplified fans perfectly attuned to the call and response structure built into hip hop's aesthetics. Even my niece and nephew, fourteen and twelve, who come from a small, mostly white town in Northern California can feel the pulse of the music and the stakes in the words being projected on lit-up buildings. Phrases like "Impeach Snyder," "Water is a Human Right," and "Fuck Water Shutoffs" pan above the heads of every fan in the park. All night my niblings fire questions about the artists they meet and the water situation. They are also swept up in the innovative dance moves they see younger folks in the audience executing. T. Miller, an award-winning local poet, hosts the show featuring Miz Korona and Invincible/ill Weaver among the night's line up. My niece and nephew meet nearly all of the artists who performed that night and they are blown away when Miz Korona knows their names. Between each of their sets the performers share updates about the water shutoff crisis and the recently displaced residents who have been subject to the Little Caesars Arena construction. This is also the night that Miz Korona first performs her track "Set Fire" in public. Her ever-supportive mother attends the show and storms the stage when Korona raps about her mother's strength and perseverance. That act moves the audience; family reaches for one another when Korona's mother hugs her on stage.

This moment is a snapshot of one among many shows that we attended during the course of our traveling encounters with the Foundation. It showcases the way that artistry produces urgency; affect and idea move through speech, beats, lyrics, and poetry, and they course through the hearts and minds of audiences. In this sense, artists mobilize audiences to: (1) feel the energy and sonic pleasure of live performance; and (2) to engage the content and expressive forms that invite fans to think about immediate politics, high stakes economic policy, and corporatized practices of urban renewal. The collective performances also demonstrate how artists reclaim public space to challenge state and corporate interests. At New Center Park hosts and performers moved through music, poetry, and public speaking to motivate fans to take action. This event is illustrative of not only the political messages that course through these artists' lyrical content but also the community work they do. In effect, we contend that the cultural organizing that happens through performance constitutes political work. Our thinking here is in sync with that of other scholars who have documented the myriad ways in which African American women in urban areas like Detroit and Newark, New Jersey create resistance movements to deal with social marginality.[2] Given Detroit's long-term race battles, its current state of urban renewal, uneven population shifts, corporate design, and resource-challenged neighborhoods outside the city's 7.2 miles of business investment, artists and cultural organizers have a great deal to contribute to the state of the city and its people's well-being. They are one node in the mobilizing efforts of residents who are pushing back against the neoliberal governmentality that is guiding city policies and development.

For over a century Detroit has maintained a steady fascination in the imaginations of national news outlets, niche filmmakers, scholars across disciplines, and the general public. Its economic booms and busts and race-based conflicts, along with its technological and artistic innovations, have kept Detroit in the public eye since the Ford Motor Company unveiled the first Model T in 1908. Over the past hundred years the Motor City has undergone extraordinary changes and survived innumerable challenges. Illuminating the ways in which Foundation artists, organizers, and networks employ hip hop music and culture to empower themselves and their communities, *Women Rapping Revolution* foregrounds the city's people, advancing their interests in the public consciousness. Documenting the Foundation's origins, cultural production, community-building efforts, and eventual dissolution details a moment in time (2009–2018) in the city's history. Though they are each unique, collectively the artistry, organizing efforts, politics, and perseverance of the women of the Foundation are a microcosm of the complexities and ingenuity of Detroit and its people. To borrow from Nique Love Rhodes' "Legendary" lyrics, "when we got them lemons what we do? Make that lemon pie."

Nique's lemon pie is the basis of the neoliberal hustle that is mandated by governmentality that mimics business interests at the expense of the majority of Detroit's long-term residential population. State officials and city planners have given the city over to corporate giants; it is the conglomeration of corporate and big foundation money that is responsible for redesigning Detroit—constructing its tech hub desires and its new urban loft/niche boutique look. Given this climate, it is especially important that we rethink the ways arts movements claim public space through cultural production. Collectives like the Foundation and individual artists continue to provide alternative perspectives to the dominant narratives that have defined Detroit during its bankruptcy and post-bankruptcy revival. By foregrounding everyday people, artists push back on the design-intensive decisions of a handful of key players including Mayor Mike Duggan and billionaires Dan Gilbert and Mike Ilitch. Though few in numbers, the impacts of their actions resonate far and wide.

It is common knowledge in Detroit that Dan Gilbert has a detailed miniature model of downtown Detroit and whenever one of his companies buys one of the buildings its miniature replica is illuminated.[3] As its purpose is to display Gilbert's acquisitions, the reproduction contains no people, only buildings; and yet, despite the practical reasons for their absence, the lack of any evidence of society in the model is telling. It represents a blank slate to be molded and populated as desired. As the past decade has illustrated, in the minds of some the idiom "out with the old and in with the new" seems to be applicable to not only property but also populations. According to U.S. census data, by 2018 Detroit's population had declined by over 63 percent from its peak in 1950 to 672,681 of whom 78 percent identified as African American, down from 83 percent in 2010.[4] As we have mentioned throughout this book, the two areas attracting white people back to the city are downtown and Midtown. As time wore on the lacking resources and underemployment that challenged the rest of the city and others like it across the country led

Midtown, formerly known as the Cass Corridor, to devolve into a hotbed of criminal activity and dilapidation. Over the past decade the area has changed considerably and it is now emblematic of Detroit's post-bankruptcy years of neoliberal governmentality. While the Cass Community Commons and Cass Café still stand, blocks around the corner are unrecognizable from when we first began this project in 2011. High-end stores selling baby products, home goods, books, and bicycles now populate the neighborhood, along with an influx of new restaurants. A recent outing to one of the latest food establishments reminded us of Tawana "Honeycomb" Petty's experience at a café in the area in 2014 that we recall in our introduction. In one of our conversations, she enlightened us on how gentrification transforms not only buildings but also histories and populations as schools and street signs are wiped out and newcomers impose scripts like the Angry Black Woman onto the local population. Honeycomb alerted us to what was already underway when she matter-of-factly stated, "To be a life-long resident and be treated as an invisible imposter is part of the breakdown of neighborhood continuity."[5] Hers is but one of many cautionary tales we have heard on our journey.

The Angry Black Woman, the stereotype to which Honeycomb refers above, is but one of several controlling images that have been refashioned in hip hop scholarship examining gender. We complicate the way women are represented beyond the two-dimensional subject positions they are afforded in the commercial market and studied in popular and academic discourse. We argue that both the negative scripts[6] as well as those that open more positive experiences[7] do not go far enough into the world of textual experience or material practice that we witnessed in the life of the Foundation. Players in Detroit's hip hop underground are upending the scripts and stereotypes that systematically pigeonhole both women and men in hip hop culture. We contribute the cautious category of the Vulnerable Maverick as an analytic to examine the complexity of women's experience, in and through processes of cultural production as well as their musical products. Vulnerable Mavericks see vulnerability as strength, as an experiential space where pain, fear, and struggle are worked on/out. Mavericks also rise above challenges, soaring fiercely. Imagine Aretha singing "Respect" and following it with "I Say a Little Prayer" embodied in the physical form of what Detroit Versus Everybody looks like. This is the spirit of the Vulnerable Maverick.

Along with challenging scripts that shape gender inquiry within hip hop, our work illuminates the efforts of hip hop's cultural organizers.

Practicing their art, women in the Foundation also became active in Detroit community building, networking with organizations like the Allied Media Project, Detroit Future Schools, the Detroit Water Board, Detroiters Against Emergency Management, the Boggs Center, and central actors in the urban farming movement like D-Town Farms. Until we became involved in the communities that Foundation members led us to, we knew little about the cultural organizing shaping the lives of Detroit's long-term residents, not to mention hip hop's role in it. These constituencies are invisible to most because they are not covered in mainstream news media. However, they do receive attention in alternative press publications like *Detroit Metro Times* and they use social media to promote their music, shows, and issues they care about. What is more, Detroit's activist communities have produced community-centered publications like the *Michigan Citizen* and *Riverwise* to articulate their views, calls to action, and truth-adjusting. From 1978 until 2014 the *Michigan Citizen* was a local newspaper that threw into question issues that commercial, for-profit-news avoided: the perspectives of local citizens and their investment in the city. Many of the people that created and supported the *Michigan Citizen* helped envision *Riverwise* magazine, but they also brought the next generation of community builders, like Tawana "Honeycomb" Petty and b-boy organizer Antonio Raphael, into the fold. Understanding media's power to deepen relationships, the publication focuses on local organizing efforts and provides alternative viewpoints to those that commercial media outlets regularly endorse. Activists and neighborhood associations, especially their publications, play central roles in local communities and their work is commonly unacknowledged in the public debates about Detroit's urban renewal and civic life.

Bridging lyrical content with aesthetic practice, *Women Rapping Revolution* has examined musical tracks that serve epic functions. That is, we analyzed musical anthems that artists produced to reveal the ways that hip hop aesthetics, cultural production, and textual experience bring artists into focus in central sites of Detroit, reaching for Detroiters. In the imagination of the Foundation and affiliated artists, Detroiters constitute both the extreme local as well as the translocal. Detroit activism attaches itself to the Global South; the population identifies with peoples struggling in developing nations. Some Foundation members, including Piper Carter, reach out to and partner with populations that organize and host the World Social Forum, a transnational conference that brings populations from the Global South together to resist and strategize solutions to disparities in neoliberal times. Detroiters are on the edge of the global divide. As such, artists draw fans who are identified with Detroit's past and its progressive connection with other people who face similar situations from colonization to gentrification, human rights, and water rights.

Understanding the anthems of Invincible/ill Weaver and Finale, Nique Love Rhodes, Mahogany Jones, and D.S. Sense requires listeners to contemplate and reimagine Detroit's possibilities. Here we return to Shana Redmond's work on anthems to intimate key implications of our study. Writing about music from the past but signaling towards hip hop as the latest incarnation, Redmond writes that "within the African diaspora, music functions as a method of rebellion, revolution, and future visions that disrupt and challenge the manufactured differences used to dismiss, detain, and destroy communities."[8] The anthems that we examine echo Redmond's thinking. Rebellion and revolution come through both words and aesthetics. Call and response evokes ideas and practices that produce hip hop underground fans as always already aware of Detroit's viability. They provide hope and caution, a sonic call to action employing boom-bap strategies for reclaiming a city that is being governed by actors disconnected from Detroit's grassroots organizers, citizen groups, and neighborhood associations. Anthems call citizens to action symbolically and, at times, in material ways; they can uplift as much as they provide social imaginaries for resistance. They create alternative identification anchors for long-term Black Detroiters who feel erased in the context of gentrification. Dan Gilbert will never sing the words "On My Detroit Everything" or "Locusts, never let them approach us." Certainly, nary a line in "Blue Collar Logic" would resonate in spirit or lifestyle. One has to be local, to be a Detroiter involved in community organizing, to live the lines in each anthem. They are not written for everybody, only those who know the codes and aesthetic conventions through which they speak. Anthems are historically situated epic stories; musically they create citizen soldiers in cities like Detroit with arts-movement histories.

Women Rapping Revolution is situated within a well-established history of music and politics in Detroit that, despite all that has been written about it, remains underexplored. The musical milieu that nurtured African American expressive forms and practices and community-based cultural work in the bebop era has never gone away; rather, it is ongoing. It has survived population loss, economic hardships, and racial politics. Motown, Detroit Techno, and local hip hop rose from the entanglement of these conditions. The Foundation's work fits into this palimpsest of musical history and leaves behind a historical mark on a city known for its male hip hop icons. It propelled women onto stages and into studios and their cultural productions continue to intervene in hip hop narratives beyond the local. Analogous to 1950s bebop musicians' rejection of the racist commercial industry, the women of the Foundation and the men who support them rebuff the industry's sexism and continue to push artistic and political boundaries.

Finally, this study offers a dialogic, feminist, racially conscious approach to conducting co-ethnography in neoliberal times. As white women we entered Detroit and the Foundation's community cautiously. Our economic and racial privilege matter. Second, our knowledge of hip hop prior to encountering the Foundation gave us legitimacy, and we were tested. We were asked questions like "what do you listen to?" and expected to recognize insider references like Phife Dawg's Funky Diabetic identity and women in hip hop showcases like She's So Fresh in NYC. If we had not had an awareness of hip hop's history, we might have been easily dismissed. The hip hop underground is suspicious of people who grab onto hip hop like it is a trend. Given the gentrification at work in the city, Black artists are also concerned about what white people want to know about Detroiters. To some extent we look like the people buying back Detroit. Earning trust meant being there, doing deep hanging out no matter where it took us or what was accomplished. Going all the way in meant showing up. We learned to be led and also to play the role of leader when our expertise was helpful—for example, suggesting materials for reading groups or inviting scholars for talks, both jobs we do regularly. It was a labor of love to do this organizing work for The Foundation.

When it came to processing Black women's experience in the music industry or in the local music scene we certainly did not lead. We listened so as to learn and understand. Being there quietly and listening actively were as important as offering our thoughts. In time, we developed close relationships with several Foundation artists. We share meals, attend one another's weddings, travel, and sometimes make art together. It was normal, but never comfortable when tensions flared. Tension emerged most often over competing considerations of time. As academics, being on time is a given for us, a normative practice. In the art world, time is more fatalistic. Detroit hip hop heads experience time like the Arabic saying *Inshallah*— God willing, I will be there on time. So if God deems it necessary people will be on time; if not, oh well. Waiting for people who set the time frames for meetings drove us crazy, just as our need to manage time frustrated artists. Even toward the end of the project we continued to arrive on time, but we learned to laugh at ourselves for our hyperpunctuality.

Member checks happened whenever we wrote about particular artists. They read drafts and provided comments, approved or disapproved. We had so much opportunity to text, tweet, or chat with artists that many potential misunderstandings were addressed before we wrote up field notes and biographical information about their lives. Some of our most engaging conversations were about feminism, who claims it, and whether or not it is relevant to Black women's lives. To this day, Piper says she is not a feminist. Still, we have to pause to take in that statement. Years of notetaking at all the feminist conferences she attends, after countless conversations about all the hip hop feminists she reads and mingles with, after watching her create platforms for women and the battles she fights to expose misogyny leaves us with a different impression. Identity is indeed complex and unpredictable. The questions of what is in a name and who decides remain relevant when women make culture across race, class, gender, and sexuality lines that both converge and diverge. Who are we to name Piper?

If we had launched this study in an exclusive, feminist lens we would have missed crucial frameworks for understanding the relationships between music, politics, and social identity. Relations of gender play out in a broad range of cultural and social practices. As such, practice theory's assertion that music is both a cultural product and social process also shaped this project.[9] Advancing Simon Frith's understanding of the relationship between music and identity, we highlighted many occasions and tactics through which music making, listening, and performing produces subjects—audiences that move on beat and bust moves like the hustle or the Errol Flynn collectively. Hip hop's call and response musical structure means audiences don't listen quietly, they are compelled to participate. Improvisation and freestyling are not only experienced by artists, but all in the room. And yet, improvisation is not random; it emerges from a history of sense and practice. It is an assemblage of past practices, erupting in the moment. "Throw your hands in the air, wave 'em like you just don't care" is not a rhetorical statement. It is a call to action. Identities and social relations are always in flux, being made, remade, and contested through cultural activity. Music, Frith writes, "articulates in itself an understanding of both group relations and individuality, on the basis of which ethical codes and social ideologies are understood."[10] The Foundation's music and cultural organizing challenge dominant ideologies, particularly those that presuppose that

Detroit's revival requires the erasure of working-class Black people. Hip hop's phallocentric/male identified worldview is also wrenched open, so as to create space for women to command stages, dance floors, turntables, paint cans, and podiums. In so doing, the artists create anthems, tracks, music videos, b-girl battles, even conferences. All of these cultural productions are rife with revolutionary ideas; they reshape the very form of social ideology.

The Foundation's members support and claim collective action on a national scale. Black populations living in urban contexts are painfully aware of issues like police brutality, racism, and the prison industrial complex. Detroit's social justice advocates have been organizing campaigns against violence and systemic racism since long before the Black Lives Matter Movement that emerged towards the end of the Foundation's active period. The Black Power movement was not born in Detroit, but it was enriched and advanced through the theorizing of Jimmy Boggs and Grace Lee Boggs, yet another reason why Detroit has such a rich history of Black cultural resistance. This history is not lost on Foundation artists. So too, the Foundation highlighted and developed the creative artistry of Black and Brown women before Black Girl Magic was popularized as a concept and movement in 2013. Elsewhere, we have articulated the ways this new identifier captures the spirt of D.S. Sense's "On My Detroit Everything."[11] What is more, the #MeToo movement also started as our study drew to a close. Long before sexual assault climbed to the top of the media's attention, before public figures were arrested and shamed, Foundation artists were doing battle with sexual violence. Calling out misogynist practices is daily work for organizers like Piper Carter and artists like Mahogany Jones. The threating climate that Trump's election created led to the organization of the National Women's March in January 2017. The women who organized the international day of protest came to Detroit in the fall of 2017 for the National Women's Conference. Piper was a key local organizer who put women from around the country in conversation with one another. All this is to say that collectives work on national, state, and local levels, and when they meet their goals they often grow into new formations and/or dissolve; sometimes new entities take their place.

BUILDING RELATIONSHIPS/TEMPERING DISSOLUTIONS

"It is only in relationship to other bodies and many somebodies that anybody is somebody."[12] This simple, profound statement captures

Jimmy Boggs's ruminations about self–other relations. It is the basis of what adrienne maree brown conceptualizes as "simple interactions" that change lives. As such, ethical communication is the basis for community work, imagination, and hope. brown and Tawana "Honeycomb" Petty are the next generation of Boggsian thinkers, activists, and cultural organizers. Their work is situated locally but has global reach. Tawana does work that ranges from data justice community research to organizing conferences, performing poetry, giving public talks, mentoring youth, and of course, writing books. Artists/activists like Invincible/ ill Weaver, brown, and Petty have deep roots in the Allied Media Project which gives them insight on how youth activists use media as liberation tools. Foundation artists mobilize the worldviews that they share with these organizers. The Boggsian philosophy of social change has traction in Detroit, particularly in hip hop and spoken word poetry circles.

In the history of social movements and small activist formations there are cycles of formation and dissolution. Keeping the Foundation active was an uphill battle that required extensive time and effort. Hosting a weekly open mic night was particularly exhausting. Piper was continuously promoting the next week's event and creating unique flyers for nights when headliners were featured. She also used a range of social media platforms to help advertise shows that Foundation artists did around the city. Changes in venue from the first 5e Gallery to the Old Miami, the second gallery space, and then the Cass Corridor Commons required engaging in social media blitzes and other tactics to inform supporters of the change and build up participants and audiences again. The work also involved constant battles with misogyny and those who did not want a women in hip hop night to succeed in Detroit. Managing the breadth of personalities invested in the work was also a challenge. Some artists came and went and others remained dedicated throughout. Over the course of our study we watched artists develop their skills, create new projects, and expand their networks. They became headlining performers, overseas travelers, and community leaders. The collective's trajectory reminded us of Bekka's earlier work with women DJ collectives. Once they fulfilled their ultimate purpose of helping women develop their artistry and support systems they organically came to an end as members moved on.[13] Similarly, in the years following the end of the weekly open mic nights the Foundation splintered; some artists went their own way while others formed new collectives.

While we were a part of the Foundation we experienced many slices of relational and organizational life that both energized and exhausted its members. On an organizational level, the Foundation and the 5e Gallery faced a chronic lack of resources. This reality created the need for what Lester Spence calls the neoliberal hustle. In his view, having to hustle is undesirable because the state is failing to do its job to support its citizenry. Sparring with Spence, Piper Carter calls herself a serial entrepreneur. The hustle gives Piper autonomy on the one hand; stress over cash flow, on the other. The organization felt these financial tensions. When Piper and DJ Sicari imagined the Gallery, they saw it as a free space where artists in the making could develop and youth would be mentored. They were both artists in their own right but they identified more as promoters. They loved getting young artists on stage. Artists also appreciated the vibe and performance opportunities that the Foundation provided. They viewed the Foundation as a networking space, a cool, community gathering hub, and a place where women's art was respected. In time, when artists developed skills to get on paid bills, they also expected to be paid when they performed at the Foundation. This unstated set of understandings and expectations led to many relational crashes, some damaged beyond the point of repair. It is ironic that the most vocal group of women one can imagine experienced fundamental communication trouble vocalizing their expectations, feelings, and concerns. Expectations were unstated and often misunderstood. Some folks operated from a "we're all good" sentiment verbally, while passive-aggressive comportment told another non-verbal story. Founding and longtime Foundation members believed that they should have been the first invited to headline major events like the collective's annual anniversary parties. The last anniversary party and the Women in Hip Hop conference concert were cases in point. One of the pioneering artists attended a collective meeting when the group was planning the concert program. Mama Sol, a legendary Flint emcee, was suggested for the last anniversary party; Rapsody was the pick for the conference concert. Some members were upset when they were not asked to headline or perform. This led to a slow-fuse blow-up. Several people felt strongly about the issue but said little at the planning meetings. By the time the Women in Hip Hop concert occurred several artists had left the Foundation and set out to create their own collectives.

Organizational structure and procedural practices like Roberts' Rules of Order were also negotiated regularly. Piper worked from a horizontal theory of leadership and a collective economics model. This orientation to organizing did not square well with people in the business world who were members of the Foundation. They wanted more structure, hierarchy, and delegation of duties. Piper did not operate that way. Also, getting 501(c)(3) status took a long time and many disagreements occurred as to why that was an issue. The people who ran businesses or who worked in community service industries wanted a different kind of organizing and shared governance where each person had defined roles. Piper resisted finite structure and labels. These differences overtaxed a group that had a tall order of goals and a short order of resources.

Time was also always a factor. All of the artists we came to know worked multiple jobs, a steady 9-to-5 plus their performance lives. This workload put pressure on their schedules. Piper was also spread thin; her time was in demand across organizations and she held multiple jobs to get by. Nobody had time to spare. Taxed timelines and little money meant most artists competed for limited pools of money when they applied for every grant available. More than one Foundation artist applied for a prestigious Kresge Foundation grant; some were successful, others were not. This too was a structural problem that was personally felt. Even when Piper was awarded a Knight Foundation grant she was competing against kindred collectives like Allied Media Project. The hustle for resources led comrades to be competitors.

Complicating these issues, earlier in the year Piper and Sicari's breakup split the community. Some were loyal to Sicari, others to Piper. Many longtime members and supporters attended the last ever Foundation anniversary party—with the exception of Piper. Her absence was deeply felt even though Sicari shouted her out throughout the night. We were sad to watch it end, even more teary-eyed when Mahogany Jones began crying as she left the stage singing "We Gonna Keep On Keeping On." Seeing the space go away was one thing, but when the whole collective as we knew it came to an end we had to pause and "clear our throats"; lumps took over. We felt something historic disappear.

NEW TRAJECTORIES

In 2017, Piper Carter rebirthed the Foundation as We Found Hip Hop. She reimagined the scope of the organization to focus more directly on cultural organizing and pop-up events. Rather than open mics, We Found Hip Hop is setting up mobile hip hop learning jams—mini Dilla Youth Days that bring music, culture, and technology to schools in different neighborhoods. Having earned 501(c)(3) status more quickly, Piper is now fundraising and gathering sponsors. Over the past few years she has brought R&B and hip hop artists together; produced a fashion show; and hosted a kick-off film/concert at the Charles Wright Museum of African American History, where she premiered a documentary in the making from Foundation footage she had recorded and compiled over the years. The Eastern Michigan Environmental Council [EMEAC] is We Found Hip Hop's fiduciary sponsor. Over the years, the organization has come to play an instrumental role in Piper's growth as a cultural organizer. She is now invested in attending conferences with transnational, Indigenous footprints and EMEAC has sponsored Piper's attendance at conferences about Indigenous peoples, feminists, and the Global South. At the It Takes Roots conference in 2018 Piper orchestrated a hip hop cypher that she recorded and shared with us along with videos of ancestral ceremonies, dances, chants, and drumming circles from throughout the weekend.

In 2018 Piper also launched two other media ventures—thestudioArena, an online sustainable fashion magazine, and the Piper Carter podcast. The magazine "uses fashion and contemporary art to encourage awareness of a cultural worldview, improve attitudes towards cultural differences, and develop cultural competence."[14] At her pre-launch workshop, we witnessed the progressive content and broad mix of people drawn to Piper's work, including fashion designers, students, dyemakers, models, and retail employers. All of Piper's events require mingling and conversation. What she does in hip hop, she brings to fashion—managing meetings, leading workshops, and performing at conferences. Piper continues to be a force in Detroit's community of cultural organizers. In addition to building up thestudioArena as a brand, Piper hosts a monthly podcast on the Detroit is Different platform. Khary Frazier created Detroit is Different as an online space where he could share his music and connect people in his community to one another, but it has since grown to be much more than that, providing the world with citizen-driven content about the city. Piper's podcast features dynamic people and places shaping the city, from water warriors to hip hop entrepreneurs. Many of her guests are educators, artists, and cultural organizers. Recognized by hip hop activists and artists for her work in New York and Detroit, in 2018 she was invited to serve on the Hip Hop Congress's national executive board. This new position is just another of the many accolades that stem from her knowledge, expertise, and commitment to entertainment justice.

Mahogany Jones's international hip hop diplomacy is another kind of cultural citizenship that former Foundation artists and networks perform. From North Africa, Central Asia to South America, Mahogany has shared her music and politics with fans globally. Her *Pure* movement platform gives fans opportunities for discussion and provides fashion news, sustainable business tips, life lessons, and musical snap shots that cut across her catalogue. The album bore a movement of hip hop fans who want and reach for more than what the commercial industry offers. She has also helped other local artists network and explore this kind of hip hop activism and invited Foundation singer/producer Jaci Caprice to join her band and become a cultural diplomat for the U.S. State Department. Both Jaci and Deidre "D.S. Sense" Smith have participated in the Next Level program, a similar joint venture between the State Department, the University of North Carolina at Chapel Hill, and the Meridian International Center.

Other Foundation members expanded their networks, formulated new crews, tours, and projects. In 2015, Insite the Riot and Nique Love Rhodes teamed up with another local artist, Junni, to form the D.Cipher collective. In 2017, they received a Knight Arts Grant to help independent artists grow their careers so that they are able to participate in Detroit's growing economy. In 2018, D.Cipher partnered with the Detroit Riverfront Conservancy to program a summer concert series featuring local artists from different genres.

Miz Korona now performs with a band as The Korona Effect. They headlined a music festival in Berlin in 2018. In June of 2018, they performed at the Allied Media Conference's concert and packed the Diego Rivera court at the Detroit Institution of Arts. Miz Korona is constantly in demand as a host and at the time of this writing, was busy planning events at the Modern and Contemporary Art Museum of Detroit, her daytime employer. Questlove came to MOCAD to promote his book about food justice. Miz Korona assisted with the planning and production of the events that structured his visit. She has also launched her own photography business, Trigger Finger Photography. Every artist in Detroit hustles. Korona's life of three jobs is the new normal for Detroiters.

Invincible/ill Weaver commands success in their multimedia work with the Complex Movements collective. Grace Lee Boggs and local grassroots networks inspire their exploration of the connections between complex science and social justice movements. ill is also the founding director of the Detroit Narrative Agency [DNA] within Allied Media Projects. The agency supports the development of arts-based projects that offer counternarratives to popular accounts that attribute the city's resurgence post-bankruptcy to white billionaires and pioneering artists.

Focusing on the people who have been here doing the work all along, the DNA is creating stories with the intent of shifting the dominant narratives about Detroit towards liberation and justice.[15]

The men we discuss at length in chapter 6—Los, Bryce Detroit, Will See, Supa Emcee, and Valid—continue to produce music and in Los's case, also DJ. Together, Bryce and Will See host a conversational open mic monthly at the Cass Corridor Commons building. They are kindred cultural organizers. In addition to their music, all of the men with whom we worked also engage in vital community work. They support one another, featuring and collaborating across projects. They belong to neighborhood associations, and support local community centers, particularly Black-identified institutions like Nandi's Knowledge Café and the Charles Wright African American Museum. Dismantling food deserts and fighting for environmental justice are commitments that all of the men share.

NO EASY OUTS: REFLECTIONS ON "CLOSURE"

As we documented and ruminated on all the changes that we witnessed artists, the hip hop underground, and the city of Detroit experience over the course of our research, we talked at length about how we too feel transformed as a result of our experiences. Identity is messy and dynamic. For one, at the start of this project we did not know what we did not know about Detroit and the long-term residents who fight for its future. Community organizing and cultural activism accounts for crucial political labor that most outside the exact sites of work cannot see. With the exception of feel-good stories, only elite actors are engaged on the news. Activists are rarely seen in their natural environments—working in small groups, showing films, organizing, and making decisions. Protests and sit-ins, which do occasionally make news, are a tiny portion of the work that gets accomplished. We came to know the part of the hip hop underground that has an activist orientation and learned to navigate the interdependence of the networking that holds this portion of the underground together. Collectively, their relational work provides a model for reimagining citizens' rights to the city.

We also learned about patience, empathy, and accepting our cultural learning curves. Before 2012, we needed tools to understand the codes that mark hip hop's lexicon. We did not know the idiomatic language of the underground or the richness of Detroit's hip hop history. Urban Dictionary and genius.com were resources we turned to while the Foundation was acculturating us to hip hop's underground lexicon. The underground is certainly connected to the broader culture of idiomatic hip hop; however, Detroit's local flavor is woven into the overall texture of language use. "What up Doe" may be a phrase that many say, but Detroiters own it as theirs. Now we catch ourselves taking for granted that people know what we mean when we talk about b-girls, emcees, dope music, and joints—a slang term for rap songs.

As researchers we bonded; after seven years of close working practices we have become like extended family. We looked after one another during stressful times, illnesses, loss, and we became better thinkers and writers from our collaborations. Our libraries and our literacies have expanded, but ethnography also changes hearts. We were unaware of how much we would also bond with key collaborators. The completion of *Women Rapping Revolution* defines the end of a moment of this project—and yet, the people and our work together are ongoing facets of our lives. There is no exit for us. We continue to listen to hip hop, attend shows, and keep up with the busy lives of Foundation and other related artists. This academic inquiry may be complete, but we remain a part of the community that has changed our worldviews, our lives. Our key collaborators afforded us the opportunity to gain a better understanding of what it means to hustle, what it takes to make an album, the inner workings of the political economy of the hip hop underground, and how hard it is to earn a living as an artist. We learned the exacting details through which cultural production unfolds within an equally collaborative, politically motivated methodological framework.

Feminist activist ethnography is a methodology that fosters collaboration across researcher/researched relationships but also in the world of political action. Throughout this book we have sought to illuminate the cultural production of women in Detroit's hip hop underground: their efforts, their time, their dedication to their own artistry, and their relationship to the Foundation. We tracked the struggles they dealt with, especially as women who chose not to conform to confining industry norms for women in hip hop because they are so much more than that. We also came to understand that community-building constitutes political work.

For far too long the hip hop industry has taught us that there is only room for one "exceptional" woman at the top. When we asked our students to name women rappers, for years they were quick to shout out Nicki Minaj, then silence would fill the room. Cardi B's rise to fame in 2017 has only exacerbated the "exceptional woman" narrative as entertainment publications continue to pit the two rappers against one another. This kind of cat-fight framing of successful women is not new to hip hop. Tammy L. Kernodle explores the professional collaborations and personal relationships between jazz trombonist/arranger Melba Liston and peer Black women musicians like Mary Lou Williams in the 1950s and 1960s. She argues that "the narrative of the competitive personality or the inability to 'get along' among black women musicians has become paramount to the mythologies that have shaped the public understandings of the culture of jazz."[16] Unlike the male competitive spirit which produced moments of genius, the competitiveness that women exhibited in jazz spaces was labeled "disruptive" and women were characterized as battling to be the "one" that survived. These framing practices were used to justify the invisibility of numerous women jazz musicians under the guise that they were not good enough. In actuality, Liston and Williams created support systems and networks that were instrumental to their success in male-defined jazz environments.[17] Half a century later, the Nicki Minaj/Cardi B feud suggests that little has changed.

When Piper Carter returned to Detroit from New York she found the lack of women on stages and in audiences at local hip hop shows disappointing, so she set out to change these conditions. *Women Rapping Revolution* is the story of women working together and getting things done. Their ongoing artistic production and collaborations in the community that started with the Foundation for some, prior to the collective for others, and has continued after its dissolution for most, challenge the exceptional-woman narrative that justifies women's invisibility in not only hip hop but across many other music genres, arts, and professions. These artists also demonstrate how women working together can make change in meaningful ways. Experience is the bedrock of theory. Each artist that we came to know draws on their lived experience as Detroiters to create innovative, provocative ideas and strategies to speak back to the city and neoliberal state politics. The Foundation put women on the map, along with Detroit and its Black-identified citizenry. Collectively, its members create hip hop that returns cultural forms to their roots in knowledge production, aesthetics, and social practices. If Detroit is coming back from anything, its citizens and cultural organizers must figure into the conversations over who has the right to shape the vision, materiality, and future of the city.

Notes

PREFACE

1. DJing, emceeing, b-boying/b-girling, and graffiti writing are widely known to have been hip hop's first four elements. Afrika Bambaataa and the Universal Zulu Nation added Knowledge (of self and community) as the fifth element.

2. See Nelson George, *Hip Hop America* (New York: Penguin, 1998), for a detailed discussion about the racial politics tied to crossover music in the major label music industry.

3. Christa Craven and Dána-Ain Davis, eds., *Feminist Activist Ethnography: Counterpoints to Neoliberalism in North America* (Lanham, MD: Lexington Books, 2014).

4. Craven and Davis, *Feminist Activist Ethnography.*

5. Lila Abu-Lughod, "Can There Be A Feminist Ethnography?," *Women & Performance: A Journal of Feminist Theory* 5, no. 1 (1990): 9.

6. Anthony Kwame Harrison, *Ethnography: Understanding Qualitative Research* (New York: Oxford University Press, 2018), 29.

7. Harrison, *Ethnography,* 30.

8. Richard D. Sawyer, Joe Norris, and Darren E. Lund, eds., *Duoethnography: Dialogic Methods for Social, Health, and Educational Research* (Walnut Creek, CA: Left Coast Press, 2012).

9. Dina Perrone, "Gender and Sexuality in the Field: A Female Ethnographer's Experience Researching Drug Use in Dance Clubs," *Substance Use and Misuse* 45, no. 5 (2010): 717–35; Bina Bhardwa, "Alone, Asian and Female: The Unspoken Challenges of Conducting Fieldwork in Dance Settings," *Dancecult: Journal of Electronic Dance Music Culture* 5, no. 1 (2013): 39–60; Kaitlyne A. Motl, "Fear in the Festival Field: Threat, Apprehension and Apathy,"

Dancecult: Journal of Electronic Dance Music Culture 9, no. 1 (2017), https:// dj.dancecult.net/index.php/dancecult/article/view/942/869.

10. Craven and Davis, *Feminist Activist Ethnography*, 8.

INTRODUCTION

1. "Outer Spaces," Emergence Media. September 14, 2018, https:// emergencemedia.org/pages/outer-spaces.

2. H. Samy Alim, Jooyoung Lee, and Lauren Mason Carris, "Moving the Crowd, 'Crowding' the Emcee: The Corproduction and Contestation of Black Normativity in Freestyle Rap Battles," *Discourse & Society* 22, no. 4 (2011): 422–39.

3. Simon Frith, "Music and Identity," in *Questions of Cultural Identity,* ed. Stuart Hall and Paul du Gay, Reprint Edition (Thousand Oaks, CA: Sage, 1996), 108–27.

4. Dina Dunham breaks down the history of the Errol Flynn: "The first innovators of this new type of 'jitting' were the 'Errol Flynns,' [the] east side of Detroit's most notorious gang, who gathered at full capacity with common-folk in basement parties and clubs, skylarking their signature hand signs called the 'Errol Flynn'. The 'Errol Flynn' was simply characterized by twisting the wrists with open-handed, tightly clasped fingers, both arms staircase-bouncing up and down in the air in tempo to popular songs they proclaimed as their anthem" ("Jit' On. . .Detroit's Legacy Dance Represents," *Hardcore Detroit,* 2005, http://www.hardcoredetroit.biz/jit/jit.html).

5. This phrase appears in the hook of Dead Prez's track "Hip Hop" (2000). Molefi K. Asante's book *It's Bigger Than Hip Hop: The Rise of the Post-Hip-Hop Generation* (New York: St. Martin's Griffin, 2009) borrows from and is an ode to the song. While this is an important text, Asante's views on gender and sexuality are not consistent with ours.

6. Sara Ahmed, "Selfcare As Warfare," *Feminist Killjoys,* August 25, 2014, https://feministkilljoys.com/2014/08/25/selfcare-as-warfare.

7. The late community activist and environmental guru Charity Hicks coined the phrase "waging love." It is an ethic of care where one has to love enemies and know them to engage change. Many, but not all, Foundation artists share this view and support her legacy.

8. Deidre "D.S. Sense" Smith created this slogan and many Detroit hip hop heads deeply identify with its message. It is also the name and hook of her famous anthem/poem.

9. Grace Lee Boggs and Scott Kurashige, *The Next American Revolution: Sustainable Activism for the Twenty-First Century* (Berkeley: University of California Press, 2012), 17.

10. Jeff Chang, *Can't Stop Won't Stop: A History of the Hip Hop Generation* (New York: St. Martin's Press, 2005), 141.

11. Gwendolyn D. Pough, *Check It While I Wreck It: Black Womanhood, Hip-Hop Culture, and the Public Sphere* (Boston: Northeastern University Press, 2004); Marcyliena Morgan, *The Real Hip Hop: Battling for Knowledge, Power, and Respect in the LA Underground* (Durham, NC: Duke University

Press, 2009); Jessica Nydia Pabón-Colón, "Writin', Breakin', Beatboxin': Strategically Performing 'Women'in Hip-Hop," *Signs: Journal of Women in Culture & Society* 43, no. 1 (2017): 175–200.

12. Nelson George, *Hip Hop America* (New York: Penguin Books, 2005), 184.

13. Jessica Nydia Pabón-Colón, "Writin', Breakin', Beatboxin': Strategically Performing 'Women' in Hip-Hop," *Signs: Journal of Women in Culture & Society* 43, no. 1 (2017): 176.

14. Nancy Guevara, "Women Writin' Rappin' Breakin'," in *Droppin' Science: Critical Essays on Rap Music and Hip Hop Culture,* ed. William Eric Perkins (Philadelphia: Temple University Press, 1996), 49–62.

15. While the commercial rap industry is a profit-driven, exclusive, structured corporate institution, the hip hop underground is local, community-driven, and consists mainly of independent artists who sell their products directly to fans.

16. Barbara Ransby, *Making All Black Lives Matter: Reimagining Freedom in the Twenty-First Century* (Berkeley: University of California Press, 2018).

17. Ransby, *Making All Black Lives Matter,* 159.

18. We take Gramsci's (1971) term "organic intellectual" and put it in conversation with Boggs and Kurashige's (2012) notion that everyday ordinary people have the power to reimagine the possibilities of social life. Detroit emcee Will See stakes claim to the identity of "Detroit Diplomat." Sharing this move, members of the Foundation engage in cultural production and community work like cultural diplomats.

19. We purposefully employ the term "rebellion" in reference to the uprising of 1967 in place of the more commonly used "riot." Grace Lee Boggs explains that *riot* refers to a simple breakdown in law and order. "A rebellion, we decided, is an important massive uprising and protest of the oppressed. Therefore, it not only begets reforms but also throws into question the legitimacy and supposed permanence of existing institutions" (James Boggs and Grace Lee Boggs, *Revolution and Evolution in the Twentieth Century* [New York: Monthly Review Press, 2008], viii).

20. For further commentary on the aestheticization of poverty in Detroit and its affects see John Patrick Leary, "Detroitism," *Guernica: A Magazine of Art and Politics,* January 15, 2011, https://www.guernicamag.com/features/leary_1_15_11. Furthermore, the year 2010 alone saw the publication of several books documenting Detroit's urban decay, including Dan Austin and Sean Doerr, *Lost Detroit: Stories Behind the Motor City's Majestic Ruins* (Charleston, SC: The History Press, 2010); Yves Marchand and Romain Meffre, *Yves Marchand and Romain Meffre: The Ruins of Detroit* (Göttingen, Germany: Steidl, 2010); and Andrew Moore and Philip Levine, *Andrew Moore: Detroit Disassembled* (New York: Damiani/Akron Art Museum, 2010).

21. Ceara O'Leary, "Detroit's Vacant Land: Strategies and Support," *Funders' Network for Smart Growth and Livable Communities,* November 1, 2013, http://www.fundersnetwork.org/blog/detroits-vacant-land-strategies-and-support.

22. Devon G. Peña, "Detroit Food Justice Activists Resist a Land Grab," *Environmental and Food Justice,* December 7, 2012, http://ejfood.blogspot.com/2012/12/land-grabs-not-limited-to-global-south.html.

23. Nancy Kaffer, "Watching Dan Gilbert's Watchmen," *Detroit Free Press,* May 18, 2015, http://www.freep.com/story/opinion/columnists/nancy-kaffer /2015/05/18/quicken-detroit-security/27521889.

24. Antonio Rafael and Matthew Irwin, "Gilbert's Trojan Horse: Capturing the City Core," *Riverwise,* Summer 2017, 10.

25. Interview, November 30, 2014, Detroit, MI.

26. Interview, December 14, 2015, Detroit, MI.

27. Shana L. Redmond, *Anthem: Social Movements and the Sounds of Solidarity in the African Diaspora* (New York: New York University Press, 2014), 1.

28. Redmond, *Anthem,* 10.

29. Reiland Rabaka, *Hip Hop's Amnesia: From Blue and the Black Women's Club Movement to Rap and the Hip Hop Movement* (Lanham, MD: Lexington Books, 2012), xix.

30. Redmond, *Anthem.*

31. Jayna Brown, "Buzz and Rumble: Global Pop Music and Utopian Impulse," *Social Text* 28, no. 1 (2010): 125–46.

32. Mahogany Jones, Nique Love Rhodes, and Piper Carter in conversation with Mark Pedelty, Rebekah Farrugia, and Kellie Hay, November 9, 2013.

33. Anthony Macías, "'Detroit Was Heavy': Modern Jazz, Bebop, and African American Expressive Culture," *The Journal of African American History* 95, no. 1 (2010): 56.

34. Macías, "'Detroit Was Heavy,'" 50.

35. Suzanne E. Smith, *Dancing in the Street: Motown and the Cultural Politics of Detroit* (Cambridge, MA: Harvard University Press, 1999), 222.

36. Smith, *Dancing in the Street,* 230.

37. Sean Albiez, "Post-Soul Futurama: African American Cultural Politics and Early Detroit Techno," *European Journal of American Culture* 24, no. 2 (2005): 137.

38. Christopher Schaub, "Beyond the Hood? Detroit Techno, Underground Resistance, and African American Metropolitan Identity Politics," *Forum for Inter-American Research* 2, no. 2 (2009), http://interamerica.de/volume-2–2 /schaub.

39. Schaub, "Beyond the Hood?"

40. Carleton S. Gholz, "Welcome to Tha D: Making and Re-Making Hip Hop Culture in Post-Motown Detroit," in *Hip Hop in America: A Regional Guide.,* ed. Mickey Hess (Santa Barbara, CA: Greenwood Press, 2010), 393–428.

41. The Foundation, "About," March 2, 2017, http://5egallery.org/about.

CHAPTER ONE. DETROIT HIP HOP AND THE RISE OF THE FOUNDATION

1. Carleton S. Gholz, "Welcome to Tha D: Making and Re-Making Hip Hop Culture in Post-Motown Detroit," in *Hip Hop in America: A Regional Guide.,* ed. Mickey Hess (Santa Barbara, CA: Greenwood Press, 2010), 394.

2. Gholz, "Welcome to Tha D."

3. Gholz, "Welcome to Tha D."

4. Gholz, "Welcome to Tha D," 400.

5. Kahn Santori Davison, "Remembering Notable Locales Among Detroit's Hip-Hop History," *Detroit Metro Times*, November 15, 2018, https://www.metrotimes.com/detroit/remembering-notable-locales-among-detroits-hip-hop-history/Content?oid=10184070.

6. Interview, February 17, 2018, Detroit, MI.

7. Interview, February 17, 2018, Detroit, MI.

8. Tricia Rose, *The Hip Hop Wars: What We Talk about When We Talk about Hip Hop—and Why It Matters* (New York: Basic Books, 2008).

9. Interview, July 17, 2018, Detroit, MI.

10. Interview, August 20, 2015, Detroit, MI.

11. Interview, January 14, 2012, Detroit, MI.

12. Interview, January 14, 2012, Detroit, MI.

13. Bakari Kitwana, *The Hip Hop Generation: Young Blacks and the Crisis in African American Culture* (New York: Verso, 2003).

14. Bettina L. Love, "A Ratchet Lens: Black Queer Youth, Agency, Hip Hop, and the Black Ratchet Imagination," *Educational Researcher* 46, no. 9 (2017): 539–47.

15. Interview, January 14, 2012, Detroit, MI.

16. Interview, May 14, 2012, Detroit, MI.

17. Rebekah Farrugia and Magdalena Olszanowski, "Women and Electronic Dance Music Culture: Introduction," *Dancecult: Journal of Electronic Dance Music Culture* 9, no. 1 (2017): 1–8.

18. Nitasha Tamar Sharma, *Hip Hop Desis: South Asian Americans, Blackness, and a Global Race Consciousness* (Durham, NC: Duke University Press, 2010).

19. Rebekah Farrugia, *Beyond the Dance Floor: Female DJs, Technology, and Electronic Dance Music Culture* (Wilmington, NC: Intellect, 2012); Marion Leonard, *Gender in the Music Industry: Rock, Discourse and Girl Power* (Burlington, VT: Ashgate, 2007).

20. Interview, January 14, 2012, Detroit, MI.

21. Interview, January 14, 2012, Detroit, MI.

CHAPTER TWO. HIP HOP SOUNDS AND SENSIBILITIES IN POST-BANKRUPTCY DETROIT

A version of this chapter was published previously in *The Oxford Handbook of Hip Hop Music,* edited by Justin D. Burton and Jason Lee Oakes. We are grateful to Oxford University Press for permission to expand and republish this work.

1. Deidre "D.S. Sense" Smith, "'On My Detroit Everything' is a brand, initiative and movement," Facebook, January 27, 2015, https://www.facebook.com/D.S.SENSE/posts/on-my-detroit-everything-is-a-brand-an-initiative-and-a-movement-that-focuses-on/826978170697247.

2. Lester Spence, *Knocking the Hustle: Against the Neoliberal Turn in Black Politics* (Brooklyn, NY: Punctum Books, 2015).

3. Sara Ahmed, "Selfcare As Warfare," *Feminist Killjoys,* August 25, 2014, https://feministkilljoys.com/2014/08/25/selfcare-as-warfare.

4. Peter Moskowitz, "The Two Detroits: A City Both Collapsing and Gentrifying at the Same Time," *The Guardian,* February 5, 2015, http://www.theguardian.com/cities/2015/feb/05/detroit-city-collapsing-gentrifying.

5. Laura Gottesdiener, "A Tale of Two Detroits, Separate and Unequal," *In These Times,* November 18, 2014, http://inthesetimes.com/article/17372/inequality_in_detroit.

6. Nelson George, *Hip Hop America* (New York: Penguin, 2005).

7. Tricia Rose, *Black Noise: Rap Music and Black Culture in Contemporary America* (Middletown, CT: Wesleyan University Press, 1994), 125–26.

8. Marc Lamont Hill, *Nobody: Casualties of America's War on the Vulnerable, from Ferguson to Flint and Beyond* (New York City: Atria Books, 2016), 67.

9. Byron Hurt, *Hip Hop: Beyond Beats and Rhymes* (Independent Lens, 2006).

10. Nadia Ellis, "New Orleans and Kingston: A Beginning, A Recurrence," *Popular Music Studies* 27, no. 4 (2015): 392.

11. David Font-Navarrete, "Bass 101: Miami, Rio, and the Global Music South," *Journal of Popular Music Studies* 27, no. 4 (2015): 488–517.

12. June Manning Thomas, *Redevelopment and Race: Planning a Finer City in Postwar Detroit* (Detroit, MI: Wayne State University Press, 2013).

13. Thomas J. Sugrue, *The Origins of the Urban Crisis: Race and Inequality in Postwar Detroit* (Princeton, NJ: Princeton University Press, 2005).

14. U.S. Census Bureau, "U.S. Census Bureau, Census 2000 Summary File 1," Profile of General Demographic Characteristics (United States Census Bureau, 2000), https://factfinder.census.gov/faces/tableservices/jsf/pages/productview.xhtml?src=CF, accessed December 10, 2019.

15. Diane Bukowski, "Brush Park Historical Area—Can We Trust Those Who Wrecked It to Restore It?," *Voice of Detroit,* June 25, 2015, http://voiceofdetroit.net/2015/06/25/brush-park-historic-area-can-we-trust-those-who-wrecked-it-to-restore-it; Dianne Feeley, "Applying the Shock Doctrine in Detroit," *Solidarity,* December 5, 2013, http://www.solidarity-us.org/site/node/4050.

16. Mingo is the former head of the Brush Park Citizens District Council and also the Coordinating Council of all Detroit district councils. Scott was a founder of the Detroit chapter of the Black Panthers and the most public face of the Detroit Coalition Against Police Brutality until his death in 2015.

17. Leonidas Murembya and Eric Guthrie, "Demographic and Labor Market Profile: Detroit City," State of Michigan (Department of Technology, Management, and Budget, April 2015), http://milmi.org/admin/uploadedPublications/2343_Detroit_City_Demographic_and_Labor_Mkt_Profile.pdf.

18. Complete lyrics for "Locusts" are available at https://genius.com/Invincible-locusts-lyrics. The video is available at *https://vimeo.com/13196691.*

19. Hill, *Nobody.*

20. Bukowski, "Brush Park Historical Area."

21. David Harvey, "Neoliberalism as Creative Destruction," *The Annals of the American Academy* 610 (2007): 28.

22. See Audre Lorde, *A Burst of Light: and Other Essays* (Mineola, NY: Ixia Press, 2017).

23. Interview, January 28, 2016.

24. Deborah Willis and Carla Williams, *The Black Female Body: A Photographic History* (Philadelphia: Temple University Press, 2002); Kimberly Juanita Brown, *The Repeating Body: Slavery's Visual Resonance in the Contemporary* (Durham, NC: Duke University Press, 2015).

25. Mereille Miller-Young, *A Taste for Brown Sugar: Black Women in Pornography* (Durham, NC: Duke University Press, 2014).

26. Gottesdiener, "A Tale of Two Detroits"; Moskowitz, "The Two Detroits."

27. Cacildia Cain, "The Necessity of Black Women's Standpoint and Intersectionality in Environmental Movements," *Medium* (blog), April 14, 2016, https://medium.com/black-feminist-thought-2016/the-necessity-of-black-women-s-standpoint-and-intersectionality-in-environmental-movements-fc52d4277616; Valerie Ann Kaalund, "Witness to Truth: Black Women Heeding the Call for Environmental Justice," in *New Perspectives on Environemntal Justice: Gender, Sexuality and Activism,* ed. Rachel Stein (New Brunswick, NJ: Rutgers University Press, 2004), 78–92; Dorceta E. Taylor, "Women of Color, Environmental Justice, and Ecofeminism," in *Ecofeminism: Women, Culture, Nature* (Bloomington: Indiana University Press, 1997), 38–81.

28. Cain, "The Necessity of Black Women's Standpoint and Intersectionality in Environmental Movements."

29. Michele Tracy Berger, *Workable Sisterhood: The Political Journey of Stigmatized Women with HIV/AIDS* (Princeton, NJ: Princeton University Press, 2006).

30. Interview, March 26 2017, Detroit, MI.

31. Andrew Templeton, "'Detroit Hustles Harder' Phrase Is Key to Aptemal Clothing's XXL Growth," *Crain's Detroit Business,* May 5, 2013, http://www.crainsdetroit.com/article/20130505/NEWS/305059991/detroit-hustles-harder-phrase-is-key-to-aptemal-clothings-xxl.

32. It is somewhat ironic that it has become commonplace to see the merchandise for sale in expensive boutiques in predominantly white suburbs such as downtown Birmingham where homes are valued at over $1 million. While they may only superficially relate to the concept of hustling, these consumers still identify with the sense of community the slogan creates because of its working-class roots and the extent to which the metro Detroit area is so often depicted as undesirable.

33. Complete lyrics for "Blue Collar Logic" are available at https://mahoganyjonz.bandcamp.com/track/blue-collar-logic. Video available at *https://www.youtube.com/watch?v=bEGGj6T64uo.*

34. Interview, August 5 2015, Detroit, MI.

35. Nique Love Rhodes, "Detroit Made," December 2015, https://soundcloud.com/nlrmusic/detroit-made-live.

36. Interview, January 14 2016, Detroit, MI.

37. Shea Howell, "Water, Dispossession, and Resistance," {r}evolution: James and Grace Lee Boggs Center for Community Leadership, June 10, 2014. http://boggscenter.org/?p=6086.

38. Howell, "Water, Dispossession, and Resistance."

39. Harvey, "Neoliberalism as Creative Destruction," 35.

40. Interview, January 14 2016, Detroit, MI.

41. Adrienne Brown, "Drive Slow: Rehearing Hip Hop Automotivity," *Journal of Popular Music Studies* 24, no. 3 (2012): 265–75.

42. Brown, "Drive Slow," 266.

43. Brown, "Drive Slow," 266.

44. Brown, "Drive Slow," 267.

45. Spence, *Knocking the Hustle,* passim.

46. Henri Lefebvre advocates for practical solutions to the crises impacting many urban cities in France (see *Right to the City,* edited and translated by Eleonore Kofman and Elizabeth Lebas [Malden, MA: Blackwell, 1996/1967]). He contends that the presence and actions of the working class, and to this we add all marginalized populations, are essential to the materialization of any and all reconstruction strategies.

CHAPTER THREE. NEGOTIATING GENDERQUEER IDENTITY FORMATION

1. adrienne maree brown, *Emergent Strategy: Shaping Change, Changing Worlds* (Chico, CA: AK Press, 2017).

2. Tawana "Honeycomb" Petty, *Towards Humanity: Shifting the Culture of Anti-Racism Organizing* (CreateSpace Independent Publishing Platform, 2018).

3. Lisa Allardice, "Chimamanda Ngozi Adichie: 'This Could Be the Beginning of a Revolution,'" *The Guardian,* April 28, 2018, https://www.theguardian.com/books/2018/apr/28/chimamanda-ngozi-adichie-feminism-racism-sexism-gender-metoo.

4. Hip hop artist and professional photographer Miz Korona made this statement one night while we chatted with her at the Old Miami, the place where the Foundation once held its weekly open mic. She was talking about all the men she knows who are emcees that tell her, "I get a stack," meaning "I get paid well for my work rapping across the city." Miz Korona was explicit in her assessment: "skill level is not what gets paid." Only then did she make the claim, "if you got a rack you ain't getting a stack" (Interview, May 28, 2015, Detroit, MI).

5. bell hooks, *Feminism Is for Everybody* (Cambridge, MA: South End Press, 2000).

6. See Aisha Smith Durham, *Home with Hip Hop Feminism: Performances in Communication and Culture* (New York: Peter Lang, 2014); Joan Morgan, *When Chicken-Heads Come Home to Roost* (New York: Touchstone, 1999); Tricia Rose, *Black Noise: Rap Music and Black Culture in Contemporary America* (Middletown, CT: Wesleyan University Press, 1994).

7. Unless stated otherwise, the interview data we cite in this section is from a focus group we held on October 7, 2013.

8. Michael Kaufman and Michael Kimmel, *The Guy's Guide to Feminism* (Berkeley, CA: Seal Press, 2011).

9. Patricia Hill Collins, *Black Feminist Thought: Knowledge, Consciousness, and the Politics of Empowerment* (New York: Routledge, 2000).

10. Chimamanda Ngozi Adichie, *Dear Ijeawele, or A Feminist Manifesto in Fifteen Suggestions* (New York: Anchor Books, 2018).

11. Phoenix and Janus, interview, February 17, 2012.

12. Morgan, *When Chicken-Heads Come Home to Roost.*

13. Interview, June 9, 2012, Detroit, MI.

14. Interview, March 13, 2013, Detroit, MI.

15. Interview, April 22, 2015, Detroit, MI.

16. Patricia Hill Collins, *Black Sexual Politics* (New York: Routledge, 2004).

17. Morgan, *When Chicken-Heads Come Home to Roost.*

18. Interview, April 22, 2015, Detroit MI.

19. Interview, April 22, 2015, Detroit, MI.

20. Crunk Feminist Collective, "Where Crunk Meets Conscious and Feminism Meets Cool," February 20, 2018, http://www.crunkfeministcollective.com.

21. Whitney A. Peoples, "'Under Construction': Identifying Foundations of Hip-Hop Feminism and Exploring Bridges Between Second-Wave and Hip-Hop Feminisms," *Meridians* 8, no. 1 (2008): 19–52.

22. Peoples, "Under Construction," 20; Kristal Brent Zook, "A Manifesto of Sorts for a Black Feminist Movement," *New York Times Magazine,* December 3, 1995; Morgan, *When Chicken-Heads Come Home to Roost;* Shani Jamila, "Can I Get a Witness? Testimony from a Hip Hop Feminist," in *Colonize This!: Young Women of Color on Today's Feminism,* ed. Daisy Hernandez, Bushra Rehman, and Cherrie Moraga (Berkeley, CA: Seal Press, 2002), 382–94.

23. Jamila, "Can I Get a Witness?," 392.

24. Aisha Durham, Brittany C. Cooper, and Susana M. Morris, "The Stage Hip-Hop Feminism Built: A New Directions Essay," *Signs* 38, no. 3 (2013): 721–37.

25. Maisha Z. Johnson, "5 Ways 'Respectability Politics' Blame Black Women for Their Own Oppression," *Everyday Feminism,* November 5, 2015, https://everydayfeminism.com/2015/11/respectability-politics-black-women/.

26. Joel Penney, "'We Don't Wear Tight Clothes': Gay Panic and Queer Style in Contemporary Hip Hop," *Popular Music and Society* 35, no. 3 (2012): 326.

27. Penney, "'We Don't Wear Tight Clothes.'"

28. Durham, Cooper, and Morris, "The Stage Hip-Hop Feminism Built," 726.

29. Durham, *Home with Hip Hop Feminism;* Rose, *Black Noise.*

30. Peoples, "'Under Construction,'" 46.

31. The Foundation, "About," March 2, 2017, http://5egallery.org/about.

32. Gwendolyn D. Pough, *Check It While I Wreck It: Black Womanhood, Hip-Hop Culture, and the Public Sphere* (Boston: Northeastern University Press, 2004).

33. Ruth Nicole Brown, *Black Girlhood Celebration: Toward a Hip Hop Feminist Pedagogy* (New York: Peter Lang, 2009), 7.

34. Interview, May 28, 2015, Detroit, MI.

35. Robin R. Means Coleman and Jasmine Cobb, "No Way of Seeing: Mainstreaming and Selling the Gaze of Homo-Thug Hip Hop," *Popular Com-*

munication 5, no. 2 (2007): 89–108; Imani Perry, *Prophets of the Hood: Politics and Poetics in Hip Hop* (Durham, NC: Duke University Press, 2004); Rose, *Black Noise.*

36. Rose, *Black Noise,* 39.

37. Adam Krims, *Rap Music and the Poetics of Identity* (Cambridge, UK: Cambridge University Press, 2000).

38. Interview, June 27, 2013, Detroit, MI.

39. Rose, *Black Noise,* 80.

40. Perry, *Prophets of the Hood,* 54–55.

41. Interview, June 27, 2013, Detroit, MI.

42. Interview, June 27, 2013, Detroit, MI.

43. Interview, June 27, 2013, Detroit, MI.

44. Coleman and Cobb, "No Way of Seeing"; Shinsuke Eguchi and Myra N. Roberts, "Gay Rapping and Possibilities: A Quare Reading of 'Throw That Boy P***y'," *Text and Performance Quarterly* 35, no. 2–3 (2015): 142–57; Bettina Love, "A Ratchet Lens: Black Queer Youth, Agency, Hip Hop, and the Black Ratchet Imagination," *Educational Researcher* 46, no. 9 (2017): 539–47; Jeffery Q. McCune Jr., "Out in the Club: The Down Low, Hip-Hop, and the Architecture of Black Masculinity," *Text and Performance Quarterly* 28, no. 3 (2008): 298–314.

45. Rinaldo Walcott, "Boyfriends with Clits and Girlfriends with Dicks: Hip Hop's Queer Future," *Palimpsest: A Journal on Women, Gender, and the Black International* 2, no. 2 (2013): 168–73.

46. Walcott, "Boyfriends with Clits," 171.

47. Perry, *Prophets of the Hood,* 1.

48. Georgetown University, *A Conversation with Nas and Michael Eric Dyson* (Washington, DC, 2014), https://www.georgetown.edu/news/rapper-nas-says-hip-hop-artists-need-to-be-more-responsible.

49. Michael Eric Dyson and Sohail Daulatzai, *Born To Use Mics: Reading Nas's Illmatic* (New York: Civitas Books, 2009); Rose, *Black Noise.*

50. Murray Forman, *The 'Hood Comes First: Race, Space, and Place in Rap and Hip-Hop* (Hanover, NH: Wesleyan University Press, 2002).

51. Richard T. Craig, "'I Know What Them Girls Like': A Rhetorical Analysis of Thug Appeal in Rap Lyrics," *Journal of Communication Inquiry* 40, no. 1 (2016): 25–45.

52. Coleman and Cobb, "No Way of Seeing"; Byron Hurt, *Hip Hop: Beyond Beats and Rhymes* (Independent Lens, 2006); Mark Anthony Neal, *Looking for Leroy: Illegible Black Masculinities* (New York: New York University Press, 2013); Jeffrey Ogbar, *Hip-Hop Revolution: The Culture and Politics of Rap* (Lawrence, KS: University of Kansas Press, 2007); Perry, *Prophets of the Hood;* Kevin Powell, *The Education of Kevin Powell: A Boy's Journey Into Manhood* (New York: Atria Books, 2016); Miles White, *From Jim Crow to Jay-Z: Race, Rap and the Performance of Masculinity* (Urbana: University of Illinois Press, 2011).

53. Toby S. Jenkins, "A Beautiful Mind: Black Male Intellectual Identity and Hip-Hop Culture," *Journal of Black Studies* 42, no. 8 (2011): 1231–51.

54. Anthony Kwame Harrison, *Hip Hop Underground: The Integrity and Ethics of Racial Identification* (Philadelphia: Temple University Press, 2009); Marcyliena Morgan, *The Real Hip Hop: Battling for Knowledge, Power, and Respect in the LA Underground* (Durham, NC: Duke University Press, 2009); James Braxton Peterson, *The Hip-Hop Underground and African American Culture: Beneath the Surface* (New York: Palgrave MacMillan, 2015); Joseph G. Schloss, *Foundation: B-Boys, B-Girls, and Hip-Hop Culture in New York* (New York: Oxford University Press, 2009); Nitasha Tamar Sharma, *Hip Hop Desis: South Asian Americans, Blackness, and a Global Race Consciousness* (Durham, NC: Duke University Press, 2010).

55. Michael Eric Dyson, *Know What I Mean?: Reflections on Hip Hop* (New York: Basic Books, 2007); Herman Gray, *Cultural Moves: African Americans and the Politics of Representation* (Berkeley: University of California Press, 2005).

56. Ogbar, *Hip-Hop Revolution*, 43.

57. Ogbar, *Hip-Hop Revolution*, 92.

58. Michael P. Jeffries, *Thug Life: Race, Gender and the Meaning of Hip Hop* (Chicago: University of Chicago Press, 2011).

59. Hurt, *Hip Hop*.

60. Perry, *Prophets of the Hood*, 1–2.

61. Perry, *Prophets of the Hood*, 3.

62. Craig, "'I Know What Them Girls Like.'"

63. Destiny's Child featuring T.I. & Lil' Wayne, "Soldier," *Destiny Fulfilled*, Columbia Records, 2004.

64. Neal, *Looking for Leroy*.

65. Interview, March 2, 2018, Detroit, MI.

66. Interview, February 17, 2018, Detroit, MI.

67. Interview, February 21, 2018, Detroit, MI.

68. Interview, February 21, 2018, Detroit, MI.

69. William Jelani Cobb, *To the Break of Dawn: A Freestyle on the Hip Hop Aesthetic* (New York: New York University Press, 2008).

70. Interview, May 16 2018, Detroit, MI.

71. Interview, May 16, 2018, Detroit, MI.

72. Interview, May 16, 2018, Detroit, MI.

73. Ogbar, *Hip-Hop Revolution*.

74. Interview, January 25, 2018, Detroit, MI. All quotations in this section are from this interview.

75. Ethridge Knight, *Belly Song and Other Poems* (Detroit, MI: Broadside Press, 1973).

76. Krims, *Rap Music and the Poetics of Identity*.

77. Valid, "risen from Detroit's legendary hip hop scene," Facebook, November 30, 2017, https://www.facebook.com/Valid313.

78. Ogbar, *Hip-Hop Revolution*, 59.

79. Facebook post, November 30, 2017.

80. Ogbar, *Hip-Hop Revolution*, 102.

81. Interview, May 28, 2015, Detroit, MI.

82. David R. Roediger, *Working Toward Whiteness: How America's Immigrants Became White: The Strange Journey from Ellis Island to the Suburbs* (New York: Basic Books, 2006).

83. Roediger, *Working Toward Whiteness*, 43.

84. Durham, Cooper, and Morris, "The Stage Hip-Hop Feminism Built"; Love, "A Ratchet Lens."

85. Kyra Gaunt, "Foreword," in *Wish to Live: The Hip Hop Feminism Pedagogy Reader,* ed. Ruth Nicole Brown and Chamara Jewel Kwakye (New York: Peter Lang, 2012), xiii.

86. Mark Anthony Neal, "Foreword," in *Homegirls Make Some Noise! Hip-Hop Feminism Anthology,* ed. *Gwendolyn D. Pough, Elaine Richardson, Aisha Durham,* and *Rachel Raimist* (Mira Loma, CA: Parker Publishing, 2007), i–iii.

CHAPTER FOUR. VULNERABLE MAVERICKS WRECK RAP'S CONVENTIONS

A version of this chapter was published previously in *Popular Music*. We are grateful to the journal for permission to expand and republish this work.

1. Gwendolyn D. Pough, *Check It While I Wreck It: Black Womanhood, Hip-Hop Culture, and the Public Sphere* (Boston: Northeastern University Press, 2004), 176.

2. Tricia Rose, *Black Noise: Rap Music and Black Culture in Contemporary America* (Middletown CT: Wesleyan University Press, 1994).

3. Patricia Hill Collins, *Black Feminist Thought: Knowledge, Consciousness, and the Politics of Empowerment* (New York: Routledge, 2000); Patricia Hill Collins, *From Black Power to Hip Hop: Racism, Nationalism, and Feminism* (Philadelphia: Temple University Press, 2006); Jeffrey Ogbar, *Hip-Hop Revolution: The Culture and Politics of Rap* (Lawrence: University of Kansas Press, 2007).

4. Cheryl L. Keyes, "Empowering Self, Making Choices, Creating Space: Black Female Identity via Rap Music Performance," *The Journal of American Folklore* 113, no. 449 (2000): 255–69; Reiland Rabaka, *Hip Hop's Amnesia: From Blue and the Black Women's Club Movement to Rap and the Hip Hop Movement* (Lanham, MD: Lexington Books, 2012).

5. Aisha Durham, "Hip Hop Feminist Media Studies," *International Journal of Africana Studies* 16, no. 1 (2010): 117–40.

6. T.M. Adams and D.B. Fuller, "The Words Have Changed but the Ideology Remains the Same: Misogynistic Lyrics in Rap Music," *Journal of Black Studies* 36, no. 6 (2006): 938–57; Collins, *From Black Power to Hip Hop;* bell hooks, *We Real Cool: Black Men and Masculinity* (New York: Routledge, 2003); Margaret Hunter, "Shake It, Baby, Shake It: Consumption and the New Gender Relation in Hip-Hop," *Sociological Perspectives* 54, no. 1 (2011): 15–36; Imani Perry, *Prophets of the Hood: Politics and Poetics in Hip Hop* (Durham, NC: Duke University Press, 2004); Tricia Rose, *The Hip Hop Wars: What We Talk about When We Talk about Hip Hop—and Why It Matters* (New York: Basic Books, 2008); T. Denean Sharpley-Whiting, *Pimps Up, Ho's*

Down: Hip Hop's Hold on Young Black Women (New York: New York University Press, 2008).

7. Rose, *The Hip Hop Wars*, 1.

8. Sharpley-Whiting, *Pimps Up, Ho's Down.*

9. Adams and Fuller, "The Words Have Changed but the Ideology Remains the Same." "Sapphire" was used to describe a socially aggressive woman who uses manipulation to try to control her man and "Jezebel" to describe a loose, sexually aggressive woman.

10. Lakeyta M. Bonnette, *Pulse of the People: Political Rap Music and Black Politics* (Philadelphia: University of Pennsylvania Press, 2015); Keyes, "Empowering Self, Making Choices, Creating Space"; Rose, *Black Noise.*

11. Rabaka, *Hip Hop's Amnesia*, 75.

12. Rabaka, *Hip Hop's Amnesia*, 75.

13. Perry, *Prophets of the Hood,* 159.

14. Joan Morgan, *When Chicken-Heads Come Home to Roost* (New York: Touchstone, 1999); Mark Anthony Neal, "Hip Hop Feminist," in *That's the Joint: The Hip Hop Studies Reader,* ed. Murray Forman and Mark Anthony Neal (London: Routledge, 2012), 413–18.

15. Dionne P. Stephens and Layli D. Phillips, "Freaks, Gold Diggers, Divas, and Dykes: The Sociohistorical Development of Adolescent African American Women's Sexual Scripts," *Sexuality & Culture* 7, no. 1 (2003): 3–49.

16. Stephens and Phillips, "Freaks, Gold Diggers, Divas, and Dykes," 31.

17. Interview, July 27, 2015, Royal Oak, MI.

18. Insite the Riot, "Winner," *Girl Meets Beat* EP, October 2, 2015, https://insitetheriot.bandcamp.com/track/winner.

19. Adam Krims, *Rap Music and the Poetics of Identity* (Cambridge, UK: Cambridge University Press, 2000).

20. Jerry Herron, *AfterCulture: Detroit and the Humiliation of History* (Detroit: Wayne State University Press, 1993), 13.

21. Interview, May 28, 2015, Detroit, MI. Other quotations in this section are from this interview.

22. Interview, April 26, 2015, Detroit, MI.

23. The video for "Skin Deep" is available at www.youtube.com/watch?v = zrckVMb1mkQ.

24. Interview, May 28, 2015, Detroit, MI.

25. Interview, July 27, 2015, Detroit, MI.

26. Interview, November 16, 2015, Detroit, MI.

27. Interview, July 17, 2018, Detroit, MI.

28. Krims, *Rap Music and the Poetics of Identity,* 50.

29. Interview, July 30, 2018, Detroit, MI.

30. There are, however, a handful of women who crossover from the underground to the commercial markets who do speak on issues like manhood, vulnerability, and resistance. They include artists like Bahamadia, Rapsody, and Noname.

31. Interview, July 27, 2015, Royal Oak, MI.

32. Interview, July 27, 2015, Royal Oak, MI.

33. Interview, January 16, 2018, Detroit, MI.

34. Miz Korona, "Set Fire," November 9, 2017, https://mizkorona.band-camp.com/track/set-fire.

35. Interview, January 16, 2018, Detroit, MI.

36. Interview, January 16, 2018, Detroit, MI.

37. Jeff Milo, "Hip-Hop Emcee Miz Korona, of '8 Mile' Fame, Knows Something about Persevering," *Detroit Free Press*, August 10, 2017, https://www.freep.com/story/entertainment/music/2017/08/10/miz-korona-best-friends-forever-fest/547431001.

38. Rabaka, *Hip Hop's Amnesia*.

39. Ruth Nicole Brown, *Black Girlhood Celebration: Toward a Hip Hop Feminist Pedagogy* (New York: Peter Lang, 2009), 139.

40. Interview, May 28, 2015, Detroit, MI.

41. In *The Next American Revolution: Sustainable Activism for the Twenty-First Century* (Berkeley: University of California Press, 2012), Grace Lee Boggs (with Scott Kurashige) conceptualizes revolutionaries as "solutionaries." This is a more people-centered view of revolution as empowerment rather than a struggle for political power. Viewing revolutionaries as solutionaries is about encouraging people to work together to solve practical problems. It is in the process of working together that we build community and grow our souls.

CHAPTER FIVE. "LEGENDARY," ENVIRONMENTAL JUSTICE, AND COLLABORATIVE CULTURAL PRODUCTION

A version of this chapter was published previously in *Music and Politics*. We are grateful to the journal for permission to expand and republish this work.

1. Travis D. Stimeling, "Music, Place, and Identity in the Central Appalachian Mountaintop Removal Mining Debate," *American Music* 30, no. 1 (2012): 1–29.

2. Aaron S. Allen, "Prospects and Problems for Ecomusicology in Confronting a Crisis of Culture," *Journal of the American Musicology Association* 64, no. 2 (2011): 417.

3. Rebekah Farrugia and Kellie D. Hay, "The Politics and Place of a 'Legendary' Hip Hop Track," *Music and Politics* 8, no. 2 (2014), http://dx.doi.org/10.3998/mp.9460447.0008.203. The video for "Legendary" is embedded in this article and available at: https://quod.lib.umich.edu/m/mp/9460447.0008.203/—politics-and-place-of-a-legendary-hip-hop-track-in-detroit?rgn=main;view=fulltext;q1=farrugia.

4. Emery Petchauer, "Starting With Style: Toward a Second Wave of Hip-Hop Education Research and Practice," *Urban Education* 50, no. 1 (2015): 79.

5. Dominic Capeci Jr. and Martha Wilkerson critique the established mythology as to what caused the riots in Detroit during World War II in *Layered Violence: The Detroit Riots of 1943* (Jackson: University of Mississippi Press, 1991). In *Detroit Divided* (New York: Russell Sage Foundation, 2000), Reynolds Farley, Sheldon Danziger, and Harry Holzer investigate the roots of contemporary inequality in Detroit, focusing on labor force issues and economic

equality. In *Social Justice and the City* (Baltimore: Johns Hopkins University Press, 2009), David Harvey reconceptualizes urban development, looking at larger issues of economic development and the use of space. See also Heather Ann Thomson, *Whose Detroit? Politics, Labor, and Race in a Modern American City* (Ithaca, NY: Cornell University Press, 2000). Thompson examines the causes of the 1967 rebellion as well as the attempts to reconstruct frameworks of power in the city's economy. The primary focus is the UAW but there are implications for larger re-imaginings of the city.

6. Susan McClary, "Terminal Prestige: The Case of Avant-Garde Music Composition," *Cultural Critique* 12 (Spring 1989): 57–81; Susan McClary, *Feminine Endings: Music, Gender, and Sexuality* (Minneapolis: University of Minnesota Press, 1991); Lawrence Kramer, *Music as Cultural Practice: 1800–1900* (Berkeley: University of California Press, 1993).

7. Mark Pedelty, *Ecomusicology: Rock, Folk, and the Environment* (Philadelphia, PA: Temple University Press, 2012).

8. Nancy Guy, "Flowing Down Taiwan's Tamsui River: Towards an Ecomusicology of the Environmental Imagination," *Ethnomusicology* 53, no. 2 (Spring/Summer 2009): 218–48; Pedelty, *Ecomusicology*; Stimeling, "Music, Place, and Identity in the Central Appalachian Mountaintop Removal Mining Debate."

9. Denise Von Glahn, *Music and the Skillful Listener* (Bloomington, IN: Indiana University Press, 2013): 1.

10. Von Glahn, *Music and the Skillful Listener*, 321.

11. The following texts make a strong case for these lines of inquiry: David Ingram, *The Jukebox in the Garden: Ecocriticism and American Popular Music Since 1960* (Amsterdam: Rodopi, 2010); Debra J. Rosenthal, "Hoods and the Woods: Rap Music as Environmental Literature," *The Journal of Popular Culture* 39, no. 4 (Summer 2006): 661–76; and Pedelty, *Ecomusicology*.

12. Philip Bohlman, "Musicology as a Political Act," *The Journal of Musicology* 11, no. 4 (Autumn 1993): 434.

13. Pedelty, *Ecomusicology*, 67.

14. Allen, "Prospects and Problems for Ecomusicology in Confronting a Crisis of Culture," 419.

15. Alexander Rehding, "Ecomusicology between Apocalypse and Nostalgia," *Journal of the American Musicological Society* 64, no. 2 (2011): 409–414.

16. R. Murray Schafer, *The Tuning of the World* (Philadelphia: University of Pennsylvania Press, 1980).

17. Jacques Attali, *Noise: The Political Economy of Music,* trans. Brian Massumi (Manchester: Manchester University Press, 1985), 4.

18. See for example, Attali, *Noise;* Steven Feld, "From Ethnomusicology to Echo-Muse-Ecology: Reading R. Murray Schafer in the Papua New Guinea Rainforest," *The Soundscape Newsletter* 8 (June 1994): 9–13; Jonathan Sterne, ed., *The Sound Studies Reader* (New York: Routledge, 2012); Georgina Born, ed. *Music, Sound and Space: Transformations of Public and Private Experience* (Cambridge: Cambridge University Press, 2013).

19. Susan J. Smith, "Soundscape," *Area* 26, no. 3 (1994): 234.

20. Jonathan Sterne, "Sonic Imaginations," in *The Sound Studies Reader,* ed. Jonathan Sterne (New York: Routledge, 2012), 1–18.

21. Marina Peterson, *Sound, Space, and the City: Civic Performances in Downtown Los Angeles* (Philadelphia: University of Pennsylvania Press, 2012), 3.

22. See for example, John Connell and Chris Gibson, *Sound Tracks: Popular Music Identity and Place* (New York: Routledge, 2003); Brian Cross, *It's Not About a Salary: Rap, Race and Resistance in Los Angeles* (London: Verso, 1993); Anthony Kwame Harrison, *Hip Hop Underground: The Integrity and Ethics of Racial Identification* (Philadelphia: Temple University Press, 2009); Murray Forman, *The 'Hood Comes First: Race, Space and Place in Rap and Hip Hop* (Hanover, NH: Wesleyan University Press, 2002); Adam Krims, *Music and Urban Geography* (London: Routledge, 2007); Ali Colleen Neff, *Let the World Listen Right: The Mississippi Delta Hip Hop Story* (Jackson, MS: University Press of Mississippi, 2011); Tricia Rose, *Black Noise: Rap Music and Black Culture in Contemporary America* (Hanover, NH: Wesleyan University Press, 1994).

23. Forman, *The 'Hood Comes First,* xvii.

24. Forman, *The 'Hood Comes First,* xxvii.

25. Connell and Gibson, *Sound Tracks,* 192.

26. June Manning Thomas, *Redevelopment and Race: Planning a Finer City in Postwar Detroit* (Detroit: Wayne State University Press, 1997), 36.

27. *Detroit Future City: 2012 Detroit Strategic Framework Plan* (Detroit: Inland Press, 2013), https://detroitfuturecity.com/wp-content/uploads/2014/02/DFC_ExecutiveSummary_2ndEd.pdf.

28. Peter Hammer, "The Impacts of Detroit Future City," paper presented at the Martin Luther King Youth Celebration, Cass Community Commons, Detroit, MI, January 20, 2014.

29. Interview, April 11, 2014, Detroit, MI.

30. Sierra Club, "The State of Detroit's Environment: An Initial Assessment Using the Framework of Environmental Justice," accessed January 13, 2014, http://www.SierraClub.org.

31. Kevin Petersen, "Room to Grow: Detroit Takes the First Steps to Legalize Urban Agriculture," *Michigan Journal of Environmental and Administrative Law,* February 8, 2013, http://www.mjeal-online.org/room-to-grow-detroit-takes-the-first-steps-to-legalize-urban-agriculture.

32. Krims, *Music and Urban Geography,* xxix.

33. Krims, *Music and Urban Geography.*

34. Rose Gray, "Red, Black, and Green: A More Inclusive Environmental Movement Takes the Stage," *Orion Magazine,* April 2014, http://www.orion-magazine.org/index.php/articles/article/8050.

35. At the time of the video's production, Piper did not identify as "Mama Piper." Over time she has grown into the role of a wise elder who is respected in the community. Elder is relative, as Piper is not yet fifty; however, for the youth she mentors she has earned the status of Mama. In March 2019, we witnessed her refer to herself as Mama Piper. She is part of the latest generation of community organizers who follows the lead of the most revered women community leaders in the city.

36. Emery Petchauer, "Back to the Lab With Hip Hop Education: An Introduction," *Urban Education* 50, no. 1 (2015): 4.

37. George Lipsitz, "The Possessive Investment in Whiteness: Racialized Social Democracy and the 'White' Problem in American Studies," *American Quarterly* 47, no. 3 (1995): 371.

38. For extended discussions of race and housing see Thomas Sugrue, *The Origins of the Urban Crisis: Race and Inequity in Postwar Detroit* (Princeton, NJ: Princeton University Press, 1996) and Karen A.J. Miller, "Living in the Arsenal of Democracy: Workers and the Problem of Housing," paper presented at the North American Labor History Conference, Wayne State University, Detroit, Michigan (October 2012).

39. John Gallagher, "When Detroit Paved Over Paradise: The Story of I-375," *Detroit Free Press,* December 15, 2013, http://www.freep.com/article/20131215/OPINION05/312150060/Black-Bottom-Detroit-I-375-I-75-paradise-valley-removal.

40. Patricia Hill Collins, *Black Feminist Thought: Knowledge, Consciousness, and the Politics of Empowerment* (New York: Routledge, 2000).

41. Interview, Nique Love Rhodes, November 9, 2013, Pittsburgh, PA.

42. Kevin R. Cox and Andrew Mair, "Locality and Community in the Politics of Local Economic Development," *Annals of the Association of American Geographers* 78, no. 2 (June 1998): 307–25.

43. Hazel Carby, "It Jus Be's Dat Way Sometime: The Sexual Politics of Women's Blues," in *The Jazz Cadence of American Culture,* ed. Robert O'Meally (New York: Columbia University Press, 1988), 470–82.

44. Connell and Gibson, *Sound Tracks,* 85.

45. Connell and Gibson, *Sound Tracks,* 209.

46. Krims, *Music and Urban Geography,* xxxv.

47. Mark Pedelty, *Ecomusicology,* 12.

48. Folk musicians, such as Woody Guthrie, Bob Dylan, and Peter Seeger, wrote music that aimed to open up spaces for listeners to think about the relationship between the self and the kinds of community these artists envisioned. Hip hop is a genre that is ripe for inquiry, as it is rooted in uprising, knowledge of self, and community.

49. H. Bernard Hall, "Deeper than Rap: Expanding Conceptions of Hip-Hop Culture and Pedagogy in the English Language Arts Classroom," *Research in the Teaching of English* 51, no. 3 (2017): 341–50; Marc Lamont Hill and Emery Petchauer, *Schooling Hip-Hop: Expanding Hip-Hop Based Education Across the Curriculum* (New York: Teachers College Press, 2013); Emery Petchauer, "Starting With Style: Toward a Second Wave of Hip-Hop Education Research and Practice," *Urban Education* 50, no. 1 (2015): 78–105; Elaine Richardson, "Developing Critical Hip Hop Feminist Literacies: Centrality and Subversion of Sexuality in the Lives of Black Girls," *Equity & Excellent in Education* 46, no. 3 (2013): 327–41.

50. Grace Lee Boggs and Scott Kurashige, *The Next American Revolution: Sustainable Activism for the Twenty-First Century* (New York: Monthly Review Press, 2008), xxi.

51. Margaret J. Wheatley, *Leadership and the New Science: Discovering Order in a Chaotic World* (San Francisco: Berrett-Koehler Publisher, 2006), 40.

CHAPTER SIX. HIP HOP ACTIVISM IN ACTION

1. Will See's 2018 album *Detroit Diplomat* inspired our use of the phrase "cultural diplomacy."

2. Reiland Rabaka, *Hip Hop's Inheritance: From the Harlem Renaissance to the Hip Hop Feminist Movement* (Lanham, MD: Lexington Books, 2011).

3. adrienne maree brown, *Emergent Strategy: Shaping Change, Changing Worlds* (Chico, CA: AK Press, 2017).

4. Stephen M. Ward, *In Love and Struggle: The Revolutionary Lives of James and Grace Lee Boggs* (Chapel Hill: University of North Carolina Press, 2016).

5. Boggs Center, "Detroit Summer," {r}evolution: James and Grace Lee Boggs Center for Community Leadership, September 4, 2018, http://boggs-center.org/html/detroit_summer.htm.

6. Grace Lee Boggs and Scott Kurashige, *The Next American Revolution: Sustainable Activism for the Twenty-First Century* (New York: Monthly Review Press, 2008), 36.

7. Mesfin Fekadu, "MTV, Save the Music Launch Grant Named after Rapper-Producer J Dilla," *Detroit Free Press,* August 29, 2019, https://www.freep.com/story/entertainment/music/2019/08/29/j-dilla-music-tech-grant-mtv-save-the-music/2157503001.

8. Interview, January 4, 2018, Detroit, MI.

9. Marc Lamont Hill and Emery Petchauer, *Schooling Hip-Hop: Expanding Hip-Hop Based Education Across the Curriculum* (New York: Teachers College Press, 2013), 28.

10. Ruth Nicole Brown, *Black Girlhood Celebration: Toward a Hip Hop Feminist Pedagogy* (New York: Peter Lang, 2009), 7.

11. Interview, March 2, 2014, Detroit, MI.

12. brown, *Emergent Strategy.*

13. American Music Therapy Association, "History of Music Therapy," April 13, 2019, https://www.musictherapy.org/about/history.

14. Don Elligan, "Rap Therapy: A Culturally Sensitive Approach to Psychotherapy with Young African American Men," *Journal of African American Men* 5, no. 3 (2000): 27–36; Don Elligan, *Rap Therapy: A Practical Guide for Communicating with Youth and Young Adults Through Rap Music* (New York: Kensington, 2004); Susan Hadley and George Yancy, eds., *Therapeutic Uses of Rap and Hip-Hop* (New York: Routledge, 2012); Marc Lamont Hill, "Wounded Healing: Forming a Storytelling Community in Hip-Hop Lit," *Teachers College Record* 111, no. 1 (2009): 248–93; Ian Levy, Christopher Emdin, and Edmund S. Adjapong, "Hip-Hop Cypher in Group Work," *Social Work with Groups* 41, no. 1–2 (2018): 103–10; Carrie Louise Sheffield, "Native American Hip-Hop and Historical Trauma: Surviving and Healing Trauma on the 'Rez,'" *Studies in American Indian Literatures* 23, no. 3 (2011): 94–110.

15. Elligan, *Rap Therapy;* Tiphanie Gonzales and B. Grant Hayes, "Rap Music in School Counseling Based on Don Elligan's Rap Therapy," *Journal of Creativity in Mental Health* 4, no. 2 (2009): 161–72.

16. Elligan, *Rap Therapy.*

17. Sheffield, "Native American Hip-Hop and Historical Trauma."

18. Hill, "Wounded Healing."

19. Levy, Emdin, and Adjapong, "Hip-Hop Cypher in Group Work."

20. Linda Archibald and Jonathan Dewar, "Creative Arts, Culture, and Healing: Building an Evidence Base," *Pimatisiwin: A Journal of Aboriginal and Indigenous Community Health* 8, no. 3 (2010): 20.

21. Elaine Richardson, "Developing Critical Hip Hop Feminist Literacies: Centrality and Subversion of Sexualy in the Lives of Black Girls," *Equity & Excellent in Education* 46, no. 3 (2013): 327–41.

22. Richardson attributes the concept of "literate witnessing" to Jeanine M. Staples, "'There Are Two Truths': African American Women's Critical, Creative Ruminations on Love through New Literacies," *Pedagogy, Culture & Society* 20, no. 3 (2012): 451–83.

23. Richardson, "Developing Critical Hip Hop Feminist Literacies," 328.

24. Douglas Kellner and Jeff Share, "Toward Critical Media Literacy: Core Concepts, Debates, Organizations, and Policy," *Discourse: Studies in the Cultural Politics of Education* 26, no. 3 (2005): 369–86.

25. Kellner and Share, "Toward Critical Media Literacy," 269.

26. Allied Media Projects, "Cultivating Media for Liberation," June 12, 2018, https://www.alliedmedia.org/about/story.

27. Interview, July 24, 2012, Detroit, MI.

28. Allied Media Projects, "A Vision for Digital Justice," June 12, 2019, http://www.alliedmedia.org/ddjc/story.

29. Richardson, "Developing Critical Hip Hop Feminist Literacies," 239.

30. Detroit Future (DF) is an initiative of the Detroit Digital Justice Coalition (DDJC) and consists of three areas: DF Schools, DF Media, and DF Youth. The DDJC was launched in 2010 after receiving federal grant money from the Broadband Technology Opportunities Program. The DDJC was a citywide movement to build a more just, creative, and collaborative Detroit through broadband adoption activities. The coalition was initiated in 2009 by Allied Media Projects. For more information, see Allied Media Projects, "A Vision for Digital Justice."

31. Interview, January 14, 2012, Detroit, MI.

32. Andreana Clay, *The Hip-Hop Generation Fights Back: Youth, Activism, and Post-Civil Rights Politics* (New York: New York University Press, 2012), 162.

33. Clay, *The Hip-Hop Generation Fights Back*, 162.

34. Interview, June 20, 2012, Detroit, MI.

35. Emergence Media, "About," May 2, 2018, https://emergencemedia.org/pages/about-us.

36. Interview, May 28, 2015, Detroit, MI.

37. Interview, April 26, 2015, Detroit, MI.

38. Interview, May 14, 2015, Detroit, MI.

39. Interview, November 30, 2014, Detroit, MI.

40. Clay, *The Hip-Hop Generation Fights Back*.

41. Zenzele Isoke, *Urban Black Women and the Politics of Resistance* (New York: Palgrave MacMillan, 2012).

42. Reiland Rabaka, *Hip Hop's Amnesia: From Blue and the Black Women's Club Movement to Rap and the Hip Hop Movement* (Lanham, MD: Lexington Books, 2012).

CONCLUSION

1. We borrow this gender-neutral term from adrienne maree brown who, in *Emergent Strategy: Shaping Change, Changing Worlds* (Chico, CA: AK Press, 2017), 25, attributes it to Chicago based healer/writer Tanuja Jagernauth.

2. See Michele Tracy Berger, *Workable Sisterhood: The Political Journey of Stigmatized Women with HIV/AIDS* (Princeton, NJ: Princeton University Press, 2006); Zenzele Isoke, *Urban Black Women and the Politics of Resistance* (New York: Palgrave McMillan, 2013); and Aimee Meredith Cox, *Shapeshifters: Black Girls and the Choreography of Citizenship* (Durham, NC: Duke University Press, 2015).

3. The model was profiled in "Detroit on the Edge," *60 Minutes,* October 13, 2013, https://www.cbsnews.com/video/detroit-on-the-edge.

4. "American Community Survey Demographic and Housing Estimates," Table ID: DP05. U.S. Census Bureau, https://data.census.gov/cedsci/all?q=detroit&g=1600000US2622000&hidePreview=false&table=DP05&tid=ACSD P1Y2018.DP05&vintage=2018&layer=place&cid=DP05_0001E&lastDisplay edRow=51, accessed December 16, 2019.

5. Interview, November 30, 2014, Detroit, MI.

6. T. M. Adams and D. B. Fuller, "The Words Have Changed but the Ideology Remains the Same: Misogynistic Lyrics in Rap Music," *Journal of Black Studies* 36, no. 6 (2006): 938–57; T. Denean Sharpley-Whiting, *Pimps Up, Ho's Down: Hip Hop's Hold on Young Black Women* (New York: New York University Press, 2008).

7. Cheryl Keyes, "Empowering Self, Making Choices, Creating Space: Black Female Identity via Rap Music Performance," *The Journal of American Folklore* 113, no. 449 (2000): 255–69; Mereille Miller-Young, *A Taste for Brown Sugar: Black Women in Pornography* (Durham, NC: Duke University Press, 2014).

8. Shana L. Redmond, *Anthem: Social Movements and the Sounds of Solidarity in the African Diaspora* (New York: New York University Press, 2014), 1.

9. Simon Frith, "Music and Identity," in *Questions of Cultural Identity,* ed. Stuart Hall and Paul du Gay (Thousand Oaks, CA: Sage, 1996), 108–27; Maureen Mahon, "The Visible Evidence of Cultural Producers," *Annual Review of Anthropology* 29 (2000): 467–92.

10. Frith, "Music and Identity," 111.

11. Kellie D. Hay, Rebekah Farrugia, and Deidre "D.S. Sense" Smith, "D.S. Sense's 'On My Detroit Everything': Self-Articulating Black Girl Magic," *Arts* 7, no. 2 (2018), https://www.mdpi.com/2076-0752/7/2/17.

12. Stephen Ward, *In Love and Struggle: The Revolutionary Lives of James and Grace Lee Boggs* (Chapel Hill: University of North Carolina Press, 2016), ix.

13. Rebekah Farrugia, *Beyond the Dance Floor: Female DJs, Technology, and Electronic Dance Music Culture* (Wilmington, NC: Intellect, 2012).

14. "The Studio Arena," September 28, 2019, https://thestudioarena.com.

15. Allied Media Projects, "Detroit Narrative Agency," January 15, 2019, https://www.alliedmedia.org/dna.

16. Tammy L. Kernodle, "Black Women Working Together: Jazz, Gender, and the Politics of Validation," *Black Music Research Journal* 34, no. 1 (2017): 28.

17. Kernodle notes that Liston and Williams also benefited from relationships with male musicians like Dizzy Gillespie who chose Melba Liston to be part of his State Department jazz diplomacy band ("Black Women Working Together," 37). Mahogany Jones's work as a hip hop ambassador is the latest version of State-Department endorsed cultural diplomacy.

Bibliography

Abu-Lughod, Lila. "Can There Be A Feminist Ethnography?" *Women & Performance: A Journal of Feminist Theory* 5, no. 1 (1990): 7–27.

Adams, T.M., and D.B. Fuller. "The Words Have Changed but the Ideology Remains the Same: Misogynistic Lyrics in Rap Music." *Journal of Black Studies* 36, no. 6 (2006): 938–57.

Adichie, Chimamanda Ngozi. *Dear Ijeawele, or A Feminist Manifesto in Fifteen Suggestions.* New York: Anchor Books, 2018.

Ahmed, Sara. "Selfcare As Warfare." *Feminist Killjoys,* August 25, 2014. https://feministkilljoys.com/2014/08/25/selfcare-as-warfare.

Albiez, Sean. "Post-Soul Futurama: African American Cultural Politics and Early Detroit Techno." *European Journal of American Culture* 24, no. 2 (2005): 131–52.

Alim, H. Samy, Jooyoung Lee, and Lauren Mason Carris. "Moving the Crowd, 'Crowding' the Emcee: The Corproduction and Contestation of Black Normativity in Freestyle Rap Battles." *Discourse & Society* 22, no. 4 (2011): 422–39.

Allardice, Lisa. "Chimamanda Ngozi Adichie: 'This Could Be the Beginning of a Revolution.'" *The Guardian,* April 28, 2018. https://www.theguardian.com/books/2018/apr/28/chimamanda-ngozi-adichie-feminism-racism-sexism-gender-metoo.

Allen, Aaron S. "Prospects and Problems for Ecomusicology in Confronting a Crisis of Culture." *Journal of the American Musicology Association* 64, no. 2 (2011): 414–24.

Archibald, Linda, and Jonathan Dewar. "Creative Arts, Culture, and Healing: Building an Evidence Base." *Pimatisiwin: A Journal of Aboriginal and Indigenous Community Health* 8, no. 3 (2010): 1–25.

Asante, Molefi K. *It's Bigger Than Hip Hop: The Rise of the Post-Hip-Hop Generation*. New York: St. Martin's Griffin, 2009.

Attali, Jacques. *Noise: The Political Economy of Music*. Translated by Brian Massumi. Manchester, UK: Manchester University Press, 1985.

Austin, Dan, and Sean Doerr. *Lost Detroit: Stories Behind the Motor City's Majestic Ruins*. Charleston, SC: The History Press, 2010.

Berger, Michele Tracy. *Workable Sisterhood: The Political Journey of Stigmatized Women with HIV/AIDS*. Princeton, NJ: Princeton University Press, 2006.

Bhardwa, Bina. "Alone, Asian and Female: The Unspoken Challenges of Conducting Fieldwork in Dance Settings." *Dancecult: Journal of Electronic Dance Music Culture* 5, no. 1 (2013): 39–60.

Boggs Center. "Detroit Summer." {r}evolution: James and Grace Lee Boggs Center for Community Leadership, September 4, 2018. http://boggscenter .org/html/detroit_summer.htm.

Boggs, Grace Lee, and James Boggs. *Revolution and Evolution in the Twentieth Century*. New York: Monthly Review Press, 2008.

Boggs, Grace Lee, and Scott Kurashige. *The Next American Revolution: Sustainable Activism for the Twenty-First Century*. Berkeley: University of California Press, 2012.

Bolhman, Philip. "Musicology as a Political Act." *The Journal of Musicology* 11, no. 4 (Autumn 1993): 411–36.

Bonnette, Lakeyta M. *Pulse of the People: Political Rap Music and Black Politics*. Philadelphia: University of Pennsylvania Press, 2015.

Born, Georgina, ed. *Music, Sound and Space: Transformations of Public and Private Experience*. Cambridge, UK: Cambridge University Press, 2013.

Bradley, Regina N. "Barbz and Kings: Explorations of Gender and Sexuality in Hip-Hop." In *The Cambridge Companion to Hip Hop*, edited by Justin A. Williams, 181–91. Cambridge, UK: Cambridge University Press, 2015.

Brown, Adrienne. "Drive Slow: Rehearing Hip Hop Automotivity." *Journal of Popular Music Studies* 24, no. 3 (2012): 265–75.

brown, adrienne maree. *Emergent Strategy: Shaping Change, Changing Worlds*. Chico, CA: AK Press, 2017.

Brown, Jayna. "Buzz and Rumble: Global Pop Music and Utopian Impulse." *Social Text* 28, no. 1 (2010): 125–46.

Brown, Kimberly Juanita. *The Repeating Body: Slavery's Visual Resonance in the Contemporary*. Durham, NC: Duke University Press, 2015.

Brown, Ruth Nicole. *Black Girlhood Celebration: Toward a Hip Hop Feminist Pedagogy*. New York: Peter Lang, 2009.

Bukowski, Diane. "Brush Park Historical Area—Can We Trust Those Who Wrecked It to Restore It?" *Voice of Detroit,* June 25, 2015. http://voiceofdetroit.net/2015/06/25/brush-park-historic-area-can-we-trust-those-who-wrecked-it-to-restore-it.

Cain, Cacildia. "The Necessity of Black Women's Standpoint and Intersectionality in Environmental Movements." *Medium* (blog), April 14, 2016. https://medium.com/black-feminist-thought-2016/the-necessity-of-black-women-s-standpoint-and-intersectionality-in-environmental-movements-fc52d4277616.

Capeci, Dominic Jr., and Martha Wilkerson. *Layered Violence: The Detroit Riots of 1943.* Jackson: University of Mississippi Press, 1991.

Carby, Hazel. "It Jus Be's Dat Way Sometime: The Sexual Politics of Women's Blues." In *The Jazz Cadence of American Culture,* edited by Robert O'Meally, 470–82. New York: Columbia University Press, 1988.

Chang, Jeff. *Can't Stop Won't Stop: A History of the Hip Hop Generation.* New York: St. Martin's Press, 2005.

Clay, Andreana. *The Hip-Hop Generation Fights Back: Youth, Activism, and Post-Civil Rights Politics.* New York: New York University Press, 2012.

Cobb, William Jelani. *To the Break of Dawn: A Freestyle on the Hip Hop Aesthetic.* New York: New York University Press, 2008.

Coleman, Robin R. Means, and Jasmine Cobb. "No Way of Seeing: Mainstreaming and Selling the Gaze of Homo-Thug Hip Hop." *Popular Communication* 5, no. 2 (2007): 89–108.

Collins, Patricia Hill. *Black Feminist Thought: Knowledge, Consciousness, and the Politics of Empowerment.* New York: Routledge, 2000.

———. *Black Sexual Politics.* New York: Routledge, 2004.

———. *From Black Power to Hip Hop: Racism, Nationalism, and Feminism.* Philadelphia: Temple University Press, 2006.

Connell, John, and Chris Gibson. *Sound Tracks: Popular Music, Identity and Place.* New York: Routledge, 2003.

Cox, Aimee Meredith. *Shapeshifters: Black Girls and the Choreography of Citizenship.* Durham, NC: Duke University Press, 2015.

Cox, Kevin R., and Andrew Mair. "Locality and Community in the Politics of Local Economic Development." *Annals of the Association of American Geographers* 78, no. 2 (June 1998): 307–25.

Craig, Richard T. "'I Know What Them Girls Like': A Rhetorical Analysis of Thug Appeal in Rap Lyrics." *Journal of Communication Inquiry* 40, no. 1 (2016): 25–45.

Craven, Christa, and Dána-Ain Davis, eds. *Feminist Activist Ethnography: Counterpoints to Neoliberalism in North America.* Lanham, MD: Lexington Books, 2014.

Cross, Brian. *It's Not About a Salary: Rap, Race and Resistance in Los Angeles.* London: Verso, 1993.

Davison, Kahn Santori. "Remembering Notable Locales Among Detroit's Hip-Hop History." *Detroit Metro Times,* November 15, 2018. https://www.metrotimes.com/detroit/remembering-notable-locales-among-detroits-hip-hop-history/Content?oid=10184070.

"Detroit Future City: 2012 Detroit Strategic Framework Plan." 2012. https://detroitfuturecity.com/wp-content/uploads/2014/02/DFC_ExecutiveSummary_2ndEd.pdf.

Durham, Aisha. "Hip Hop Feminist Media Studies." *International Journal of Africana Studies* 16, no. 1 (2010): 117–40.

Durham, Aisha Smith. *Home with Hip Hop Feminism: Performances in Communication and Culture.* New York: Peter Lang, 2014.

Durham, Aisha, Brittany C. Cooper, and Susana M. Morris. "The Stage Hip-Hop Feminism Built: A New Directions Essay." *Signs* 38, no. 3 (2013): 721–37.

Dyson, Michael Eric. *Know What I Mean?: Reflections on Hip Hop.* New York: Basic Books, 2007.

———, and Sohail Daulatzai. *Born To Use Mics: Reading Nas's Illmatic.* New York: Civitas Books, 2009.

Eguchi, Shinsuke, and Myra N. Roberts. "Gay Rapping and Possibilities: A Quare Reading of 'Throw That Boy P***y.'" *Text and Performance Quarterly* 35, no. 2–3 (2015): 142–57.

Elligan, Don. "Rap Therapy: A Culturally Sensitive Approach to Psychotherapy with Young African American Men." *Journal of African American Men* 5, no. 3 (2000): 27–36.

———. *Rap Therapy: A Practical Guide for Communicating with Youth and Young Adults Through Rap Music.* New York: Kensington, 2004.

Ellis, Nadia. "New Orleans and Kingston: A Beginning, A Recurrence." *Popular Music Studies* 27, no. 4 (2015): 387–407.

Farley, Reynolds, Sheldon Danziger, and Harry Holzer. *Detroit Divided.* New York: Russell Sage Foundation, 2000.

Farrugia, Rebekah. *Beyond the Dance Floor: Female DJs, Technology, and Electronic Dance Music Culture.* Wilmington, NC: Intellect, 2012.

Farrugia, Rebekah, and Kellie D. Hay. "The Politics and Place of a 'Legendary' Hip Hop Track." *Music and Politics* 8, no. 2 (2014). http://dx.doi.org/10.3998/mp.9460447.0008.203.

Farrugia, Rebekah, and Magdalena Olszanowski. "Women and Electronic Dance Music Culture: Introduction." *Dancecult: Journal of Electronic Dance Music Culture* 9, no. 1 (2017): 1–8.

Feeley, Dianne. "Applying the Shock Doctrine in Detroit." *Solidarity,* December 5, 2013. http://www.solidarity-us.org/site/node/4050.

Fekadu, Mesfin. "MTV, Save the Music Launch Grant Named after Rapper-Producer J Dilla." *Detroit Free Press,* August 29, 2019. https://www.freep.com/story/entertainment/music/2019/08/29/j-dilla-music-tech-grant-mtv-save-the-music/2157503001.

Feld, Steven. "From Ethnomusicology to Echo-Muse-Ecology: Reading R. Murray Schafer in the Papua New Guinea Rainforest." *The Soundscape Newsletter* 8 (June 1994): 9–13.

Font-Navarrete, David. "Bass 101: Miami, Rio, and the Global Music South." *Journal of Popular Music Studies* 27, no. 4 (2015): 488–517.

Forman, Murray. *The 'Hood Comes First: Race, Space, and Place in Rap and Hip-Hop.* Hanover, NH: Wesleyan University Press, 2002.

Frith, Simon. "Music and Identity." In *Questions of Cultural Identity,* edited by Stuart Hall and Paul du Gay, 108–27. Thousand Oaks, CA: Sage, 1996.

Gallagher, John. "When Detroit Paved Over Paradise: The Story of I-375." *Detroit Free Press,* December 15, 2013. http://www.freep.com/article/20131215/OPINION05/312150060/Black-Bottom-Detroit-I-375-I-75-paradise-valley-removal.

Gaunt, Kyra. "Foreword." In *Wish to Live: The Hip Hop Feminism Pedagogy Reader*, edited by Ruth Nicole Brown and Chamara Jewel Kwakye, ix–xv. New York: Peter Lang, 2012.

George, Nelson. *Hip Hop America*. New York: Penguin Books, 2005.

Georgetown University. *A Conversation with Nas and Michael Eric Dyson*. Washington, DC, 2014. https://www.georgetown.edu/news/rapper-nas-says-hip-hop-artists-need-to-be-more-responsible.

Gholz, Carleton S. "Welcome to Tha D: Making and Re-Making Hip Hop Culture in Post-Motown Detroit." In *Hip Hop in America: A Regional Guide.*, edited by Mickey Hess, 393–428. Santa Barbara, CA: Greenwood Press, 2010.

Gonzales, Tiphanie, and B. Grant Hayes. "Rap Music in School Counseling Based on Don Elligan's Rap Therapy." *Journal of Creativity in Mental Health* 4, no. 2 (2009): 161–72.

Gottesdiener, Laura. "A Tale of Two Detroits, Separate and Unequal." *In These Times*, November 18, 2014. http://inthesetimes.com/article/17372/inequality_in_detroit.

Gray, Herman. *Cultural Moves: African Americans and the Politics of Representation*. Berkeley: University of California Press, 2005.

Gray, Rose. "Red, Black, and Green: A More Inclusive Environmental Movement Takes the Stage." *Orion Magazine*, April 2014. http://www.orionmagazine.org/index.php/articles/article/8050.

Guevara, Nancy. "Women Writin' Rappin' Breakin'." In *Droppin' Science: Critical Essays on Rap Music and Hip Hop Culture*, edited by William Eric Perkins, 49–62. Philadelphia: Temple University Press, 1996.

Guy, Nancy. "Flowing Down Taiwan's Tamsui River: Towards an Ecomusicology of the Environmental Imagination." *Ethnomusicology* 53, no. 2 (Spring/Summer 2009): 218–48.

Hadley, Susan, and George Yancy, eds. *Therapeutic Uses of Rap and Hip-Hop*. New York: Routledge, 2012.

Hall, H. Bernard. "Deeper than Rap: Expanding Conceptions of Hip-Hop Culture and Pedagogy in the English Language Arts Classroom." *Research in the Teaching of English* 51, no. 3 (2017): 341–50.

Harrison, Anthony Kwame. *Ethnography: Understanding Qualitative Research*. New York: Oxford University Press, 2018.

———. *Hip Hop Underground: The Integrity and Ethics of Racial Identification*. Philadelphia: Temple University Press, 2009.

Harvey, David. "Neoliberalism as Creative Destruction." *The Annals of the American Academy of Political and Social Science* 610 (2007): 22–44.

———. *Social Justice and the City*. Baltimore: Johns Hopkins University Press, 2009.

Hay, Kellie D., Rebekah Farrugia, and Deidre "D.S. Sense" Smith. "D.S. Sense's 'On My Detroit Everything': Self-Articulating Black Girl Magic." *Arts* 7, no. 2 (2018). https://doi.org/10.3390/arts7020017.

Herron, Jerry. *AfterCulture: Detroit and the Humiliation of History*. Detroit: Wayne State University Press, 1993.

Hill, Marc Lamont. *Nobody: Casualties of America's War on the Vulnerable, from Ferguson to Flint and Beyond*. New York City: Atria Books, 2016.

———. "Wounded Healing: Forming a Storytelling Community in Hip-Hop Lit." *Teachers College Record* 111, no. 1 (2009): 248–93.

———, and Emery Petchauer. *Schooling Hip-Hop: Expanding Hip-Hop Based Education Across the Curriculum*. New York: Teachers College Press, 2013.

hooks, bell. *Feminism Is for Everybody*. Cambridge, MA: South End Press, 2000.

———. *We Real Cool: Black Men and Masculinity*. New York: Routledge, 2003.

Howell, Shea. "Water, Dispossession, and Resistance." {r}evolution: James and Grace Lee Boggs Center for Community Leadership, June 10, 2014. http://boggscenter.org/?p=6086.

Hunter, Margaret. "Shake It, Baby, Shake It: Consumption and the New Gender Relation in Hip-Hop." *Sociological Perspectives* 54, no. 1 (2011): 15–36.

Hurt, Byron. *Hip Hop: Beyond Beats and Rhymes*. DVD. Independent Lens, 2006.

Ingram, David. *The Jukebox in the Garden: Ecocriticism and American Popular Music Since 1960*. Amsterdam: Rodopi, 2010.

Isoke, Zenzele. *Urban Black Women and the Politics of Resistance*. New York: Palgrave MacMillan, 2012.

Jamila, Shani. "Can I Get a Witness? Testimony from a Hip Hop Feminist." In *Colonize This! Young Women of Color on Today's Feminism*, edited by Daisy Hernandez, Bushra Rehman, and Cherrie Moraga, 382–94. Berkeley, CA: Seal Press, 2002.

Jeffries, Michael P. *Thug Life: Race, Gender, and the Meaning of Hip Hop*. Chicago: University of Chicago Press, 2011.

Jenkins, Toby S. "A Beautiful Mind: Black Male Intellectual Identity and Hip-Hop Culture." *Journal of Black Studies* 42, no. 8 (2011): 1231–51.

Johnson, Maisha Z. "5 Ways 'Respectability Politics' Blame Black Women for Their Own Oppression." *Everyday Feminism*. November 5, 2015. https://everydayfeminism.com/2015/11/respectability-politics-black-women.

Kaalund, Valerie Ann. "Witness to Truth: Black Women Heeding the Call for Environmental Justice." In *New Perspectives on Environmental Justice: Gender, Sexuality, and Activism*, edited by Rachel Stein, 78–92. New Brunswick, NJ: Rutgers University Press, 2004.

Kaffer, Nancy. "Watching Dan Gilbert's *Watchmen*." *Detroit Free Press*, May 18, 2015. http://www.freep.com/story/opinion/columnists/nancy-kaffer/2015/05/18/quicken-detroit-security/27521889.

Kaufman, Michael, and Michael Kimmel. *The Guy's Guide to Feminism*. Berkeley, CA: Seal Press, 2011.

Kellner, Douglas, and Jeff Share. "Toward Critical Media Literacy: Core Concepts, Debates, Organizations, and Policy." *Discourse: Studies in the Cultural Politics of Education* 26, no. 3 (2005): 369–86.

Kernodle, Tammy L. "Black Women Working Together: Jazz, Gender, and the Politics of Validation." *Black Music Research Journal* 34, no. 1 (2017): 27–55.

Keyes, Cheryl L. "Empowering Self, Making Choices, Creating Space: Black Female Identity via Rap Music Performance." *The Journal of American Folklore* 113, no. 449 (2000): 255–69.

Kitwana, Bakari. *The Hip Hop Generation: Young Blacks and the Crisis in African American Culture.* New York: Verso, 2003.

Knight, Ethridge. *Belly Song and Other Poems.* Detroit: Broadside Press, 1973.

Kramer, Lawrence. *Music as Cultural Practice: 1800–1900.* Berkeley: University of California Press, 1993.

Krims, Adam. *Music and Urban Geography.* London: Routledge, 2007.

———. *Rap Music and the Poetics of Identity.* Cambridge, UK: Cambridge University Press, 2000.

Leary, John Patrick. "Detroitism." *Guernica: A Magazine of Art and Politics,* January 15, 2011. https://www.guernicamag.com/features/leary_1_15_11.

Lefebvre, Henri. 1996 (1967). *Writings on Cities.* Edited and translated by Eleonore Kofman and Elizabeth Lebas. Malden, MA: Blackwell.

Leonard, Marion. *Gender in the Music Industry: Rock, Discourse and Girl Power.* Burlington, VT: Ashgate, 2007.

Levy, Ian, Christopher Emdin, and Edmund S. Adjapong. "Hip-Hop Cypher in Group Work." *Social Work with Groups* 41, no. 1–2 (2018): 103–10.

Lipsitz, George. "The Possessive Investment in Whiteness: Racialized Social Democracy and the 'White' Problem in American Studies." *American Quarterly* 47, no. 3 (1995): 369–87.

Lorde, Audre. *A Burst of Light: and Other Essays.* Mineola, NY: Ixia Press, 2017.

Love, Bettina L. "A Ratchet Lens: Black Queer Youth, Agency, Hip Hop, and the Black Ratchet Imagination." *Educational Researcher* 46, no. 9 (2017): 539–47.

Macías, Anthony. "'Detroit Was Heavy': Modern Jazz, Bebop, and African American Expressive Culture." *The Journal of African American History* 95, no. 1 (2010): 44–70.

Mahon, Maureen. "The Visible Evidence of Cultural Producers." *Annual Review of Anthropology* 29 (2000): 467–92.

Marchand, Yves, and Romain Meffre. *Yves Marchand and Romain Meffre: The Ruins of Detroit.* Göttingen, Germany: Steidl, 2010.

McClary, Susan. *Feminine Endings: Music, Gender, and Sexuality.* Minneapolis: University of Minnesota Press, 1991.

———. "Terminal Prestige: The Case of Avant-Garde Music Composition." *Cultural Critique* 12 (Spring 1989): 57–81.

McCune, Jeffery Q., Jr. "Out in the Club: The Down Low, Hip-Hop, and the Architecture of Black Masculinity." *Text and Performance Quarterly* 28, no. 3 (2008): 298–314.

Miller-Young, Mereille. *A Taste for Brown Sugar: Black Women in Pornography.* Durham, NC: Duke University Press, 2014.

Milo, Jeff. "Hip-Hop Emcee Miz Korona, of '8 Mile' Fame, Knows Something about Persevering." *Detroit Free Press,* August 10, 2017. https://www.freep.com/story/entertainment/music/2017/08/10/miz-korona-best-friends-forever-fest/547431001.

Moore, Andrew, and Philip Levine. *Andrew Moore: Detroit Disassembled.* New York: Damiani/Akron Art Museum, 2010.

Morgan, Joan. *When Chicken-Heads Come Home to Roost.* New York: Touchstone, 1999.

Morgan, Marcyliena. *The Real Hip Hop: Battling for Knowledge, Power, and Respect in the LA Underground.* Durham, NC: Duke University Press, 2009.

Moskowitz, Peter. "The Two Detroits: A City Both Collapsing and Gentrifying at the Same Time." *The Guardian,* February 5, 2015. http://www.theguardian.com/cities/2015/feb/05/detroit-city-collapsing-gentrifying.

Motl, Kaitlyne A. "Fear in the Festival Field: Threat, Apprehension and Apathy." *Dancecult: Journal of Electronic Dance Music Culture* 9, no. 1 (2017). https://dj.dancecult.net/index.php/dancecult/article/view/942/869.

Neal, Mark Anthony. "Hip Hop Feminist." In *That's the Joint: The Hip Hop Studies Reader,* edited by Murray Forman and Mark Anthony Neal, 413–18. London: Routledge, 2012.

———. *Looking for Leroy: Illegible Black Masculinities.* New York: New York University Press, 2013.

Neff, Ali Colleen. *Let the World Listen Right: The Mississippi Delta Hip Hop Story.* Jackson, MS: University Press of Mississippi, 2011.

Ogbar, Jeffrey. *Hip-Hop Revolution: The Culture and Politics of Rap.* Lawrence: University of Kansas Press, 2007.

O'Leary, Ceara. "Detroit's Vacant Land: Strategies and Support." *Funders' Network for Smart Growth and Livable Communities,* November 1, 2013. http://www.fundersnetwork.org/blog/detroits-vacant-land-strategies-and-support.

Pabón-Colón, Jessica Nydia. "Writin', Breakin', Beatboxin': Strategically Performing 'Women' in Hip-Hop." *Signs: Journal of Women in Culture & Society* 43, no. 1 (2017): 175–200.

Pedelty, Mark. *Ecomusicology: Rock, Folk, and the Environment.* Philadelphia, PA: Temple University Press, 2012.

Peña, Devon G. "Detroit Food Justice Activists Resist a Land Grab." *Environmental and Food Justice,* December 7, 2012. http://ejfood.blogspot.com/2012/12/land-grabs-not-limited-to-global-south.html.

Penney, Joel. "'We Don't Wear Tight Clothes': Gay Panic and Queer Style in Contemporary Hip Hop." *Popular Music and Society* 35, no. 3 (2012): 321–32.

Peoples, Whitney, A. "'Under Construction': Identifying Foundations of Hip-Hop Feminism and Exploring Bridges Between Second-Wave and Hip-Hop Feminisms." *Meridians* 8, no. 1 (2008): 19–52.

Perrone, Dina. "Gender and Sexuality in the Field: A Female Ethnographer's Experience Researching Drug Use in Dance Clubs." *Substance Use and Misuse* 45, no. 5 (2010): 717–35.

Perry, Imani. *Prophets of the Hood: Politics and Poetics in Hip Hop.* Durham, NC: Duke University Press, 2004.

Petchauer, Emery. "Back to the Lab With Hip Hop Education: An Introduction." *Urban Education* 50, no. 1 (2015): 3–6.

———. "Starting With Style: Toward a Second Wave of Hip-Hop Education Research and Practice." *Urban Education* 50, no. 1 (2015): 78–105.

Petersen, Kevin. "Room to Grow: Detroit Takes the First Steps to Legalize Urban Agriculture." *Michigan Journal of Environmental and Administrative Law*, February 8, 2013. http://www.mjeal-online.org/room-to-grow-detroit-takes-the-first-steps-to-legalize-urban-agriculture.

Peterson, James Braxton. *The Hip-Hop Underground and African American Culture: Beneath the Surface.* New York: Palgrave MacMillan, 2015.

Peterson, Marina. *Sound, Space, and the City: Civic Performances in Downtown Los Angeles.* Philadelphia: University of Pennsylvania Press, 2012.

Petty, Tawana Honeycomb. *Towards Humanity: Shifting the Culture of Anti-Racism Organizing.* CreateSpace Independent Publishing Platform, 2018.

Pough, Gwendolyn D. *Check It While I Wreck It: Black Womanhood, Hip-Hop Culture, and the Public Sphere.* Boston: Northeastern University Press, 2004.

Powell, Kevin. *The Education of Kevin Powell: A Boy's Journey Into Manhood.* New York: Atria Books, 2016.

Rabaka, Reiland. *Hip Hop's Amnesia: From Blue and the Black Women's Club Movement to Rap and the Hip Hop Movement.* Lanham, MD: Lexington Books, 2012.

———. *Hip Hop's Inheritance: From the Harlem Renaissance to the Hip Hop Feminist Movement.* Lanham, MD: Lexington Books, 2011.

Ransby, Barbara. *Making All Black Lives Matter: Reimagining Freedom in the Twenty-First Century.* Berkeley: University of California Press, 2018.

Rafael, Antonio, and Matthew Irwin. "Gilbert's Trojan Horse: Capturing the City Core." *Riverwise*, Summer 2017, 8–10.

Redmond, Shana L. *Anthem: Social Movements and the Sounds of Solidarity in the African Diaspora.* New York: New York University Press, 2014.

Rehding, Alexander. "Ecomusicology between Apocalypse and Nostalgia." *Journal of the American Musicological Society* 64, no. 2 (2011): 409–14.

Richardson, Elaine. "Developing Critical Hip Hop Feminist Literacies: Centrality and Subversion of Sexualy in the Lives of Black Girls." *Equity & Excellent in Education* 46, no. 3 (2013): 327–41.

Roediger, David R. *Working Toward Whiteness: How America's Immigrants Became White: The Strange Journey from Ellis Island to the Suburbs.* New York: Basic Books, 2006.

Rose, Tricia. *Black Noise: Rap Music and Black Culture in Contemporary America.* Middletown, CT: Wesleyan University Press, 1994.

———. *The Hip Hop Wars: What We Talk about When We Talk about Hip Hop—and Why It Matters.* New York: Basic Books, 2008.

Rosenthal, Debra J. "Hoods and the Woods: Rap Music as Environmental Literature." *The Journal of Popular Culture* 39, no. 4 (Summer 2006): 661–76.

Sawyer, Richard D., Joe Norris, and Darren E. Lund, eds. *Duoethnography: Dialogic Methods for Social, Health, and Educational Research.* Walnut Creek, CA: Left Coast Press, 2012.

Schafer, R. Murray. *The Tuning of the World.* Philadelphia: University of Pennsylvania Press, 1980.

Schaub, Christopher. "Beyond the Hood? Detroit Techno, Underground Resistance, and African American Metropolitan Identity Politics." *Forum for*

Inter-American Research 2, no. 2 (2009). http://interamerica.de/volume-2-2
/schaub.

Schloss, Joseph G. *Foundation: B-Boys, B-Girls, and Hip-Hop Culture in New
York*. New York: Oxford University Press, 2009.

Sharma, Nitasha Tamar. *Hip Hop Desis: South Asian Americans, Blackness,
and a Global Race Consciousness*. Durham, NC: Duke University Press,
2010.

Sharpley-Whiting, T. Denean. *Pimps Up, Ho's Down: Hip Hop's Hold on
Young Black Women*. New York: New York University Press, 2008.

Sheffield, Carrie Louise. "Native American Hip-Hop and Historical Trauma:
Surviving and Healing Trauma on the 'Rez.'" *Studies in American Indian
Literatures* 23, no. 3 (2011): 94–110.

Sierra Club. "The State of Detroit's Environment: An Initial Assessment Using the
Framework of Environmental Justice." April 4, 2013. https://studyres.com
/doc/23404868/the-state-of-detroit-s-environment.

Smith, Susan J. "Soundscape." *Area* 26, no. 3 (1994): 232–40.

Smith, Suzanne E. *Dancing in the Street: Motown and the Cultural Politics of
Detroit*. Cambridge, MA: Harvard University Press, 1999.

Spence, Lester. *Knocking the Hustle: Against the Neoliberal Turn in Black Politics*. Brooklyn, NY: Punctum Books, 2015.

Stephens, Dionne P., and Layli D. Phillips. "Freaks, Gold Diggers, Divas, and
Dykes: The Sociohistorical Development of Adolescent African American
Women's Sexual Scripts." *Sexuality & Culture* 7, no. 1 (2003): 3–49.

Sterne, Jonathan. "Sonic Imaginations." In *The Sound Studies Reader,* edited
by Jonathan Sterne, 1–18. New York: Routledge, 2012.

Stimeling, Travis D. "Music, Place, and Identity in the Central Appalachian
Mountaintop Removal Mining Debate." *American Music* 30, no. 1 (2012):
1–29.

Sugrue, Thomas J. *The Origins of the Urban Crisis: Race and Inequality in
Postwar Detroit*. Princeton, NJ: Princeton University Press, 2005.

Taylor, Dorceta E. "Women of Color, Environmental Justice, and Ecofeminism." In *Ecofeminism: Women, Culture, Nature,* edited by Karen J. Warren,
38–81. Bloomington: Indiana University Press, 1997.

Templeton, Andrew. "'Detroit Hustles Harder' Phrase Is Key to Aptemal Clothing's XXL Growth." *Crain's Detroit Business,* May 5, 2013. http://www
.crainsdetroit.com/article/20130505/NEWS/305059991/detroit-hustles-
harder-phrase-is-key-to-aptemal-clothings-xxl.

Thomas, June Manning. *Redevelopment and Race: Planning a Finer City in
Postwar Detroit*. Detroit: Wayne State University Press, 2013.

Thomson, Heather Ann. *Whose Detroit? Politics, Labor, and Race in a Modern
American City*. Ithaca, NY: Cornell University Press, 2000.

Von Glahn, Denise. "American Women and the Nature of Identity." *Journal of
The American Musicological Society* 64, no. 2 (2011): 399–403.

Walcott, Rinaldo. "Boyfriends with Clits and Girlfriends with Dicks: Hip Hop's
Queer Future." *Palimpsest: A Journal on Women, Gender, and the Black
International* 2, no. 2 (2013): 168–73.

Ward, Stephen M. *In Love and Struggle: The Revolutionary Lives of James and Grace Lee Boggs*. Chapel Hill: University of North Carolina Press, 2016.

Wheatley, Margaret J. *Leadership and the New Science: Discovering Order in a Chaotic World*. San Francisco: Berrett-Koehler, 2006.

White, Miles. *From Jim Crow to Jay-Z: Race, Rap and the Performance of Masculinity*. Urbana: University of Illinois Press, 2011.

Willis, Deborah, and Carla Williams. *The Black Female Body: A Photographic History*. Philadelphia: Temple University Press, 2002.

Zook, Kristal Brent. "A Manifesto of Sorts for a Black Feminist Movement." *New York Times Magazine*, December 3, 1995. https://www.nytimes.com/1995/12/03/magazine/l-a-manifesto-of-sorts-for-a-black-feminist-movement-079081.html.

Index

Founded in 1893,
UNIVERSITY OF CALIFORNIA PRESS
publishes bold, progressive books and journals
on topics in the arts, humanities, social sciences,
and natural sciences—with a focus on social
justice issues—that inspire thought and action
among readers worldwide.

The UC PRESS FOUNDATION
raises funds to uphold the press's vital role
as an independent, nonprofit publisher, and
receives philanthropic support from a wide
range of individuals and institutions—and from
committed readers like you. To learn more, visit
ucpress.edu/supportus.